# FEARLESS *in* TIBET

# ALSO BY MATTEO PISTONO

*In the Shadow of the Buddha:*
*One Man's Journey of Discovery in Tibet*

# FEARLESS
# *in* TIBET

*The Life of the* **Mystic Tertön Sogyal**

## Matteo Pistono

**HAY HOUSE, INC.**
Carlsbad, California • New York City
London • Sydney • Johannesburg
Vancouver • Hong Kong • New Delhi

**Published and distributed in the United States by:** Hay House, Inc.: www
.hayhouse.com® • **Published and distributed in Australia by:** Hay House Australia
Pty. Ltd.: www.hayhouse.com.au • **Published and distributed in the United Kingdom by:** Hay House UK, Ltd.: www.hayhouse.co.uk • **Published and distributed in
the Republic of South Africa by:** Hay House SA (Pty), Ltd.: www.hayhouse.co.za •
**Distributed in Canada by:** Raincoast Books: www.raincoast.com • **Published in
India by:** Hay House Publishers India: www.hayhouse.co.in

*Indexer:* Jay Kreider
*Cover design:* Amy Rose Grigoriou • *Interior design:* Riann Bender

*Map:* Drawn by Jocelyn Slack

*Mirror section break image:* Line drawing from *The Encyclopedia of Tibetan Symbols
and Motifs,* courtesy of Robert Beer (www.tibetanart.com)

*Title page image:* Retraced from the original at Kalzang Temple and digitized by
Jamyang Dorjee Chakrishar (www.tibetancalligraphy.com)

**Library of Congress Cataloging-in-Publication Data**

Pistono, Matteo, author.
  Fearless in Tibet : the life of the mystic Terton Sogyal / Matteo Pistono ; foreword
by Sogyal Rinpoche. -- 1st edition.
     pages cm
  ISBN 978-1-4019-4146-8 (paperback)
  1.  Las-rab-glin-pa, 1856-1926. 2.  R?in-ma-pa lamas--China--Tibet Autonomous
Region--Biography.  I. Title.
  BQ970.A87P58 2014
  294.3'923092--dc23
  [B]
                              2013050163

ISBN: 978-1-4019-4146-8

17  16  15  14   4  3  2  1
1st edition, May 2014

Printed in the United States of America

SUSTAINABLE
FORESTRY
INITIATIVE
Certified Chain of Custody
Promoting Sustainable Forestry
www.sfiprogram.org
SFI-01268
SFI label applies to the text stock

# CONTENTS

# FOREWORD

It was just over 50 years ago that the world suddenly became aware of Tibet and its culture, when His Holiness the Dalai Lama and a hundred thousand Tibetan people fled into exile, escaping the destruction in our homeland. Since that time, people in the wider world have discovered our extraordinary living tradition of Tibetan Buddhism, which has prevailed for more than a thousand years in Tibet and the Himalayan regions and has often been called one of the last ancient wisdom cultures on earth. With its remarkable knowledge of the mind and its profound disciplines of study and practice, the Buddhist tradition of Tibet produced countless outstanding masters and spiritually realized practitioners. One of these was Tertön Sogyal, or Lerab Lingpa, an exceptional figure who lived more than a century ago during the lifetime of the Thirteenth Dalai Lama.

As I write these words, I can see the sun gleaming on the copper roof of the temple here at Lerab Ling, the retreat center in France that I founded in the name of Tertön Sogyal. Thinking about him now, I realize that he was someone whose life embraced many different facets and dimensions. To begin with, you could say that he was a spiritual leader, deeply concerned with the future well-being of the world and its inhabitants, as well as with the spiritual progress of humanity. From the perspective of the ancient Nyingma tradition of Tibetan Buddhism, he stood out as a great master, mystic, visionary, and prophet, and a *tertön*, or treasure revealer, with more than 20 large volumes of revelations to his name. From the viewpoint of the historian, he was a teacher, friend, and ally of the Thirteenth Dalai Lama (1876–1933) and a defender of the realm, who, through his revelations, prophecies, and spiritual presence, played a crucial part in striving to ensure the survival of Tibet as a sanctuary for the study and practice of Vajrayana Buddhism.

To understand what drove and inspired Tertön Sogyal, we ought to step back for a moment into the eighth century, a time when the Buddhist teachings were established in Tibet by the extraordinary master Guru Padmasambhava, affectionately called "Guru Rinpoche," meaning "Precious Master," by the Tibetan people. Along with the great Indian abbot Shantarakshita and the King of Tibet Trisong Detsen, he presided over the construction of the first temple at Samye, the ordination of the first seven Tibetan monks, and the translation of the Buddhist teachings into Tibetan. To his closest 25 disciples, who included his consort, Yeshe Tsogyal, and King Trisong Detsen, he transmitted the innermost secret mantra teachings of Vajrayana, and then, blessing the whole land of Tibet and the Himalayas, he concealed countless spiritual treasures, or *terma*, destined to be discovered by successive incarnations of his chief disciples at precisely the most potent time in the future for them to be of maximum benefit. These treasures can take the form of statues, sacred objects and texts, or teachings revealed from within the minds of the treasure revealers. Once deciphered, they bring to light entire cycles of spiritual practice and teaching. One of these close disciples of Guru Rinpoche was Nanam Dorje Dudjom, a trusted minister of the king and an accomplished practitioner, who had been one of the original delegation sent to invite Padmasambhava to Tibet. Tertön Sogyal, or to give him his name as a tertön, Lerab Lingpa, was the incarnation of Nanam Dorje Dudjom.

I believe I must have first heard about Tertön Sogyal from my own beloved master, Jamyang Khyentse Chökyi Lodrö, who raised me as his son, gave me the name "Sogyal," and recognized me as an incarnation of Lerab Lingpa. This was because Jamyang Khyentse was one of the "heart sons," the closest disciples, of Tertön Sogyal. He used to say that, before he had even seen the great tertön, the very first time he heard his name, he was overcome by an uncanny sense of yearning, a spontaneous surge of devotion. He met him a number of times, the first occasion being in 1920, and was struck by Tertön Sogyal's incredible qualities of learning and realization. Tertön Sogyal authorized Jamyang Khyentse to be the holder of all his treasure teachings, and he would appear to him in vivid dreams and visions.

After Jamyang Khyentse passed away in exile in Sikkim in 1959, I continued to study with other great masters of the tradition, and I learned more about Tertön Sogyal. I also heard stories about him as I grew up among my family, the Lakartshang, who had been one of the most generous benefactors of Buddhism in Tibet, sponsoring the monasteries and masters of all traditions. As time went by, I became increasingly aware of and inspired by Tertön Sogyal's revelations, so much so that they became the cornerstone of my life, my practice, and my teachings.

Tertön Sogyal's masters had included the most prominent lamas of his age, exceptional figures like Jamyang Khyentse Wangpo and Jamgön Kongtrul, and he had received the famous Patrul Rinpoche's oral lineage of Dzogpachenpo, "the Great Perfection," which is the deepest stream of teachings within the Tibetan Buddhist tradition. If you look into Tertön Sogyal's life story, you can see that he experienced an almost continuous series of visions, predictions, and revelations from Padmasambhava, and his entire life was lived to the full within the sacred vision and pure perception of the Vajrayana teachings.

The end of the 19th and beginning of the 20th centuries was a precarious period in history, an era of constant unrest, when the Dalai Lama and Tertön Sogyal struggled to preserve the integrity of Tibet, a country menaced on all sides by the great powers of China, Russia, and British India. Summoned by the Dalai Lama, between 1888 and 1904, Tertön Sogyal made five visits to Lhasa, the capital city, from his homeland in eastern Tibet. Working closely with the State Oracle's monastery at Nechung and drawing on all the depth, power, and intricacy of the Vajrayana's vast range of skillful methods, he performed rituals to defend Tibet. He discovered terma treasures and received prophecies related to the Dalai Lama or Tibet, which would often give specific directions, for example, about the building of temples and stupas, so as to protect the country from invasion. Two of the most well-known of his terma connected with the welfare of Tibet are "The Wish-fulfilling Jewel" statue, now in the Jokhang Cathedral, and the "Heart Life" stone, which I have seen in the Fourteenth Dalai Lama's possession. I sometimes think there was an almost conscious reenactment of the events one thousand years before, as the Dalai Lama, who was considered to be an incarnation of King Trisong Detsen, aided by Tertön Sogyal, the incarnation of Dorje Dudjom, once again followed Padmasambhava's guidance and instructions, this time to safeguard Tibet at a delicate and dangerous moment.

One of Tertön Sogyal's terma that focused on the deity Vajrakilaya, the wrathful embodiment of enlightened action, came to have particular importance. It was called "The Razor of the Innermost Essence," *Yang Nying Pudri*. The heir to this cycle of teaching and practices, the prediction said, was the Thirteenth Dalai Lama, and it was adopted by both him and his personal chapel, the Namgyal Monastery. The Yang Nying Pudri is associated with removing obstacles, both worldly and spiritual, warding off misfortune and negativity, and, above all, protecting the Dalai Lamas and Tibet. It is one of the main practices of the Fourteenth Dalai Lama. In 2000, in fact, he granted the initiation and led an intensive group practice of this treasure teaching at Lerab Ling, blessing the site of the future temple. Another unique terma of Tertön Sogyal, of which the Dalai Lama was the destined holder, is the *Tendrel Nyesel*, "Eliminating Flaws in Interdependence," a practice dedicated specifically to creating harmony and peace in the world by eliminating, preventing, protecting against, and transforming harm and conflict.

The more I have learned and understood about Tertön Sogyal, the more I have come to feel his presence and sensed the atmosphere of his life. Twenty years ago, I met the other incarnation of Tertön Sogyal, the great scholar and visionary Khenpo Jigmey

Phuntsok Rinpoche (1933–2004). With his Buddhist Institute at Larung Gar, Khenpo Jikphun set in motion nothing less than a renaissance of Buddhist teaching and practice in eastern Tibet. It has attracted thousands of students, among them many Chinese men and women, and proved to be the most extraordinary center of education. When he visited Lerab Ling in France, he spoke at length about Tertön Sogyal's life and mission. "There was a prediction," he explained, "that Tibet was to suffer twelve invasions, and that the ninth would take place during the lifetime of Tertön Sogyal. The Thirteenth Dalai Lama entrusted him with the task of averting this ninth invasion, and of dispelling the perils that faced Tibet. In fact, Tertön Sogyal went through unthinkable hardships for the sake of the teachings and to help sentient beings in Tibet." Khenpo Jigmey Phuntsok also quoted a number of prophecies that predicted Tertön Sogyal would reappear in his next life in two main incarnations: one was to be an ordained monk with pure vows, and one was to be a yogin, a mantra practitioner. One of the prophecies read:

> Nanam Dorje Dudjom will certainly ripen into two fruits: One, a turquoise dragon holding up a jewel for all to see, the other, his voice resounding everywhere like a lion's roar.

Khenpo Jigmey Phuntsok identified us as the two incarnations and declared that his mind and mine were inseparable.

When so little is known in general about Tertön Sogyal, it is timely indeed that Matteo Pistono has written this book about him. Matteo is a student of mine and has for many years received teachings with some of the most senior Tibetan Buddhist lamas in both Tibet and in exile. In this book, he throws light on a whole world and period of history and brings Tertön Sogyal's story to life, based on his own tireless research, for which I congratulate him, and on the biography written by the great tertön's disciple, the remarkable Tulku Tsullo, one of the present Dalai Lama's favorite writers.

These days, I often think about Tertön Sogyal's legacy, and I like to imagine that he continues still to protect the life of the Dalai Lama and must have foreseen that His Holiness would become a world leader, loved and respected by millions. Tertön Sogyal also predicted that his teachings would not spread so much during his own lifetime, but during the life of his next reincarnation that "they would spread throughout the entire world, their impact, power, and blessing would multiply a hundredfold, and they would remain, without ever declining, for five hundred years." Certainly they endure in the extraordinary work of Khenpo Jigmey Phuntsok Rinpoche in Tibet, who trained an entire generation of Tibetan scholars. In its first 20 years, for example, his center at Larung Gar produced 600 fully trained *khenpos*, or professors, who returned to their home areas and other parts of Asia to teach. Then there are also my own humble efforts, holding the name at least of Tertön Sogyal, to uphold the teachings of which he was such a sublime example.

But above all, I pray that Tertön Sogyal's blessing continues to radiate throughout the world, to inspire and strengthen the Dalai Lama and ensure his long life; to make the precious teachings of Buddha flourish and spread; to pacify conflict, suffering, and negativity all over the world; to bring peace and tranquillity to Tibet; and to ensure the welfare and happiness of living beings everywhere.

— Sogyal Rinpoche

# AUTHOR'S NOTE

My first encounter with Tertön Sogyal was seeing the striking photograph of him at the Rigpa meditation center in London; that evening I also met Sogyal Rinpoche for the first time. I had just arrived in England for a master's degree program in Buddhist philosophy at the School of Oriental and African Studies at the University of London. After seeing the photograph, I started asking questions about Tertön Sogyal's life; though I spoke with lamas, Western scholars, and Tibetan historians, no one could tell me much about him except that Tertön Sogyal was the Thirteenth Dalai Lama's teacher and a Vajrakilaya adept. Despite knowing so little about him, I felt an inexplicable connection to the tertön. I was also drawn to Tertön Sogyal's teachings by observing Sogyal Rinpoche's extraordinary embodiment and example of a Dzogchen yogi, and his immense kindness in revealing Tibet's wisdom tradition through his own teachings.

After receiving my degree in London, I went to Tibet to follow in Tertön Sogyal's footsteps, to sit where he meditated in hermitages and caves, and to speak to lineage holders, including Khenpo Jikme Phuntsok, who helped me to visit some of the tertön's holy sites. From the late 1990s to 2008, I traveled to Tibet a dozen times, each trip lasting from one to three months. Riding rickety buses to Golok, Nyarong, and Rebkong; hitchhiking to Lhasa from Kham and Amdo; and walking for weeks to arrive at ancient pilgrimage sites across the Tibetan Plateau, I visited nearly every location where Tertön Sogyal had lived and taught. I carried letters of introduction, and offerings, from Sogyal Rinpoche to lamas in Tibet, which opened to me a world that I would not have otherwise had access to. In 2006 Sogyal Rinpoche encouraged me to write Tertön Sogyal's biography.

The narrative in *Fearless in Tibet* is my chronicle of the life of Tertön Sogyal based on a number of authoritative sources. My primary source was Tulku Tsultrim Zangpo's (Tsullo's) lengthy spiritual biography of Tertön Sogyal that was carved onto woodblocks in the 1940s, about 15 years after Tertön Sogyal's passing. Entitled *The Marvelous Garland of White Lotuses*, it is the only known biography and is based upon mystical prophecies about Tertön Sogyal by Padmasambhava and other saintly persons. Little in the way of history in a Western sense exists in Tsullo's traditional hagiography, though when one reads it alongside other historical sources—Tibetan, Chinese, and Western, some of which are in this book's Reference section— it is clear that Tertön Sogyal's mystical visions and spiritual revelations occurred during very specific episodes in the tumultuous political times in late 19th- and early 20th-century Tibet. Venerable Tenzin Choephel of Nechung Monastery led me through Tsullo's 725-page biography over the course of six weeks in Dharamsala and Washington, D.C. I also benefited greatly from Lotsawa Adam Pearcey's unpublished outline of Tsullo's biography and the many conversations I had with him about Tertön Sogyal. *Fearless in Tibet* would not have appeared without Venerable Tenzin Choephel's skillful interpretations and endless patience and Lotsawa Adam's scholarship.

I have incorporated into the narrative of *Fearless in Tibet* much of the oral record recounted to me by great lamas and elderly hermits— some in their Tibetan homeland and others in exile—who hold the blessing of Tertön Sogyal. Most of the lamas in Tibet to whom I listened have since died. Their fantastic stories of Tertön Sogyal were told over butter tea and tsampa in Nyarong, Kandze, Golok, and Lhasa, and in sacred grottoes, monasteries, and wooden huts. My 15-year journey to listen to accounts of scenes from Tertön Sogyal's life also took me to meet lamas and scholars in China, India, Nepal,

France, England, and America. A few accounts about Tertön Sogyal by Dilgo Khyentse Rinpoche and other masters, I found in the Rigpa archive in Lerab Ling. I am especially indebted to the late Nyoshul Khenpo Rinpoche and Khamtrul Rinpoche in Dharamsala, whose writings and stories brought Tertön Sogyal's mysticism and yogic perseverance and grit to life.

Another thread I wove into the narrative of *Fearless in Tibet* is the sacred landscape connected to Tertön Sogyal. By traveling with devout monks and nuns and tough nomads to the most remote of power places, I learned how the inner pilgrimage creates a shift in our perception, so that the terrain we travel transforms from a wilderness into a sacred topography in which the mountains and rivers, streams and glaciers, the very pebbles that our feet touch, is part of a mandala. This was where Tertön Sogyal's visionary world unfolded, where protector guardians delivered hidden treasure to him, and where the tertön imbued the environment with profound blessings that are still palpable today despite the political upheaval of the last 60 years.

Tsullo notes in the colophon to his biography that it is nearly impossible to write about Tertön Sogyal's life because it is beyond any conceptual framework. Tsullo should know—the accomplished scholar-practitioner lived and studied with Tertön Sogyal for more than 15 years. But Tsullo also reminds us that Tertön Sogyal's life is a story that needs to be told. I carried this paradox with me while writing *Fearless in Tibet*. I know that who Tertön Sogyal is, is ultimately beyond words. The ultimate guru cannot be described, only realized. Inevitably, though, to write Tertön Sogyal's story, I had to position him against the turbulent sociopolitical backdrop, place him in a linear historical sequence, and show his apparent challenges and frustrations. Despite this, I pray that the reader still comes to know the Tertön Sogyal who is beyond concepts, to see the nonabiding mystic, and to glimpse the yogi who is deathless. For any shortcomings in *Fearless in Tibet*, especially if I have created any reified views of Tertön Sogyal, I take complete responsibility, and I ask forgiveness from the masters and lineage holders, from you the reader, and especially from guardians of Tertön Sogyal's precious teachings.

On my last research trip in 2008, I went to the sparsely populated nomadic region in Golok, to the remote valley of Nyagar, to visit the site where Tertön Sogyal passed away. A three-story-high conical-shaped stupa had just been erected in the tertön's memory; I wrote about this in my first book, *In the Shadow of the Buddha* (2011). The stupa had been filled with hundreds of volumes of sacred scriptures draped in brocade; statues of Buddha, Padmasambhava, and Vajrakilaya; mantra-infused medicines; and fragrant juniper powder. I carried with me the last items to place inside—a collection of sacred relics that I had collected from His Holiness the Dalai Lama, Sogyal Rinpoche, Khamtrul Rinpoche, Khenpo Namdrol Rinpoche, and other masters. After the silk-wrapped bundle was set inside the heart-center of the stupa, I closed a stone door, sealing in the blessings so that they might emanate outward for generations to come. Before climbing down the ladder, I placed a wooden sign by the portal, engraved with the name that Sogyal Rinpoche had bestowed upon the site: *The Enlightenment Stupa of Tertön Sogyal, Lerab Lingpa, Victorious in All Directions.*

In some ways, that was the last step in my decade-long pilgrimage; it was not unlike the way writing this book has concluded a long-held aspiration of mine to tell the life story of Tertön Sogyal. Yet, in following in the footsteps of the master—whether retracing his steps on foot or on the page—we return to the place we were before the journey began, to where the master has been pointing us all along. It is that space of innate wakefulness that is our potential for awakening, where we pray, in the words of Tertön Sogyal's aspiration nearly a century ago: "May I realize directly, here and now, the face of the ultimate guru, my very own nature of mind."

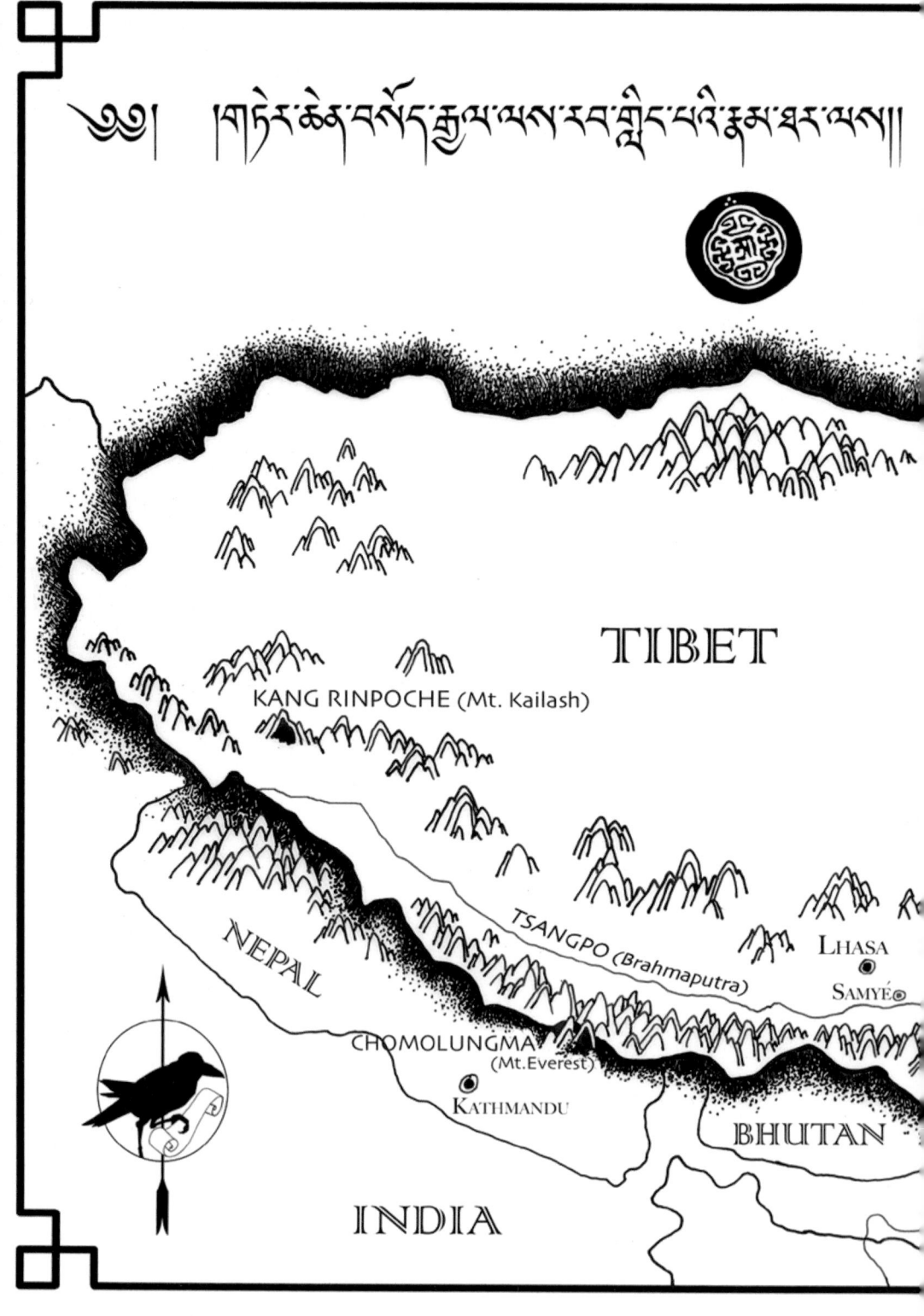

# PREFACE

In the mid-19th century, the life of a horse-riding bandit in the eastern Tibetan region of Kham took a drastic turn that would alter the future of Tibetan Buddhism. After the young man rejected his father's demands to lead a life that was harming others, he placed his trust in wise hermits and learned monks who nurtured his spiritual development in remote caves and sacred temples. As his mind turned away from worldly pursuits and toward the Buddha's instructions on how to develop boundless compassion and recognize one's inherent enlightened potential, he began a series of meditation retreats that would last more than a decade. By perfecting his meditation skills, he realized the most profound Buddhist teachings. And soon a treasure-house of visions and spiritual revelations burst forth from his wisdom mind. He became the tantric yogi par excellence. Eventually, the Thirteenth Dalai Lama asked him to become his guru, and to use his spiritual revelations to defend Tibet. This yogi's name was Tertön Sogyal.

Tertön Sogyal's emergence as a powerful spiritual figure came at a time when geopolitical pressures were pressuring Tibet and threatening the life of the Dalai Lama. Outside powers—British India, the Qing dynasty, and Tsarist Russia—were vying for control of the Buddhist country. Tibet's army in Lhasa, with only muskets and lances, and the decentralized tribes of eastern Tibet, with few rifles, would be no match for foreign militaries. Yet even more dangerous than Tibet's imperial neighbors was the internal strife that Tertön Sogyal witnessed among Tibetan Buddhists and between civil leaders in Lhasa. Religious sectarianism was rife among some influential monasteries and abbots. Cronyism and the use of funds for personal gain were prevalent. The spiritual corrosion was weakening Tibet, making the country ever more vulnerable to attacks by outside forces.

Padmasambhava had predicted that trouble would arise for Tibet at the end of the 19th century. When the Indian guru established Buddhism in Tibet in the 8th century, he had made prophecies about the age of degeneration—*kaliyuga*—when disturbing mental states such as desire, anger, pride, and jealousy would preoccupy the minds of Tibetans and lead to conflict and wars. This degenerative period would bring an overall deterioration in the quality of all things, from the sharp acumen of people to the nutritional content of food. Among the monks and lay tantric practitioners in Tibet, Padmasambhava predicted erosion in the strength of religious vows and precepts—even to the point of contravening the guidance of spiritual teachers. This degeneration, and the self-cherishing attitudes behind it, was the source of Tibet's suffering in the 19th century.

But there were antidotes to this degenerative time that could resuscitate spiritual practitioners and maintain Tibet as a realm where Buddhism could flourish. These antidotes would appear in the form of Padmasambhava's spiritual teachings. He concealed these antidotes as "treasures"—*terma*—in the form of texts describing liturgies, religious practices, and advice, sealing them with the intent that they be revealed when they would be most needed. Padmasambhava presaged future yogis to be *tertöns*, the revealers of his hidden treasures. One after another, the tertöns appeared throughout Tibet's history, becoming a garland of precious adornments for the Buddha Dharma, the teachings of Buddhism. And at the turn of the 20th century, after the passing of two great tertöns and spiritual luminaries in Jamyang Khyentse Wangpo and Jamgön Kongtrul, Tertön Sogyal was considered to be the most significant tertön. This was because the treasures he was revealing were specifically tailored by Padmasambhava to protect the Buddhist teachings, to defend Tibet against foreign invasions, and to guard the life of Tibet's spiritual and political ruler, the Dalai Lama.

Tertön Sogyal's spiritual revelations have a timeless quality and speak directly to the meditator in solitary retreat or to those engaged in the pursuit of positive social change. His teachings are as relevant and as much needed today as when the tertön first revealed them in the highlands of Tibet. And Tertön Sogyal's own life of overcoming seemingly insurmountable obstacles is an inspiring model of how to integrate skillfully the wisdom gleaned from spiritual practice with the compassionate wish to benefit all sentient beings. This is the life of a Tibetan mystic. This is the story of Tertön Sogyal.

# CHAPTER 1

# BORN
## *into a* ROUGH
## REGION

SHIWA VILLAGE, NYARONG, EASTERN TIBET

*Year of the Fire Dragon to the Iron Horse, 1856–1870*

Dargye celebrated the birth of his first son by drinking a few jugs of barley wine with his Nyarong cohorts. Flicking a bit of moonshine in the air, Dargye said, "By the power of Chieftain Amgon, may my boy, born in the Fire Dragon year, bring good fortune to this poor Shiwa Village household."

"Shall we take him to the master Nyala Pema Dündul at the monastery for a blessing and name-giving ceremony?" asked one of his cousins.

"No. I already sent some butter up to that old hermit at Purification Temple. He said the boy should be named Sonam Gyalpo. I don't want Pema Dündul getting any ideas about having my kid chanting away at his place."

Dargye had no intention of allowing his son to follow the Dharma, the teachings of the Buddha. He was counting on the boy to release him from curses that had been set upon him by locals.

"My son Sonam Gyalpo is not gonna be a monk—he's ridin' sidekick with me."

Dargye descended from a financially secure family in Upper Nyarong in Kham; however, he had not lived up to the expectations of his forefathers. Instead, it was rumored around northern Nyarong's pine-filled valleys that before taking Orgyen Drolma as his bride, Dargye rode with a group of bandits known as the Sureshots, who rambled along the north-south trade route of the Nyachu River which flowed the length of the region. Travel along the narrow canyon was slow and dangerous for caravans, making them easy targets for bandits. In a decade of late-night banditry and mule-train ambushes, the Sureshots had made off with considerable gold and silver. In the wake of their attacks, more than a dozen traders and farmers in Nyarong had been killed.

Dargye tried to convince others that he had not been a bandit with the Sureshots, but rather worked for a Chinese tea trader in the city of Chengdu in western China. His meager resources did not reflect years of high-revenue banditry. However, village gossip can make a poor tea trader into a once-profitable bandit or turn the most holy of monks into a charlatan.

"He will be a crack shot, a shrewd trader, and marry a girl from the county town. Sonam Gyalpo will carry on the spirit of our warrior chief Amgon," Dargye boasted.

Amgon was a legendary fighter and the most renowned chieftain in Nyarong, a rugged region where multigenerational blood feuds defined village relations and where scars and wounds marked its borders. Amgon's foes feared him as much as his comrades respected him. Among those he waged brutal battles against was the far-off government in central Tibet. The kingdoms in Derge and Nangchen of eastern Tibet cowered before him, and he even battled Qing military outposts. Finally, in 1863, the Tibetan government felt the Nyarong chieftain had gone too far by attacking and taking hostage the royal court in Derge, including a few incarnate lamas, and controlling the important tea trade routes to central Tibet. In a surprise attack, Tibetan government cavalry set the chieftain's fortress on fire, burning Amgon, his wife and two sons, and his lieutenants to death.

Sonam Gyalpo's youth was spent in Amgon's shadow. Dargye was keen to imbue his son with the chieftain's fierceness. It pained Sonam Gyalpo's mother, Drolma, to hear Dargye's plans for their child because she knew the boy was special. On the night of his conception, Drolma had dreamed of a beautiful celestial woman saying to her, "He shall not be with you for long. Shower him with love while you can." As the ethereal figure faded, bells and other sacred religious objects dissolved into Drolma. She awoke feeling the family had been blessed, but she feared the prediction meant her boy might die as an infant.

When Sonam Gyalpo began speaking as a toddler, he told his mother of memories of his past lives and referred to Padmasambhava, the Indian guru who established Buddhism in Tibet in the 8th century, as his father. Later, when a wandering mendicant with long hair tied atop his head and carrying a trident staff came by their home in search of a meal, a natural devotion rose in Sonam Gyalpo's heart. He asked his mother why Padmasambhava was begging for food. She just smiled and offered the mendicant tea and porridge.

When the mendicant was relaxing after tea, Sonam Gyalpo went up to him and tugged on his woolen cloak.

"What is a buddha?"

"Buddhas work for the benefit of others. Ordinary people work for the benefit of themselves. And just look at the difference between them," he said, quoting the 8th-century Buddhist saint Shantideva.

Sonam Gyalpo was only six years old, but he thought deeply about the mendicant's words. Before he left their home, the wanderer wrote a four-line verse and gave it to Sonam Gyalpo:

> *Commit not a single unwholesome action,*
> *Cultivate a wealth of virtue,*
> *To tame this mind of ours,*
> *This is the teaching of all the buddhas.*

Drolma was surprised that Sonam Gyalpo could read the verse. Dargye had prohibited their boy from learning to read, fearing it would lead him toward a religious life. Unbeknownst to his parents, Sonam Gyalpo had asked a local hermit to teach him the alphabet. The hermit taught Sonam Gyalpo from discarded prayer book pages that villagers had placed high in mountain grottoes for disposal, believing that blessings flowed out of the texts as they disintegrated into the soil. Sonam Gyalpo took advantage of these pages, decaying on the mountainside though they were, to learn to read and write. He also meditated upon verses found in the pages and contemplated them while moving sheep and yaks to pasture.

One day the great meditator and most renowned of all Nyarong lamas, Nyala Pema Dündul, passed Shiwa village. Drolma invited the respected yogi into the family's sitting room to rest. Butter tea was served, and after Pema Dündul offered a brief blessing, he drank it without speaking. Silence always made Dargye feel uncomfortable. The calm was broken when Sonam Gyalpo bounded into the room chasing a kitten.

"Hey, don't I know you?" Sonam Gyalpo blurted out.

A glowing grin spread across the master's face, like a grandfather seeing his grandchild for the first time.

"Don't you speak like that!" Drolma scolded Sonam Gyalpo. "Offer your respect to the master."

Sonam Gyalpo bowed to Pema Dündul, and when he stood straight, they looked at each other like dear friends who had not seen each other in decades. Pema Dündul saw not only a child before him but simultaneously observed Sonam Gyalpo's previous life as Prajapati Gotami, the aunt of Shakyamuni Buddha and the founder of the order of nuns, as well as his lives as past saints in Tibet and India. And Pema Dündul remembered studying together with Sonam Gyalpo in a previous life when they were both disciples of Padmasambhava. He basked in the reunion with a spiritual brother.

Sonam Gyalpo ran out of the room, following Drolma into the kitchen.

"You should know that Padmasambhava has a mission for the boy to fulfill," the master said to Dargye. "He will be of great benefit to Buddhism and to many beings."

Dargye just stared at Pema Dündul, who continued, "I suspect it will be difficult for you to make Sonam Gyalpo follow your wishes."

Dargye did not want to believe what he was hearing. If Sonam Gyalpo was sent to study the Dharma, there would be fewer hands to tend the fields and animals.

"I think it is time you go, old lama. I have to bring the yaks down the mountain."

"Although you will not let your son go with me now, in the near future I will become his guru, so what are you waiting for?"

Dargye vowed never to tell Drolma what Pema Dündul had said; instead, he tried to forget the conversation as if it were a bad dream.

# CHAPTER 2

# PADMASAMBHAVA *and* DORJE DUDJOM

CENTRAL TIBET

*Year of the Iron Tiger to the Wood Monkey, 810–864*

The Great Guru Padmasambhava had prophesied Sonam Gyalpo's birth and spiritual training. The ancient scripture *Mirror of Astonishing Manifestations* states that the 8th-century tantric master Dorje Dudjom of the Nanam clan would be reborn as Sogyal—a contraction of Sonam Gyalpo—the treasure revealer.

> *An emanation of the tantric adept Dorje Dudjom*
> *Will come in upper Nyarong region of Kham [eastern Tibet],*
> *On the right side of a great river in front of a triple-peaked snow mountain,*
> *The treasure revealer Sogyal, he of fearless conduct,*
> *Will be born in the Dragon Year and*
> *Will abide on the greatly secret, unsurpassed path [of the Vajrayana].*

Dorje Dudjom played a critical role in establishing Buddhism in Tibet. He was a minister for King Trisong Detsen at a time when Tibet's military power was at its apex. Trisong Detsen had forged alliances with many Tibetan tribal leaders, expanding both territorial and martial influence. With the world's fiercest horsemen, Tibet's cavalry overran China's capital of Xian, conquered Arab armies in northern Persia, defeated Turks in East Turkestan, and left behind victory pillars as far south as Bodhgaya in the current-day Indian state of Bihar.

During this time, King Trisong Detsen attempted to bring Buddhism to the Tibetans. Even though Tibet's tribal confederacy vowed political allegiance to the king, headstrong chieftains, strong-willed nomads, tenacious traders, and indigenous shamans resisted any new religion. Previous kings had built Buddhist temples but were unable to successfully establish the study and practice of the Dharma. This failure was largely due to resistance from Tibetans themselves, whose spiritual loyalty rested with the spirits and animistic gods of the mountains, valleys, and lakes.

When Trisong Detsen endeavored to create a monastic order and build the first Buddhist monastery, shamans commanded malevolent spirits to destroy at night any construction accomplished during the day. They used incantations and curses to cause droughts, floods, famine, and disease. The king beseeched the venerable Bengali abbot Shantarakshita, who was in Tibet on imperial patronage, "Do I not have enough merit to accomplish this task? Are your blessings not strong enough?"

The abbot replied, "It is not that the king doesn't have sufficient merit or that my blessings are not strong enough. Our way is peaceful, and the vicious Tibetan gods and demons can't be subdued peacefully. They must be subdued wrathfully."

Shantarakshita advised Trisong Detsen to search for a tantric master known as Guru Padmasambhava to come to the ruler's aid. Padmasambhava's life was one of miracles and yogic feats. He was born in Oddiyana, in the Swat Valley on the present-day

Nanam Dorje Dudjom was a close disciple of
Padmasambhava and a previous incarnation of Tertön Sogyal.

Pakistan-Afghanistan border, and at a young age he began esoteric apprenticeships with the most renowned spiritual adepts of his day. Enduring great hardships, he traveled the breadth of the Indian subcontinent to meet tantric masters and study under their tutelage. Padmasambhava also received empowerments and teachings in visions. When asked about his genealogy, Padmasambhava responded:

> *My father is the pure awareness of rigpa, Samantabhadra,*
> *My mother, the space of all things, Samantabhadri,*
> *My line, the indivisibility of awareness and space,*
> *My name, the glorious Lotus Born,*
> *My homeland, the unborn basic space of phenomena,*
> *My sustenance, consuming dualistic thoughts,*
> *My destiny, to accomplish the actions of the buddhas of the*
>     *past, present, and future.*

In the *Tantra of the Perfect Embodiment of the Unexcelled Nature*, Shakyamuni Buddha himself stated, "Eight years after I pass into nirvana, I will reappear in the country of Oddiyana bearing the name Padmasambhava. I will become lord of the teachings of Secret Mantra."

King Trisong Detsen dispatched seven envoys with offerings of gold and silk across the Himalayas to invite Padmasambhava to Tibet. Dorje Dudjom—Sonam Gyalpo's previous incarnation—led that group. Padmasambhava knew of the mission through his clairvoyance and met them on the border between Nepal and Tibet. As soon as they entered Tibet, elemental forces and spirits rose up to contest Padmasambhava's bringing the Buddhist doctrine to Tibet. Undaunted, the Indian guru took up the battle.

Padmasambhava and Shakyamuni Buddha both represent the immutable state of awakening, buddhahood, but the methods they taught differed. The historical Buddha is known for his teachings on disciplined behavior, abiding peacefully in meditation, and philosophical inquiry into the nature of reality. The Buddha's gradual approach articulated in the sutras cultivates renunciation and compassion as antidotes to the negative states of mind such as anger and aggression.

Guru Padmasambhava was more of a tough-love teacher who offered the powerful methods of Secret Mantra Vajrayana—*tantra*—to dispel obstacles on the path to awakening. The Great Guru's life and teachings demonstrate how tantric yogis' paths can transform all experiences of thoughts, words, and actions into the path to enlightenment. This is not accomplished by rejecting seemingly negative situations or suppressing unpleasant emotions; rather, through the wisdom of tantra, any and all situations in life can be transformed into spiritual insights. The path of Vajrayana does not reject anything, but instead, through purification of the yogi's mind and karma, it transforms the perception of reality and uses experience as fuel for spiritual progress. All experiences, "good" and "bad," are brought onto the spiritual path, as symbolized by the legend of the peacock, which consumes poison and transforms it into the magnificent display of its feathers, to become the most majestic of birds in the forest.

Padmasambhava subdued the myriad spirits and other animistic forces opposed to him. Tantric Buddhists do not seek to destroy maliciousness or evil absolutely, but rather to transform and redirect the energy; fierce spirits are subdued to become protectors of the Dharma, or at least assign them to worldly duties to support spiritual practitioners. In the Great Guru's supernatural duels with the spirits, Padmasambhava captured their life-force and gave them a choice: "Be destroyed or vow to support Buddhist practitioners now and in the future." The choice was clear for the weaker spirits. The multitude of spirits and ghosts in the earth, sky, and water pledged allegiance to Padmasambhava, laying the foundation for the dissemination of the Dharma in Tibet and throughout the Himalayas.

Dorje Dudjom served Padmasambhava throughout his time in Tibet, becoming one of his closest disciples. Acting true to his name, Indestructible Subduer of Demons, Dorje Dudjom gained spiritual mastery through tantric rites of the wrathful deity Vajrakilaya. It is said that he was able to slice solid stone with his *phurba* dagger as if rock were warm butter; he could fly with the speed of the wind; and near Samye Monastery he passed through a mountain unhindered. Dorje Dudjom was part of a small group of Padmasambhava's most intimate disciples, including King Trisong Detsen and Padmasambhava's consort, Lady Yeshe Tsogyal. Demonstrating their spiritual accomplishments to the general populace in order to increase their faith in Buddhist teachings, Padmasambhava and his disciples walked in the rays of the sun, brought corpses back to life, and passed through rock walls.

During Padmasambhava's time in Tibet, he hid innumerable caches of treasures, or *termas,* throughout the land. Terma treasures are ritual objects such as statues or golden scrolls upon which mystical syllables were inscribed by dakinis. The scrolls were made of tree bark, cotton, or parchment. Together with Lady Yeshe Tsogyal, Padmasambhava prepared and buried these earth treasures in caves, mountainsides, and lakes, as well as in temple pillars and inside small stone caskets. Padmasambhava also concealed mind treasures—texts, prophecies, and lists of locations of the termas—in the mind-streams of his 25 closest disciples. Padmasambhava identified future incarnations of these 25 disciples as his own representatives, charged with discovering his earth and mind treasures. They would be known as *tertöns*, the treasure revealers.

Termas serve as portals to the profound Dharma because it is through the continual revelation of such treasures, and the Dharma teachings associated with them, that the vitality and life-force of Padmasambhava's teachings are sustained. Padmasambhava had instructions for every situation. Moreover, he used this method of concealment because he recognized that not all of his instructions would be beneficial in the 8th century in Tibet. Padmasambhava determined the time and place for the revelation of every future treasure, as well as the pre-assigned tertön. The Great Guru bound specific spirits to serve as treasure guardians whose duty was to protect the terma until the future treasure revealer arrived for its discovery.

Tibetans are indebted to Padmasambhava for the country's spiritual and political foundation, and for its protection. Padmasambhava departed the land after 56 years among the Tibetans. As the king and other disciples of Padmasambhava accompanied the guru to the border of Nepal, they pleaded with him to stay in Tibet. Padmasambhava declined, invoking what Shakyamuni Buddha had told his disciples before passing into nirvana: "It is the nature of all things that take form to dissolve again. Strive with your whole being to attain perfection." Padmasambhava then gave his testament to the Tibetan people of future generations:

> *Do not forget that life flickers by and then you die.*
> *What meets must part, so do not fight and cause strife.*
> *What is gathered must be abandoned, so do not crave*
>      *intemperately for wealth.*
> *Attachment is bondage, so do not harbor unbridled clinging.*
> *What is born must die, so think of your next life.*

Padmasambhava then mounted a beam of sunlight and uttered these last instructions to the king, Dorje Dudjom, and others:

> *Have you understood this, king and subjects?*
> *If you do not feel sincere faith,*
> *The wisdom of certainty will not dawn.*
> *If the wisdom of certainty does not arise,*
> *You will not realize the master's instruction.*
> *Without realization of the instruction of the master, you*
>      *will not perceive your mind as the buddha.*
> *Practice the master's instruction*
> *With faith, devotion, and reverence.*

Padmasambhava then vanished into space. As light rays of immeasurable loving-kindness cascaded from the sky, the gathering felt blessed and had a deep confidence they could fulfill Padmasambhava's instructions. The envoys of Padmasambhava who were tasked to carry on the Great Guru's instructions were the incarnations of his principal disciples. Some 11 centuries later, it was time for the boy Sonam Gyalpo to revive memories from his previous life and fulfill his mission given to him when he was Dorje Dudjom.

# CHAPTER 3

# SCOLDING *from the* PROTECTRESS

NYARONG AND TROMGE, EASTERN TIBET

*Year of the Iron Sheep, 1871*

When Sonam Gyalpo was strong enough to hold a musket steady, his father taught him how to pack the gunpowder, aim, and reload. Sonam Gyalpo quickly gained a marksman's skill, hitting any target his father set up in the spruce and juniper forests. Yet when Dargye spotted deer or mountain sheep for Sonam Gyalpo to shoot, he would miss the mark.

"Whenever I aim at the pheasant, Father, I only see dakinis in the sights," Sonam Gyalpo said. "They are waving scarves. Sometimes all I see down the barrel of the gun are mantras standing on end."

Dargye spat, shaking his head incredulously.

The dakinis were assisting Sonam Gyalpo, urging him toward his spiritual path.

One day, as they rode past Deer Horn Junction, they could see the temple where the master Nyala Pema Dündul lived.

"Father, let's go see the precious lama."

"There's no time. We gotta get back before sundown."

"Come on, just a quick visit for a blessing. He is our buddha!"

Dargye and Sonam Gyalpo left the horses to graze and walked to the temple that was perched on the side of the mountain. They entered Pema Dündul's room, where he sat in a wooden meditation box no bigger than four feet square. When he was not camping under the stars, he sat in such meditation boxes in an upright posture throughout the day and night.

Pema Dündul invited Sonam Gyalpo to approach. The aging lama pulled a small piece of golden parchment from his prayer book. Dargye spied the leaf-like paper.

"Do you know what this means?" Pema Dündul said, pointing to a foreign script written on the parchment.

"That is the letter for *earth*," Sonam Gyalpo said.

Sonam Gyalpo recognized the letters to be of a script known as *lantsha*, often used to write Sanskrit mantras in Tibet. Dargye wondered how his son was privy to such knowledge. Pema Dündul nodded approvingly, feeling this was an early sign that the boy would develop spiritually to reign supreme throughout the land of Tibet. The lama blessed Sonam Gyalpo, gave him a piece of rock candy, and sent him out the door to retrieve the horses. Then Pema Dündul turned to Dargye to remind him that his son was an incarnate lama and that he should be sent for religious training.

"I'll think about it," Dargye lied, and walked out of the room.

As they were riding home, a small herd of musk deer was feeding in a field near their home. Dargye told Sonam Gyalpo to bag one of the larger bucks. The boy bent down on one knee and took aim.

*Smack!* Sonam Gyalpo's head snapped back.

"Padmasambhava just punched me!" the boy said, dropping his gun and holding his eye.

Dargye shook his head, disgusted.

"Get back on your horse, then."

When they arrived home, Sonam Gyalpo rushed to his friend's house to tell them he had met Pema Dündul and to share the sweets. Dargye sulked in the corner of the smoky kitchen, chewing on a piece of jerky as Drolma made cabbage soup. He told

Drolma of their son's matchlock musket target practice and how Sonam Gyalpo hit any target—any target that was not alive. He took a swig of barley beer.

"He claims to see dakinis and Padmasambhava. Foolish kid."

As Drolma stoked the earthen stove, she hid her pleasure that her son's spiritual capacity was emerging. She had always sensed a special quality in Sonam Gyalpo, though she never mentioned her intuition to her husband. Trying to calm Dargye, Drolma asked what had happened when they visited Kalzang Temple. She hoped that Dargye would not speak ill of Pema Dündul.

"Typical." Dargye smirked. "That old lama said that our boy should go to a monastery. We can't afford that. We need the boy to work the yaks here. Besides, he'll stop seeing those damn dakinis and be a good shot in no time." Dargye still chose not to tell his wife that Pema Dündul had recognized their boy as an incarnate lama and had offered to teach him.

That night Sonam Gyalpo was struck with a high fever. Dargye nursed a jug of homebrew as Drolma left the house to consult a mendicant camping near the Nyachu River. She asked him to perform a divination. Entering a deep state of concentration while repeating a mantra, the mendicant thumbed his prayer beads.

"There is nothing to be done immediately, but once the boy has recovered from the fever, he must be sent to study the Dharma."

The mendicant took out his quill pen and ink and wrote a quotation of the Buddha:

*We are what we think.*
*All that we are arises with our thoughts.*
*With our thoughts we make the world.*
*Speak or act with an impure mind*
*And trouble will follow you,*
*As the wheel follows the ox that draws the cart.*

*We are what we think.*
*All that we are arises with our thoughts.*
*With our thoughts we make the world.*
*Speak or act with a pure mind*

*And happiness will follow you*
*As your shadow, unshakable.*

"Take heed of cause and effect, Mother Drolma," the mendicant said. "Your son is ill because of handling rifles and weapons of violence. Instead, send him to train in the tradition of Padmasambhava." Drolma returned but was afraid to tell Dargye of the mendicant's message.

Sonam Gyalpo yearned to return to Pema Dündul. He wept continuously while recuperating, not because of the physical malady, but because he was disheartened by the future his father was arranging for him. It took more than two months for Sonam Gyalpo to regain his strength.

When he had fully recovered, Dargye announced it was time that Sonam Gyalpo toughen up. Dargye knew a shady character in Tromge village with whom his son could apprentice. He wanted Sonam Gyalpo to spend a season running roughshod away from Nyarong on the Tromthar Plateau. Sonam Gyalpo and his mother dared not disobey Dargye's stubborn directive.

Sonam Gyalpo was comfortable traveling by horseback and sleeping under the stars on the windy plains of Tromthar. Yet, as soon as he met the group, who were nothing more than bandits, Sonam Gyalpo knew that he was on the wrong path. They told Sonam Gyalpo of the loot they would haul in with their mule-train robberies, of yak rustling, of stolen steeds, and of the women they would bed after small-town raids.

*How can I rob, rape, and steal from innocent people and still pray for their well-being?* he thought.

That first night, as he lay near the embers of the campfire, anger toward his father burned inside the boy's heart. Trapped, Sonam Gyalpo finally fell asleep. Early the next morning, Sonam Gyalpo rode with the nine ruffians to take up positions spying down into a narrow canyon; the passage was used by travelers en route to Derge. The leader of the posse insisted that as a rite of passage, the newest among them take the first shot at the next caravan.

"No one is to shoot until I fire," Sonam Gyalpo said reluctantly, scared to defy the leader's orders.

As a caravan wove its way in single file through the canyon, Sonam Gyalpo followed one of the riders with the bead of his rifle sight. Just before he squeezed the trigger, *whack!* Sonam Gyalpo's head whipped back. As he rolled over with blood on his hands, the sound of his rifle crashing into the canyon alerted the caravan, which hightailed it out of sight.

"What the hell are you doing? You've squandered our position, you little runt!" yelled the bandits' leader.

"He just punched me in the face," Sonam Gyalpo shot back, blood running from his nose. "Padmasambhava came out of the barrel of my gun! He said, 'Until now you still haven't awakened your potential for enlightenment! You still behave like this?' And then he punched me!"

The robbers shuddered to think that Padmasambhava was watching their unrighteous behavior. Frightened that the Great Guru might turn his wrath upon them, the group rode back to town. While passing along a ridge, one of the bandits saw an elderly monk-pilgrim in the distance.

"He must have some roasted barley flour, and I'm starving," one of the bandits said while kicking his horse to quicken the pace.

"Maybe he'll have some silver pieces he gathered from Tromge village," another added.

The bandits surrounded the monk with their horses, and their leader told Sonam Gyalpo to dismount. He threw his leg over the saddle horn and jumped to the ground. They waited for Sonam Gyalpo's next move, maybe a demand for money, or perhaps just yanking the monk's satchel. The monk turned a soft gaze toward Sonam Gyalpo and, as a wave of benediction washed over him, Sonam Gyalpo fell to the pilgrim's dusty boots.

"Oh, lama, bless me with your grace."

When the monk lifted his staff above the head of Sonam Gyalpo, two of the bandits drew their swords. He turned his meditative gaze toward the bandits and arrested their thoughts and froze their hands. The monk then grazed the top of Sonam Gyalpo's head with his staff and said:

> *O sublime and precious bodhichitta,*
> *May it arise in those in whom it has not arisen;*
> *May it never decline where it has arisen*
> *But go on increasing, further and further!*

When Sonam Gyalpo stood up, the monk looked at him and said, "May you gain victory over all adverse conditions and obstacles to bring happiness and love to others."

The monk's prayer of *bodhichitta*—to attain complete awakening for the benefit of others—pierced Sonam Gyalpo's heart and held back the other bandits from doing anything that might cause harm. Clutching his walking staff, protected by his power of bodhichitta, the old monk passed through the bandits' enclosure and hobbled into the distance.

The following morning, the group of bandits milled around the general store in Tromge village. A few inspected the gunpowder, yak-hair ropes and harnesses, and Chinese copper cooking pots that hung outside on wood panels, while others tossed their lariats at fence posts. One of the bandits challenged another to a knife-throwing match. The first launched his buck knife blade over handle, hitting a wooden post dead center. The next threw his knife but missed the target. The large blade flew past the post and sliced open the belly of a pregnant mare standing by the hay bales. Sonam Gyalpo ran with others to the injured horse, to find her unborn foal hanging out of her abdomen. Trying to nuzzle and lick her dead foal back to life, the mare strained her neck. As she looked up to the staring eyes of the bandit who threw the knife, the mare's head fell to the ground and she died.

*This is what it means to act selflessly—trying to help another even while dying yourself,* Sonam Gyalpo thought as tears welled in his eyes.

Sonam Gyalpo's days as a bandit were finished. He galloped away and for the next week meandered south to Shiwa, camping along riverbanks. While sitting under the moonlight, Sogyal prayed for those he had harmed. Intense regret for recent deeds pervaded his heart. He vowed to learn methods to cleanse himself of past negative acts and continually give rise to compassion. He thought deeply about how the mare had tended to her lifeless foal even while dying herself, and arrived at a deep conviction that the only reason to live is to help others. It was as Nyala Pema Dündul had once written: "If you can pay meticulous attention to your actions and their effects, adopting virtue and abandoning non-virtue, that is a sign of finding the swift path that ascends the staircase to liberation."

Dargye could not believe his eyes when he saw his son riding back to their home. He had been away less than two months. At supper, Sonam Gyalpo told his parents that he wanted to go and live with Nyala Pema Dündul.

"You stupid boy! You don't know anything. With that lama, you'll find nothing but grass and turnips!"

Dargye scolded his son and said that the next day he must go to hunt for dinner. Dargye was firm that Sonam Gyalpo must not visit Pema Dündul.

Sonam Gyalpo departed early the next morning and headed up the mountain as ordered by his father. Before he left, Drolma gave him yogurt to take for lunch. She patted him good-bye, hoping her boy would return empty-handed with more tales of dancing dakinis blocking his rifle's sights. Maybe then her husband would understand that their son was no ordinary Nyarong yak herder.

Sonam Gyalpo knew every niche of the forests above Shiwa village. He had run up and down the mountains since he was a toddler; by the time he was seven years old, he was directing yaks to open pasture with his slingshot and whistles in Luba Drako Valley. In the summertime, Sonam Gyalpo and his friends ran barefoot through the carpet of flowers in the meadows around Puntse Monastery. Yelling, "Stop!" they dropped to their backs and kicked their legs in the air, giggling and counting the poppies and daisies stuck between their wiggling toes. On this autumn day, however, Sonam Gyalpo hiked up the mountain with a gun slung over his hunched shoulder, feeling not the joy of a teenager but the clutch of his father's will. Storms of emotion raged in his heart and drained him of energy. He did not want to upset his father, but he did not want to kill animals either.

Sonam Gyalpo walked by a pilgrimage site with a long wall of stacked slate with chiseled mantras; orange and green moss covered some of the blessed rock engravings. Mantras are sacred syllables used in Vajrayana to protect the mind of the practitioner from negativity, as well as to invoke a chosen enlightened deity. A hundred years earlier, a hermit advised a herder to devote the rest of his life to the accumulation of virtuous acts by carving mantras on rocks rather than herding and hunting. The herder complained that he would have no food or money if he did not whip his yaks in the fields or shoot a deer or boar now and again. The hermit responded that if the herder followed an authentic spiritual path, he would never need to worry about food in his belly.

"Genuine spiritual practitioners never starve," the hermit assured him.

The hermit told the herder to bring him his stock. Using a juniper branch to sprinkle blessed water on the animals, the hermit wove a red thread into their shaggy coats so all would know that the life of the yaks and goats had been ransomed—the wooly creatures would live out their days on the mountainside instead of dragging plows through barley fields, being milked continuously, or going to slaughter.

"Carve *Om Mani Padme Hum,* the mantra of the Buddha of Compassion, on the slate around here and then stack the *mani* rocks for others to see. It will remind everyone of Buddha's teachings and bless the environment."

If the herder performed these activities with compassion for his animals and carved while visualizing the Buddha of Compassion above his and the animals' heads, the herder was promised that not only sustenance would come his way but a peace of mind he had never known. Since that time, other retired herders had come to carve mantra and scriptures on rocks, adding to the half-mile-long stone prayer wall.

Sonam Gyalpo walked along the massive wall. In between two of the rocks piled above his head he saw a small scroll of golden-colored paper partially sticking out. Standing on tiptoes, he took the paper and unrolled it to see dakini script. Sensing the parchment was some sort of blessing, he opened the silver amulet that hung on his chest and placed the parchment inside among other blessed relics.

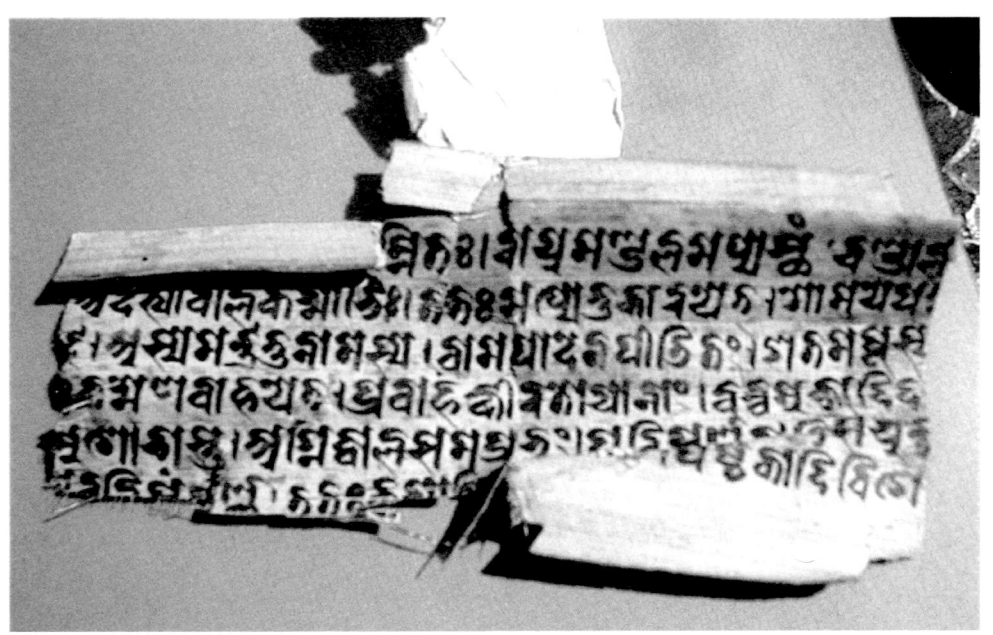

Dakini script on parchment.

Sonam Gyalpo continued trekking through the mountains until he arrived at the small Chakpur Temple. He bowed three times at the entrance and proceeded into the temple, which smelled of wood soaked with the smoke of juniper incense. A half dozen tattered felt robes lay motionless, still warm from the monks who were taking a mid-morning break from their prayers. Slanting beams of sun and the glow of oil lamps illuminated the altar. Sonam Gyalpo gazed at the shrine with statues of Avalokiteshvara, Manjushri, and Vajrapani, representing the enlightened qualities of compassion, wisdom, and power. He wanted to present an offering, but he found only buckshot in his leather satchel. He then remembered the parchment he had taken earlier in the day from the wall of prayer stones. The dakini script carried profound blessings, he knew, but he decided to offer it to the buddhas rather than keep it for himself. Reverently touching the paper to his head, he prayed for the opportunity to study with Nyala Pema Dündul and placed the paper on the shrine.

He grabbed the musket leaning against the outside temple wall as he left, wanting to walk to the master but knowing that his father demanded he hunt. Tears flowed down his cheeks as he wandered alone. When he came to the edge of a cliff, he decided to rest and quickly fell asleep. As soon as he had dozed off, a voice like an ominous echo called for him by name. He felt as though he were falling into a hole with dark clouds enveloping and constricting his arms and legs. Whirling flames vaporized the clouds, and stepping out of the inferno was the most terrifying figure Sonam Gyalpo had ever seen—the wrathful One-Eyed Protectress of Mantras, the guardian of the innermost Dzogchen teachings. As she had once said to Nyala Pema Dündul:

> *I have promised to constantly survey and accompany*
> *The yogis of the Great Perfection [Dzogchen] who have*
> *    manifested*
> *The Natural State of the Primordial Nature.*
> *I am the one who protects the practitioner's entourage*
> *    from defects.*
> *And I protect against obstacles that cause discord.*

The One-Eyed Protectress captured Sonam Gyalpo with the gaze of her single eye. Her single breast hung low, and a lone, menacing fang dripped scarlet blood. Threatening and naked, she stood on a carpet of mold-ridden, half-decayed corpses. Sonam Gyalpo turned his eyes away from the ferocity. Iron mountains shot up all around, imprisoning him.

"My mandate is not to be taken lightly," she proclaimed. "Every treasure teaching has its time, place, and revealer." Sonam Gyalpo had not realized that the parchment scroll he had taken from the stone prayer wall, and then left in the temple, was in fact a map to a treasure teaching hidden in the 8th century by Padmasambhava—and that it was intended for him.

The One-Eyed Protectress grew larger with intimidating wrath, her turquoise-colored disheveled hair blowing in all directions.

"How dare you reject the treasure map I offered to you? I shall devour your heart right now!"

Her fang grew to the size of the universe itself. As the One-Eyed Protectress thrust herself upon Sonam Gyalpo, she sank her fang directly into his heart, nailing him to the mountainside.

Sonam Gyalpo awoke drenched in sweat, looking around for someone, anyone, to help. Each heartbeat caused excruciating pain throughout his body. Stumbling to his feet, he noticed boulders had fallen around him. There, atop one of the boulders, was the same golden scroll that he had discovered earlier and left in the temple. It had once again been delivered to its rightful owner. He clutched the parchment as his own, never wanting to be separated from its blessing. He summoned all of his strength to return to his home, collapsing at the door, unconscious.

Sonam Gyalpo was unable to eat. A constant fever reduced him to skin and bones. Herbal remedies were administered from village healers, and yogis tried to remove the cause of the boy's sickness by performing fire rituals. Nothing worked. Drolma feared this was the end. A village lama suggested that, just as a wounded deer seeks solitude in which to heal, it would be beneficial for Sonam Gyalpo to move to Chopu Hermitage to recuperate. Drolma took her son there, and a monk nursed him. As his condition improved, one morning Sonam Gyalpo had a vision of Padmasambhava teaching him. Thereafter, his condition improved quickly.

When Sonam Gyalpo returned home after a month, Drolma pleaded with Dargye that their son must be allowed to receive spiritual training. She told her husband about the divination she had performed the first time Sonam Gyalpo had fallen ill. The mendicant's divination consisted of the same words that Pema Dündul had told Dargye.

"Our boy is meant to practice the Dharma. We owe it to him, and to the many people he will benefit through being a lama," she pleaded.

Dargye knew he could no longer keep his son bound to a yak herder's future.

# CHAPTER 4

# *The* BUDDHA *from* NYARONG

Nyarong and Derge Regions, Eastern Tibet

*Year of the Water Monkey to the Wood Monkey, 1872–1884*

Sonam Gyalpo scurried up the steep path to Kalzang Temple. He felt released from the shackles of his father's will. His mother followed with the horses, leather saddlebags filled with butter, dried cheese, roasted barley flour, and turnips. These offerings would accompany Drolma's request of Nyala Pema Dündul to direct her son's spiritual path.

Watching her teenage son bound ahead of her, Drolma recalled her dream on the night she conceived Sonam Gyalpo. Now she understood.

"May you be cared for now and in all your lives by our buddha from Nyarong, the accomplished master Pema Dündul," she sang.

They zigzagged their way up the mossy mountain trail to the temple below the massive shiny granite arête, Lhangdrak Peak, towering over the entire valley. Pema Dündul frequented many hermitages and caves during his lifelong wanderings, but it was this peak where he chose to spend nearly a decade in retreat in the Cave of Blazing Expanse of Great Bliss on the mountain's southeast side. He sustained himself during those years on the water that dripped in his shallow cave and the herbs that grew by the entrance. Pema Dündul's austerities mirrored those of the 11th-century Tibetan saint Milarepa. The last years of retreat in his cave, Pema Dündul perfected an alchemical practice whereby he ate only wild rhubarb flowers and berries and eventually subsisted by sucking on pebbles to extract the life essence of the substances through yogic exercises, concentration, and mantra, earning him the nickname "The Rock Eater."

One day in the Iron Monkey year (1860), soon after he had completed nine years of retreat, Pema Dündul was meditating under the cobalt sky near his home village of Khangtseg, which lies below Lhangdrak Peak. Pema Dündul rested his gaze in the space in front of the soaring peak, and soon the sky began to fill with shooting rainbows, one after another. Coils of light sprang in all directions, and a shower of five-colored effervescent spheres of light descended like a spring rain. Scintillating lights continued to arc and swirl as a crash of cymbals and trumpets filled all of Nyarong with hymns of invocation, and a mist of sandalwood fell from the heavens. In a sudden flash, the vision coalesced into a ball of light and dissolved into a grassy knoll below the peak. In the silent wake, Pema Dündul saw thousands of buddhas, enlightened deities, and past saints of India and Tibet dissolve one after another into the hillside.

Pema Dündul wasted no time in securing sponsorship to construct Kalzang Sangye Chöling Temple: Dharma Sanctuary of One Thousand Buddhas of This Fortunate Age on that very spot. He directed the sacred architecture and performed the requisite rituals that accompany temple building. Before digging in the earth, he painted sand mandalas of celestial paradises on the ground, buried in the soil vases filled with medicine and wealth as offerings to the land spirits, and asked for permission from the ruling mountain spirit to build the temple. In exchange for a long-term lease for the entire area from the local spirits, Pema Dündul offered rice wine and burnt food to the spirits, who cannot ingest

A statue of Nyala Pema Dündul at Kalzang Temple.

but can only smell. All rituals were accompanied by a vast array of visualized offerings. For the more unruly animistic forces, he commanded them to support future yogis, and if they dared not heed his directive, they risked being affixed to the monastery's door-jamb for a few painful lifetimes. The few spirits who refused Pema Dündul's presence were rounded up in the space of his meditation and buried nine body lengths underground, sealed in a vault with disassembled muskets, dulled knifes, and broken antlers.

Kalzang Temple, nestled below Lhangdrak Peak, was founded by
Nyala Pema Dündul in 1860 and later became the seat of Tertön Sogyal.

Sonam Gyalpo and Drolma tied their horses at the stable next to Kalzang Temple. Their humble arrival did not hint at the illustrious spiritual horizon toward which Sonam Gyalpo was striding. Had Pema Dündul announced to the Nyarong public that Sonam

Gyalpo was an important reincarnation, the boy would have been ceremonially escorted with incense kilns billowing smoke and long horns blowing to announce his arrival. He would have been placed on a high throne in the temple as villagers and monks prostrated before the boy and offered "the cloth of the gods" silk scarves with folded hands to request him to lead them toward enlightenment. But on this occasion there was no such welcome. Mother and son walked across a courtyard where village children played and stray dogs slept in the morning sunlight. Sonam Gyalpo knew he had arrived at his refuge, in the embrace of a buddha, in the care of Nyala Pema Dündul.

"It has taken only a short time in this life for you to sever the ties to worldly concerns," Pema Dündul said to his spiritual son, who would now be known simply as Sogyal—meaning "King of Merit."

"You shall rekindle the fire of your enlightened potential, and if the auspicious conditions ripen, a treasure-house of teachings buried deep in your mind will burst open like a shattered beehive."

Pema Dündul decided that Sogyal should first study with his heart-son, Lama Sonam Thaye. Theirs was a lineage not of ordained monks living in large monasteries but of lay tantric yogis, untethered by convention, who wandered from hermitage to cave, occasionally stopping in the towns across Tibet. Some lay tantric practitioners lived in the mountains and rambled among the remote sacred sites in Tibet, while others married and raised families, and lived in the village. While monasteries and the vows of an ordained life, such as celibacy and avoiding intoxicants, provide a protective container from the allure of worldly life's distractions, yogis like Pema Dündul and Sonam Thaye were not bound to imposed hierarchy, nor did they try to avoid provocative situations. Theirs was a river-like yoga, sustaining nonconceptual awareness, whether in meditation, during household duties, or while conducting village ceremonies. The yogi's awareness, like a mirror, allows whatever object that may present itself to appear perfectly just as it is, without attachment or aversion arising. Sights, smells, sounds, feelings, and emotions can appear without the yogis becoming particularly flustered or flattered; rather, they rest in the awareness of whatever arises.

Pema Dündul was on the move most of his life except when he was in retreat. His itinerant lifestyle reflected the Buddha's teachings on impermanence, setting up temporary encampments and then moving on before any routine could be established, habits formed, or attachment to places arose. He and his students were a hard-nosed lot, living close to the earth, cloaked in clouds, sustained by the elixir of meditation. Pema Dündul's demeanor was a manifestation of his beatific realizations; worldly pleasures held no lure. Wherever he went, white-robed, long-haired hermits and meditators gathered around him like bees following the bloom of mountain flowers. Yogis sat in the meadows, outside cliffside caves, or in large nomad tents and listened to Pema Dündul's teachings on the methods to unveil their buddha nature. Pema Dündul often sang spontaneous songs of realization and recited poems. His words were like a chisel at his students' solidified self-centeredness.

> *Whether the darkness of delusion has been eliminated*
> *Is clear whenever we lie down to sleep at night.*
>
> *Whether the flames of anger have been extinguished*
> *Is clear whenever we're struck by words of abuse.*
>
> *Whether the mountain of arrogance has been leveled*
> *Is clear whenever those of lesser learning honor us.*
>
> *Whether the lake of desire has dried up and disappeared*
> *Is clear whenever we spend time with a beautiful girl.*
>
> *Whether the tornado of envy has been brought to an end*
> *Is clear whenever our rivals gain the upper hand.*
>
> *Whether the tight knot of stinginess has been loosened*
> *Is clear whenever we gain some material wealth.*

*Whether the flower of discipline has blossomed*
*Is clear whenever we're in the midst of common folk.*

*Whether we have donned the armor of patience*
*Is clear whenever adversity suddenly strikes.*

*Whether the steed of diligence has developed to its finest*
*Is clear whenever we set about accomplishing some virtu-*
*    ous deed.*

*Whether the fortress of meditation has been secured*
*Is clear whenever serious illness befalls us.*

*And whether the sword of wisdom has been sharpened*
*Is clear whenever the destructive emotions arise and*
*    unfold.*

Nyala Pema Dündul told Sogyal to seek out Lama Sonam Thaye at a remote encampment in Drikok and to be as courageous as a lion, to pay no attention to any difficulties or bad news but, rather, "Diligently apply every instruction that Sonam Thaye gives you!"

The old teacher touched his forehead to Sogyal's and transferred his blessing and realization to him. Even at his young age, Sogyal knew that Pema Dündul's loving-kindness was so expansive that geographical distance mattered little. He waved to his mother, Drolma, as he rode away from Kalzang. She would not see him again for more than a decade.

Sogyal followed the Nyachu River north and then veered west to cross the canyons leading toward Drikok. He had never been in this area before, so when he came upon a group of hunters he asked for directions. The hunters knew Dargye and thought Sogyal was running away from home, so they did not want to tell him the route.

"You have to help me get to Drikok encampment."

"Drikok is west, over that mountain pass of Ase Tu—but people die up there. Lose their way. Freeze solid!" one of the hunters said, pointing to a saddle between two snow peaks.

"In any case, I'm shit-scared of Dargye and don't want any part of his kid running away. You'll have to get on by yourself."

Sogyal continued alone through wilderness and over the snowy passes where only the snow leopards dwelled, just like past saints who sought out abodes where others feared. For such saints who practice the pure spiritual path, assistance will always arise. Dakinis and local protectors appeared and led him to wild berries and mushrooms for sustenance and helped him pass through hazardous terrain, showing him the path to Sonam Thaye's encampment at Drikok.

Sogyal trusted that Lama Sonam Thaye's teachings would be the pillar upon which his meditation practice would be established. He bowed at the yogi's feet and requested to become his disciple. Sonam Thaye accepted and directed his new student into strict retreat to study and contemplate the fundamentals of the spiritual path. Sogyal began each of his meditation sessions with recitations from the liturgy of *The Vajra Heart Essence of the Luminous Expanse,* praying to the lineage teachers:

> *Grant your blessing so that my mind may turn toward the Dharma.*
> *Grant your blessing so that Dharma may progress along the path.*
> *Grant your blessing so that the path may clarify confusion.*
> *Grant your blessing so that confusion may dawn as wisdom.*

Sogyal contemplated the preciousness of the opportunity he possessed, and then, to fuel his resolve to diligently apply his teacher's instructions, he thought:

> *This illusory body that was born has the nature of death.*

*The movement of life of this individual is like a waterfall.*
*There are no positive or negative circumstances that*
*haven't led to death,*
*Therefore I shall cultivate meditative stability at this*
*very moment!*

After a series of visualizations with the recitations of various mantras, Sogyal prayed:

*Glorious root guru, constantly dwelling inseparable from*
*me,*
*In the center of my heart on a lotus flower,*
*Care for me with your great kindness*
*And grant me the spiritual attainments of body, speech,*
*and mind.*

With unwavering perseverance, Sogyal sat in meditation sessions month after month. In his simple hut on windswept plains and in limestone mountain caves, he discarded attachment to worldly pleasures and applied techniques to destroy his habitual patterns of self-cherishing. He followed his guru's instructions and meditated before the sun rose, throughout the day, and into the night. Such spiritual training under Sonam Thaye had been prophesied by Padmasambhava, when the Great Guru told Nanam Dorje Dudjom how he would practice the Dharma in his future incarnation as Sogyal at Drikok.

You will place no importance on home, friends, food, clothing or wealth. You will only engage in spiritual pursuits and will not hold on to the mistaken view that anything is permanent. You will not follow desires, because you will not have strong attachments. You will not try to flatter anyone with praise, nor will you retaliate impulsively against those who try to harm you—so you won't have shifty so-called friends nor will you have spiteful enemies. You will abandon negative thoughts as though they were poison and only cherish the path that leads to liberation.

While practicing the bodhisattva vehicle and the higher tantras, you will never transgress a vow; you will work only for the benefit of others. Whatever you do for others, you will not have any pride, nor will you do something in the hope for praise in return. Seeing all phenomena as the non-dual display of awareness, the activities of your body, speech and mind will be infused with bodhichitta. Seizing the stronghold of the most profound Dharma, your wisdom will shine in all directions like the rays of the sun.

The encampment at Drikok had been blessed over the centuries by many hermit meditators and tantric practitioners. Sogyal found not only a guru in Sonam Thaye at Drikok but also a community of practitioners who shared the same intention. Sogyal was another jewel in a garland of gems of yogis who stayed for long durations of retreat. As Pema Dündul had said to Sogyal, "At Drikok you will not feel you have to please the rich and famous nor will there be anyone thinking the newcomers should be bullied."

Sogyal quickly became known for accepting comfort and discomfort, and happiness and suffering, with the same stable state of mind. He did not look for the faults in those who were devoid of mindfulness and awareness, nor did he needlessly dwell in the busyness of being hopeful or fearful for anything in the future. By contemplating how his ultimate contentment was dependent on alleviating the suffering of all sentient beings, he began to genuinely regard others' well-being as more important than his own. Though he had little material wealth, as a sign of true renunciation, he adorned himself with inner contentment. Sogyal would later say, "Your material wealth will be matched by obstacles. However much you increase your riches, your downfalls and non-virtue will follow. However much you work to increase your assets, you will receive in equal amount others' scorn and evil eye. Even if you are spared such negativity in this life, your family and children will incur ceaseless illness and disturbances. So whatever wealth you accumulate, in order to benefit other beings, present it as an offering to your precious teacher. This will increase your virtue and merit. It is far superior to use wealth for the resolute intention toward enlightenment. Therefore, the constant striving to grow one's savings should be stopped immediately. Unless you have the wealth of the realization of the teachings and holy books to study, nothing else is of value. Give it all away—offer it to your guru."

For the five years he stayed in retreat at Drikok, Sogyal continually had visionary encounters of Nyala Pema Dündul. Pema Dündul bestowed tantric empowerments and meditation instructions upon him. Pema Dündul and Sonam Thaye were leading Sogyal on the path of the secret Vajrayana that involves two stages. The first stage of the tantric path is receiving empowerment, which matures a disciple and initiates him or her into a particular meditation practice. Just as a candle wick gives light when lit, an empowerment awakens the student's enlightened potential. The second stage of the path involves the instruction, the pithy know-how that liberates the disciple.

"When I saw my guru Pema Dündul in visions, whatever he told me and predicted all arose in the script of the dakinis," Sogyal said. Sogyal practiced just as the master had once sung:

> *Emaho!*
> *The View is like the sky*
> *Always afterward what it was before*
> *Forever unmoving and unchanging*
> *And Dzogchen is simply this.*

> *Emaho!*
> *Meditation is like a vast ocean*
> *Fathomless, endless*
> *Nothing to get rid of, nothing to maintain*
> *And Dzogchen is simply this.*

> *Emaho!*
> *Action is like a spear whirled through empty space*
> *Unobstructed in all direction*
> *Anything that arises liberates by itself*
> *And Dzogchen is simply this.*

*Emaho!*
*Fruition is like a great eagle soaring through the sky*
*Naturally no hope, no fear*
*Samsara and nirvana liberated in the ground of being*
*And Dzogchen is simply this.*

During the fourth month of the Water Monkey year (1872), Sogyal was continuing his meditation retreats. Early one morning, he had an unusual vision of Pema Dündul. The elder master appeared as a body of light, seated in meditation posture with his hands in his lap and a single thin cotton shawl draped around him. As if Pema Dündul's body were spiraling into his own heart, the light body dissolved. Sogyal awoke from the dream with a feeling of joy tinged with a sense of loss. A few months passed before Sogyal realized that in his vision he had presciently seen the passing of Pema Dündul. Sogyal was later told about the last days of Pema Dündul and how the master had called for his disciples to assist him in walking to a small tent on the mountainside.

"Be determined and have courage on the spiritual path," Pema Dündul told his students. "Sew up the door of my tent, and do not come near for seven days."

Fierce rainstorms came that evening and continued for a week, interspersed with rainbows. Three minor earthquakes shook the area while the sky was painted with spheres of light. Nomads in the area heard horns and cymbals, and a sweet fragrance filled the air. After a week, as the disciples climbed the hill, they saw a rainbow arc from Pema Dündul's tent all the way to his throne at Kalzang Temple. When they opened the tent door, they looked toward Pema Dündul's meditation carpet and immediately bowed their heads, because all that remained were the master's hair and fingernails in a pile. His body had vanished, dissolved into light. Pema Dündul had attained the supreme realization of a Dzogchen yogi.

The Tibetan medical tantras teach that the process of dying begins when a person's breathing stops and the five elements of the corporeal body—earth, water, fire, air, and space—progressively dissolve into one another. The death process takes anywhere from a few hours to a few days. While the death process of the body is occurring, the consciousness is suspended between death and the next rebirth. During these in-between *bardo* states, the consciousness has different kinds of visionary, auditory, and emotional experiences, which are intense and seemingly real. These visions can disturb the person's consciousness because the physical body, which is held so dear and is the source of so much attachment, is disintegrating. As the death process continues, the sense faculties that engage the world cease to function. When the final stage of death happens, the consciousness departs the corpse and is blown by the karmic wind of delusion into its next rebirth, entering the mother's womb at the time of conception. Where the karmic wind blows the consciousness to be reborn—whether among the blissful gods, demigods, humans, animals, or the extreme suffering of the hell realms—depends on one's previous actions.

The process of death and the in-between states cause great trepidation for someone unfamiliar with their own mind. The consciousness experiences an array of unfamiliar, intense visions, which tend to create fear in the dying person's mind. Accomplished yogis, however, are not perturbed; because they remain in a state of meditation while the body's elements dissolve, they are not overcome with the fear of death. The inner experiences happening at the time of death do not disorient the yogi, who has trained for this moment during life. Such yogis have the power to exert control over death's process as their consciousness departs the body. They are not simply blown into their next existence, but rather consciously direct where they will be reborn. This is how the Dalai Lamas, Dorje Dudjom, and many other meditation masters in India and Tibet have in past centuries reincarnated to continue the work from their previous lives. Reincarnation, the migration of a consciousness into another body, is analogous to the way a flame from a single candle can light another, where the second flame is both the same, yet different, from its source. These masters choose

where they will be reborn. Because the principal purpose of reincarnation is to complete the unfinished work started in a previous
life, reincarnation is a very practical way for bodhisattva yogis to
continue the job. Their job description is straightforward—to bring
about the enlightenment of all sentient beings.

Pema Dündul's realizations surpassed even those who can direct their next rebirth, for he attained a deathless state called "rainbow body." Pema Dündul's consciousness did not depart his body
at death. Instead, through the skill of specific esoteric Dzogchen
meditations, he purified the last cognitive and emotional stains in
his mind. At that point, the five coarse elements of earth, water,
fire, air, and space of Pema Dündul's body dissolved into their
pure subtlest qualities of light: yellow, white, red, green, and blue.
Then, Pema Dündul's wisdom and the lights merged indivisibly;
the union of innate awareness and appearances—the attainment
of buddhahood, the unborn primordial nature of all—leaving behind only hair and nails. Pema Dündul's potential for awakening
was fully actualized.

Enlightenment is possible in this very lifetime; yet the time
of death is uncertain. Pema Dündul's attainment of the rainbow
body motivated Sogyal more than ever to strive to realize the
depths of his teacher's instructions. As Sogyal's resolve and own
meditation deepened, his demeanor and attitude shifted from the
rambunctiously unconventional to the profoundly wise. To some
living at the hermitage, Sogyal appeared like a wide-eyed, crazed
wanderer whose actions seemed erratic, while others saw him as
a serious hermit. None of his cohorts, however, could fathom the
deep catharsis that was happening within Sogyal whereby he was
purifying his mind and heart. Nor did they know that Sogyal was
discovering mystical maps and esoteric keys to hidden treasures.

Sogyal was also beginning his lifelong relationship with the
class of beings known as treasure guardians. When Padmasambhava hid the treasure teachings in the 8th century, he entrusted

them to a class of protector dakinis—treasure guardians—whose sole job was to safeguard the teachings until the revealer they were meant for and the appropriate time coincided. These guardians' personalities, ornery and a bit jealous, was appropriate to the task of serving their role as gatekeepers to the treasure teachings. Padmasambhava most often enlisted local spirits whom he had subjugated to serve as the guardians—these were sometimes embodied as animals—while other guardians remained in the formless realm, invisible to most people. Most took mountains and other places in the Tibetan wilderness as their abodes. Treasure revealers communicated with these guardians in numerous ways, sometimes sweet-talking them and presenting offerings to obtain their help, while at other times the tertön would sternly remind them of their pledge to Padmasambhava and command them to deliver the treasure.

Though the tertön may know of the location of a treasure and the entrusted guardian, many varied causes and conditions need to be present for the revealer to bring forth a treasure either from the earth or from the depths of his mind. There are no guarantees termas will be discovered. When the interdependent factors coalesce auspiciously, a successful treasure revelation is imminent. Should there be a flaw in the circumstances, the treasure revealers will likely be unable to reveal the treasure, postponing Padmasambhava's instruction, sometimes losing the opportunity altogether.

In the first month of the Wood Dog year (1874), Sogyal was reading by a single butter lamp before dawn at Drikok. The winter morning was wrapped in a deep, frozen silence. At Drikok, the countryside mirrored the internal landscape of the yogis—vast and crystal clear. Voiced mantras and prayer accentuated the stillness of the meditators' minds. On this morning, after Sogyal supplicated Padmasambhava with the request, "Come and bless me with your grace," and while he was making prayers to propitiate the local treasure guardian, his room spontaneously filled with white light. The light began waving into colors like the aurora borealis. The scent of sandalwood permeated the room. Sogyal rested for a few moments, utterly awestruck. Then, when he looked toward the shrine, he saw that the offering tray of *torma* cakes made of barley, honey, sugar, yogurt, and butter he had earlier presented was taken and in its place was a dark stone treasure casket the size of his fist. Immense joy arose in his heart as he reached for the treasure casket to inspect, but he did not open it. He remained in meditation for the remainder of the day, with the casket placed before him.

The next day before sunrise, Sogyal was preparing to recite prayers when his normal perception again ceased. The room filled with light and perfume, and from out of the clear light, ethereal dakinis danced around him in celebration. He did not cling to the appearance of light, nor was he distracted by the surging bliss that arose from seeing the dakinis. Rather, Sogyal allowed the vision in front of him to arise and dissolve on its own accord while he remained in a state of equanimity. Sogyal prayed:

> *Hum. Padmasambhava and your hosts of dakinis, arise!*
> *Buddhas of the past, present, and future and the ten direc-*
> *tions, please pay attention.*
> *Most revered wrathful Guru Padmasambhava, please*
> *come from the land of the accomplished ones.*
> *Please think of this place with compassion and come here*
> *now.*
> *Until we gain the heart of enlightenment, please subdue*
> *the obstructers, misleaders, and obstacle makers.*
> *Please bestow supreme and general accomplishments,*
> *and take us from samsara's ocean of suffering.*

Sogyal's mind then merged with the wisdom mind of Padmasambhava, and he remained unaltered in this state until the sunlight entered his room. When he looked again at the stone treasure casket on the shrine, he saw that it had opened by itself, revealing five compartments. Inside each compartment was a rolled golden parchment with dakini script. Like steam rising from a boiling kettle spout, wrathful and peaceful deities began to emanate from the paper and took up their place in the form of a mandala in the space before Sogyal. The script on the golden paper was the key for Sogyal to open a portal in his mind to a teaching from Padmasambhava. Sogyal remembered having been initiated into these wrathful and peaceful mandalas, which were appearing before him, when he was Dorje Dudjom. Sogyal reached for a pen and paper and wrote down liturgies associated with two of the mandalas. He then took the parchment scroll from the north and south compartments and unrolled them to discover they were prophetic guides for two treasure teachings on Vajrakilaya, one entitled *The Most Secret Wrathful Vajrakilaya* and the other *The Razor of the Innermost Essence*. In the future, these guides would lead Sogyal to the location of two Vajrakilaya practices.

A few days later, Sogyal left his retreat at Drikok encampment to join Lama Sonam Thaye and a group of disciples on a pilgrimage to the famed monastic university of Katok Dorje Den, to receive teachings from its throne holders. Sogyal also visited the hermitage Dzahka Sangak Rabten Ling and received instructions from Dza Choktrul Kunzang Namgyal, who became one of his main teachers. He made sure to keep the prophetic guides hidden from others, even from the masters he met. Anticipation grew within Sogyal's mind because one of the prophecies indicated that it was at Katok Monastery where he would discover the teaching of *The Most Secret Wrathful Vajrakilaya*.

One evening at Katok, when nobody else was around, Sogyal entered a room at the monastery for receiving visitors and saw a wooden chair. He knew this was the location of the treasure. From the arm of the chair, Sogyal extracted a small parchment, the key to the teaching of *The Most Secret Wrathful Vajrakilaya*. He unrolled the parchment that had mystical dakini syllables written in the hand of Lady Yeshe Tsogyal.

The scroll's secret script was a mnemonic device that spurred Sogyal's memory of receiving *The Most Secret Wrathful Vajrakilaya* from Padmasambhava and allowed him to reveal it in the present. As if the lock on a treasure chest were clicked open with the turning of a key, the teaching flowed from Sogyal's mind. This is the special method of tertöns, which is a power arising from the wisdom of rigpa merging with memory. He ran back to his room and took

out a pen and began deciphering the meaning of the arcane script.
Words spilled forth from his wisdom mind onto the page.

> *Spontaneously perfect, illusory manifestation, the*
> *"Sixth" Buddha Vajradhara,*
> *And, inseparable from them, the all-embodying Vajrasattva,*
> *Lord of Secrets and the rest—*
> *Gurus of the lineage, to you we pray!*
> *Pema Tötreng Tsal [Padmasambhava], fully empowered*
> *with awareness-creativity,*
> *Yeshe Tsogyal, Blissful Lady of Secrets,*
> *Dorje Dudjom, empowered to practice wrathful action,*
> *and the rest—*
> *Awareness-holders of the phurba, to you we pray!*
> *Glorious lama, embodiment of all the gurus, devas, and*
> *dakinis,*
> *And deities of Vajrakilaya, magical expressions of com-*
> *passion,*
> *Together with the Vajrakilaya guardians, who weigh right*
> *and wrong, and all the treasure keepers—*
> *To all you glorious deities of the mandala, we pray!*
> *On the basis of our bodhichitta commitment to unsur-*
> *passable awakening,*
> *We cultivate the supreme wisdom of the great bliss of*
> *union—*
> *Inspire us, yogis and holders of the lineage of the Great*
> *and Glorious One,*
> *With your blessings: grant us empowerment, strength,*
> *and capacity!*
> *With the wisdom phurba, let us liberate self-clinging into*
> *all-pervading space!*
> *With the phurba of great bliss, let us overcome habitual*
> *patterns in subtle energy and mind!*
> *With the phurba of skillful means, let us transform all*
> *existence into the vajra!*
> *With the phurba of activity, let us steal the life-force of all*
> *who harm the teachings!*
> *In this way, may we gain the most supreme and wondrous*
> *of accomplishments,*

*In their entirety and at this very instant!*
*And, always inseparable from the great and glorious*
  *Heruka [Varjakilaya],*
*May we carry out the activity of spontaneously emptying*
  *samsara from its very depths!*

Sogyal one-pointedly practiced *The Most Secret Wrathful Vajrakilaya* deity yoga for five years, remembering Padmasambhava's instructions from ten centuries previous, and wrote associated esoteric liturgies, rituals, and mantras of the practice. A prophecy associated with the teaching instructed Sogyal, "Don't spread the teaching to others for five years, even if someone approaches you with a request for it." Indeed, Padmasambhava had warned tertöns, "If you divulge the instructions too early, other people will be jealous, covet the teachings, or slander them; so first bring forth the signs of accomplishment in your own *sadhana* practice."

Of the myriad deity yoga practices in Tibetan Buddhism, Vajrakilaya is central to the tantric tradition of Padmasambhava, and it was Sogyal's principal deity. Many deities of the Tibetan Buddhist pantheon are depicted as peaceful: sitting on lotus thrones with flowing silk robes, hands positioned in meditative equipoise, eyes softly cast low or inspiringly open. Such images symbolize a specific type of activity—deities such as Avalokiteshvara, Manjushri, or Tara represent the Buddha's qualities of compassion, unexcelled learning, and the granting of freedom from fear. The lineage of the Dalai Lamas embodies the Buddha of Compassion, Avalokiteshvara, who is often depicted in paintings as having a thousand helpful hands.

Vajrakilaya, on the other hand, is striding out of a raging firestorm, rolling between his hands a three-bladed ritual phurba dagger the size of the universe, grunting terrifying noises, and ornamented and clothed with various skins and animal parts. Vajrakilaya is the epitome of wrathful enlightened activity.

Wrath is differentiated from anger. The intention behind anger is to inflict pain and harm. The purpose of Vajrakilaya's wrath is to decisively remove obstacles on the spiritual path and to purify spiritual pollution, which is why Padmasambhava chose Vajrakilaya as his first instructions to his 25 closest disciples. Wrathful action and violent action may appear similar, but the motivations are diametrically opposite. Manifesting Vajrakilaya's wrathful qualities, practitioners swiftly subjugate obstacles to their inner development and defeat the enemies of compassion by destroying their own self-centered egoism and negativity. Vajrakilaya's principal armament is the phurba dagger, the great weapon of compassion, brandished to destroy demonic and negative forces. There is a particular emphasis in Vajrakilaya practice to cut through and annihilate anger and vengeance. At times when negativity is intense and pervasive, it is necessary for compassion to be accompanied by the power of the phurba.

When Sogyal practiced deity yoga, he utilized mantra, sacred hand and bodily movements, and unwavering concentration to nurture and ultimately unite with awakenend qualities of Vajrakilaya. To unite inseparably with Vajrakilaya meant that Sogyal's mind realized internally the qualities that the deity represents—fierce compassion and enlightened action. It was not as if the qualities of active compassion and wisdom that perceives reality as it is did not exist within Sogyal's being previously, but through deity yoga, such enlightened qualities manifested, just as polishing a diamond brings out the brilliant shine.

# CHAPTER 5

# TRAINING
## *with the* MASTERS

**Derge region, Eastern Tibet**

***Year of the Wood Monkey to the Wood Bird, 1884–1885***

In the autumn of the Wood Monkey year (1884), Sogyal traveled to the fertile Mesho Valley to Dzongsar Tashi Lhatse Monastery to seek out the great master Jamyang Khyentse Wangpo. Sogyal sought out Khyentse because Padmasambhava had prophesied the elder master as custodian for *The Most Secret Wrathful Vajrakilaya*. For every treasure teaching, Padmasambhava specified a holder, or custodian, whose duty was to protect and propagate the study and practice of the discovered teaching. The most important role of the treasure holder was to spread the treasure teachings. In the treasure's prophetic guide, Padmasambhava had written of the importance for Sogyal to find the guardian: "If you hand *The Most Secret Wrathful Vajrakilaya* over to Jamyang Khyentse Wangpo, it will eliminate obstacles and this profound treasure will have great benefit."

Khyentse, along with his close friend and fellow visionary, Jamgön Kongtrul, were inspiring a nonsectarian movement that was reinvigorating Buddhist scholarship across Tibet. The Rime, or ecumenical movement, was a response to the radical changes in the previous century to Tibet's religious environment when different religious traditions—namely, the Kagyu and Gelug schools—competed for political power and financial sponsors. Political and territorial competition were often conflated with doctrinal disputes of a philosophical nature, which created a twisted dynamic, and quarrels fed upon one other. The reformist Gelug school, aided by Mongolian military support, gained political supremacy and exerted its intellectual conformity throughout its vast network of monasteries. The Gelug influence permeated all levels of Tibetan government officials. Intolerance among the Tibetan Buddhist schools toward practices other than their own gained traction during this time, leading to solidified sectarianism. These divisions were most pronounced in central Tibet. It was against this backdrop of sectarianism and hardened divides among Tibetan Buddhists themselves that the Rime movement arose.

Khyentse's and Kongtrul's philosophical scholarship, encyclopedic knowledge, esoteric abilities, and spiritual insights were unmatched in the middle of the 19th century. Such authority was the backbone of their nonsectarian approach to the Dharma. The attitude of Rime honored the thousands of teaching and practice lineages in Tibet instead of proselytizing harmful biases. Rime was not so much a tradition as an attitude. Mingling all the old traditions together did not create it. Rather, Rime cultivated pure perception toward all the teachings of the Buddha, with the recognition that the different traditions are all valid means of bringing about liberation from suffering. While respecting other approaches, Rime adherents almost always follow one lineage as their main practice. As Sogyal came into his own as a treasure revealer, he developed profound spiritual relations with the senior Khyentse and Kongtrul and was himself an example of the Rime approach whereby one embodies fully one's own tradition while respecting the paths of others.

Sogyal's solo arrival at Dzongsar Monastery, two days' ride from Drikok, to see Khyentse Wangpo was unannounced. A group of monks and village boys watched him ride through the dusty town up the hill to the monastery that stretched along a ridge. His Nyarong heritage was visible in the self-assuredness with which he cast a deadpan stare at the locals. Everyone at Dzongsar remembered when, 20 years prior, they had watched most of the monastery burn to the ground by the Nyarong chieftain Amgon. Anyone whose bone-lineage came from Nyarong was suspected of allegiance to Amgon, and Sogyal's tough demeanor did not allay suspicion. As in most parts of Tibet, memories were extremely long here, especially for atrocities. Considering sending the Nyarong yogi back where he came from, three local village boys twisted fist-size rocks into their long sleeves, ready to use as an improvised mace. But nothing came of the ruffians' challenges save a few insulting words hitting Sogyal's back as he turned from the group.

From Dzongsar Monastery's hilltop, Sogyal could see the dirt path leading north toward the holy pilgrimage sites around the Crystal Lotus Cave. To the southwest, barley fields stretched as far as the eye could see. Hundreds of tents were pitched in the fields and along the river below, with horses grazing in the distance. When Khyentse was seeing visitors, the number of tents often swelled to more than a thousand, filled with pilgrims and disciples hoping for a blessing from the great master.

Sogyal was shown into the 64-year-old master's room, which was called the Joyful Grove of Immortal Accomplishment because Khyentse had experienced many visions there. Sogyal's rigid jaw and high forehead framed his leathery cheeks roughened by the wind. He prostrated and offered Khyentse a white scarf and began narrating the revelation of *The Most Secret Wrathful Vajrakilaya*. Watchful for propitious signs, he asked Sogyal about his meditative experiences and dreams after the revelation. Khyentse listened intently. Sogyal also presented the prophetic guides, the golden parchment scroll with Yeshe Tsogyal's dakini script, and the liturgies he had written thus far. Khyentse told Sogyal to return the next day. He needed to assess Sogyal's authenticity.

This would not have been the first time that a so-called tertön approached Khyentse and laid out bags full of rocks and scraps of paper and other possible self-styled treasures and asked him for authentication. Khyentse had seen fraudulent treasure scrolls; fake tertöns had been around Tibet for centuries. It was believed that some such charlatans were the reincarnations of government ministers, who, possessed by demons, had nefarious intentions toward Padmasambhava.

Sogyal returned the following morning. Khyentse, standing head and shoulders over Sogyal, pointed to a tray with various golden treasure scrolls.

"I have compared the script on the golden parchment that you presented to me yesterday with the writing on other scrolls revealed by three authentic tertöns," Khyentse said. "Your treasure scrolls and those from the past are exactly the same in quality and the handwriting of Yeshe Tsogyal is the same. That you are a revealer of Padmasambhava's treasure I can fully attest."

The great lama offered a precious terma rosary to Sogyal, along with blessed relics that he himself had revealed. With Khyentse's authorization, Sogyal was validated as one of Padmasambhava's representatives and a genuine treasure revealer. From that moment, Sogyal took the formal title of tertön. Later, when Tertön Sogyal affixed his seal to treasures he had discovered or prayers he authored, he sometimes signed with other names, including Lerab Lingpa, or the secret name of Trinley Thaye Tsal, meaning "Potential of Boundless Enlightened Activity," given to him by Khyentse.

Tertön Sogyal and Khyentse spoke about their previous incarnations. Khyentse had been King Trisong Detsen, who, in the 8th century, had tasked Dorje Dudjom to escort Padmasambhava. They spoke as if death were a mere changing of clothes. A ritual feast was prepared in Khyentse's quarters to celebrate the occasion. While prayers were being recited, a bejeweled casket spontaneously appeared on the central shrine, delivered by the treasure guardians. Khyentse told his attendant to bring it to him. He placed the casket on top of his own head as a blessing and then held it atop Tertön Sogyal's crown as he said, "Our meeting has not been by chance." At this moment, their minds and hearts mingled as one.

Just like a father would care for his only son, Khyentse gave Tertön Sogyal advice on critical matters, including how to reveal termas from his mind and the earth, finding perfect companions to accompany and inspire him, and the duties of the tertöns to mature their own disciples along the path to realization of the Dzogchen teachings.

"You will soon reach a time when your wealth and renown will increase greatly. At that time, do not follow the manner of the aristocrats. Rather, stay true to your mission."

Before the celebratory feast was concluded, Khyentse told Tertön Sogyal, "To the southwest in the province of Gonjo, in the house of Khangsar, there is a dakini of unparalleled beauty who possesses the qualities of the Queen of Bliss, Yeshe Tsogyal, the spiritual consort of Padmasambhava."

When Khyentse and others advised Tertön Sogyal on dakinis, sometimes they referred to feminine deities, other times to semi-divine female beings that could guide Tertön Sogyal on the spiritual path. Dakinis sometimes manifested to Tertön Sogyal as women possessing special qualities or meditative realizations. Tertön Sogyal would always check the dynamic physical and psychological traits of the dakinis with the descriptions in the tantras and Padmasambhava's prophecies to be certain that they were the proper individuals to assist him and with whom to practice ceremonies.

"When the time is right, venture to Gonjo with this letter," Khyentse said, handing Tertön Sogyal a note with his crimson seal affixed. "Ask the patriarch for the hand of his daughter, Pumo. Should she become your spiritual consort, the door to your storehouse of treasures will be flung wide open."

Khyentse's prophecy about Pumo in Gonjo highlighted one of the most significant factors contributing to a treasure revealer's achievements—connecting with a dakini as a spiritual consort.

Tertön Sogyal understood the great significance of finding Pumo, for wisdom consorts are ideal yogic companions for giving rise to the great bliss conducive to spiritual realization. Such consorts ensure that no obstacles arise in revealing maps to the treasures, and safeguard that the meanings of the teaching are decoded perfectly and completely. Similar to a muse who inspires the wellspring of creativity for an artist or the fire of genius for a writer, a treasure revealer's consort rouses the power and energy required for the discovery and decoding of treasures. While the guru is the source of blessings for the yogi, and the deity is the root of meditative accomplishment, the dakini consort brings the auspicious circumstances that ensure that all the interdependent factors coalesce at the right time in the right place. It is especially through this auspicious link and yogic practice with a consort that the treasures inside the mind of the tertön are unlocked.

Tibetan yogis of Tertön Sogyal's caliber use a specific understanding of the subtlest aspect of their bodies as the basis for their yogic practice with consorts. The human body has an intricate matrix of psychic-physical channels or conduits that feed into and run out of energy centers known as *chakras;* these chakras are located at the regions of the crown, throat, heart, navel, and genitals. Vertically connecting the chakras are meridians through which the body's vital energies flow. Tertön Sogyal practiced yoga to gain control over the flow of the energies, and especially the vital essence within the subtle channels, so as to attain meditative realization and stability. He mastered yogic practices in solitary retreat, including complicated breathing exercises, specific physical postures, and manipulation of energies, for example, by locking the internal energy channels. Outward signs of yogic accomplishment manifested, such as holding his breath for more than ten minutes, or remaining suspended in air while his legs were crossed in a full lotus. Nomads sometimes saw Tertön Sogyal sitting in the frozen landscape of winter in only a cotton shawl, melting snow around him in a ten-foot diameter because of the radiance from his inner-heat practice. Inner signs were evident in that Tertön Sogyal could gather all the energies and *prana* of his body into his central meridian and arrest all thoughts, leaving his unbound awareness to mingle with space. But his ability to abide effortlessly in the direct recognition of nonconceptual wakefulness, whether during the day or during a sleep state, was supreme among his attainments. Never separating from the recognition of his pure nature, Tertön Sogyal mastered his yogic training and attained complete control of his winds, energies, and vital essence.

Signs in Tertön Sogyal's dreams after Khyentse's prophecy did not indicate that he should go immediately to Gonjo to search for the dakini Pumo. Although Tertön Sogyal had been publicly recognized as a treasure revealer, he knew that his study and practice of Dzogchen still needed to be refined. He had long heard of one of the greatest meditators in eastern Tibet, named Nyoshul Lungtok Tenpe Nyima. Tertön Sogyal decided that he must search him out.

Nyoshul Lungtok served and lived with his teacher in Dzachuka, the great Patrul Rinpoche, for 28 years, receiving the quintessential teachings for Dzogchen practice. Patrul Rinpoche was direct and straightforward and known equally for asceticism and supreme erudition. He did not fall into the trend of many scholars who focused on establishing sectarian differences between various philosophical approaches found within Buddhism in Tibet, such as those between the Nyingma and Gelug schools. Often, sectarian scholars' biases and politics overshadowed their years of study. And many monks, when not creating division in monastic communities through gossip, spent their time endlessly debating the intellectual meaning of the words rather than, as Patrul Rinpoche demonstrated, living the meaning of the scriptures. Though a great scholar and master at philosophical debate, Patrul Rinpoche could nonetheless teach in a direct manner when addressing the toughest of nomads of eastern Tibet. On one occasion, when an old nomad from Golok asked him for meditation instructions, Patrul Rinpoche said:

*Don't prolong the past,*
*Don't invite the future,*
*Leave the natural mind, awareness of the present*
*moment,*
*Without modification in its open, relaxed simplicity.*
*There is nothing other than that!*
*Apart from the ordinary mind of the present moment,*
*open and relaxed,*
*There is not a damned thing!*

Though continually requested to give teachings, Patrul Rinpoche often wandered to pilgrimage places and in the mountains to practice meditation alone. Once he journeyed by himself to Katok Monastery. Nobody realized that the great Patrul Rinpoche had arrived, as he acted like an illiterate nomad. He spent his days at Katok circumambulating the reliquaries and monastery and chanting mantras. Local monks and villagers thought he was a simple old man, and he was offered a place to stay in the home of a lama from Gyarong. When asked where he was from, Patrul Rinpoche responded he was a pilgrim from Dzachuka who was seeking blessings from the venerated Katok Monastery.

"Would you like some Dharma teaching?" the Gyarong lama asked.

"Oh, of course. Who does not need to receive teachings?" Patrul Rinpoche said.

"These days there is an amazing book entitled *The Words of My Perfect Teacher* composed by a great lama called Dza Patrul Rinpoche. This will surely benefit you! You are reciting mantra and circumambulating holy sites, but without a bit of Dharma knowledge, the benefit will be limited," the Gyarong lama said with a touch of pride.

"*Ah-zi!*" exclaimed Patrul Rinpoche. "Truly, I need such a teaching. Kindly grant it to me."

The Gyarong lama then explained, chapter by chapter, *The Words of My Perfect Teacher*, the very book that Patrul Rinpoche himself had authored. When they were halfway through the text, Patrul Rinpoche moved next door to the home of an old woman, but he would return during the day to receive teachings.

Patrul Rinpoche helped the woman clean the house and emptied the chamber pots of other family members. One evening while cleaning her shrine, the old woman was praying aloud, "Oh, Patrul Rinpoche, please bless me!"

"Old mother, there are so many saintly lamas from the past and present at Katok Monastery. Why are you always calling out with devotion, 'Patrul Rinpoche, Patrul Rinpoche'? Do you think this Patrul is some sort of especially venerated lama?"

The old woman replied, "Indeed, there is not a greater saint than Patrul Rinpoche these days in Tibet! So many monks practice his teachings and study *The Words of My Perfect Teacher.*" She held her hands in prayer with her eyes closed, with Patrul Rinpoche standing before her.

"If you ask me," Patrul Rinpoche said, "I think he has just a big name. He is probably just an old nomad lama, nothing extraordinarily great or precious at all!"

"How dare you say such a thing!" the old woman retorted. "How can you have such perverted thoughts about Patrul Rinpoche? You simply lack the good fortune to recognize that Patrul Rinpoche is a buddha in person," she scolded.

One day many pilgrims from Dzachuka arrived at Katok Monastery, and being from the same area, they immediately recognized Patrul Rinpoche. "Ohh, our respected lama is here," they said, and bowed to him.

"Until now I have been staying here quite happily, chanting and even receiving teachings!" Patrul Rinpoche said, annoyed that he had been recognized. "Now you will blab that Patrul is here and my tranquillity will end."

Exactly as he had predicted, news spread around Katok Monastery that the great Patrul Rinpoche was present, although nobody could locate him.

In the afternoon, the Gyarong lama came home, where Patrul Rinpoche was waiting for teachings, and said, "Hey, everyone, Patrul Rinpoche has blessed us with his presence at Katok. He is among us!" When the old woman heard the news, she said to Patrul Rinpoche, "Can you imagine, Patrul Rinpoche is actually at the monastery!"

"You don't need to get all worked up like this. What's so special about that Patrul Rinpoche? He is just another village lama! You ought to pray to one of your own gurus from Katok," Patrul Rinpoche told both of them.

"You miserable creature," the old woman yelled while raising her fist. "How dare you say such a thing? Patrul Rinpoche is a buddha in human form; even if the radiant Buddha himself, more precious than gold, came through my door, you would feel no faith. What a wretched fellow you are!"

The next day the gong rang to summon the monks and villagers to the temple for a teaching. Patrul Rinpoche, whose identity the Gyarong lama and the old woman still did not suspect, left the house as usual, presumably to circumambulate the monastery. The old woman and her neighbor donned their best dresses and hurried to the monastery. When they entered the grand hall, sitting on the high throne was none other than Patrul Rinpoche.

The Gyarong lama was so mortified that he left the temple, embarrassed, and departed to his homeland, never to be seen again. The old woman was overwhelmed with shame and prostrated at Patrul Rinpoche's feet, saying, "What bad karma I have accumulated, scolding you, almost beating you. I might be reborn in hell. Please accept my confession!"

"There is nothing wrong," Patrul Rinpoche kindly assured her. "You don't need to confess anything. You have a pure mind, and a good heart is the root of the Dharma, the essence of the teaching that I'm going to give now. That alone will suffice for you."

Among the many disciples of Patrul Rinpoche, Nyoshul Lungtok's conviction and devotion were unmatched. Patrul Rinpoche affectionately referred to Nyoshul Lungtok as his son. In addition to studying profound treatises and meditating upon their meaning, Patrul Rinpoche introduced Nyoshul Lungtok time and again to pure awareness, the nature of mind. But Nyoshul Lungtok kept telling Patrul Rinpoche that he still had not realized fully the nature of mind. One evening, while they were staying at a hermitage a few miles from Dzogchen Monastery, Patrul Rinpoche was lying down on his back, his gaze resting in the vast sky above him, allowing his awareness to expand boundlessly. On this particular evening, the master called for Nyoshul Lungtok. The shadowed mountains surrounded them on all sides except for a narrow valley leading toward Dzogchen Monastery.

"My dear Lungtok, haven't you told me that you don't think you have got the crucial point of Dzogchen meditation? That you still have not realized the nature of mind?" Patrul Rinpoche questioned.

"I have not."

"There is nothing to it, my son."

Patrul Rinpoche told Nyoshul Lungtok to lie down next to him and look upward into the sky.

Then Patrul Rinpoche questioned, "Do you see the vault of the sky?

"Yes."

"Do you hear the dogs barking over at Dzogchen Monastery?"

"Yes."

"Do you hear what I am saying?"

"Yes."

"Well, the nature of the meditation is just like this, simply this."

At that moment, Nyoshul Lungtok's conceptual mind was extinguished. It was as if the entire construct of duality in his mind were a house of cards that came crashing down. The mind that questions, that thinks, that reifies and solidifies—the entire process—collapsed upon itself. Upon that dissolution of conceptual mind, Nyoshul Lungtok's nature of mind, its timeless awareness, effortlessly revealed itself. Nyoshul Lungtok gained total confidence in awareness free from intellectual speculation. The enlightened potential of his primordial mind, his ever-present buddha nature, shined forth like sun rays, dispelling the darkness of ignorance.

Nyoshul Lungtok later said, "Through one's total devotion combined with the blessing of an enlightened master, one can attain instantaneous realization. Practice guru yoga, pray to your lama with ardent devotion, and mingle your mind-stream with the guru's mind. This is the crucial point!"

At the end of Nyoshul Lungtok's nearly three decades of experiential-oriented training with his teacher, Patrul Rinpoche announced publicly, "With respect to the view, Nyoshul Lungtok surpasses me."

When Tertön Sogyal learned of the great Patrul Rinpoche's declaration of Nyoshul Lungtok's realization of wisdom, he knew he needed to study with him. Donning his tattered robes and white shawl, and carrying a few texts, his prayer beads, and a wooden bowl, Tertön Sogyal walked alone for well over a week to Dzongkar Nenang on the Tromthar Plateau, not far from where he had spent his days as a bandit. Tertön Sogyal's poverty protected him from harm as he begged among the very outlaws with whom he used to run. Tertön Sogyal walked with resolute intention, praying:

> *From now until I realize unsurpassed enlightenment,*
> *May I be blessed and cared for by the gurus and dakinis.*
> *And relying on the profound path of the great Mantrayana,*
> *May I and all sentient beings achieve all favorable and*
> *auspicious circumstances.*

Upon arrival at Nyoshul Lungtok's encampment, Tertön Sogyal entered the teacher's quarters and placed the crown of his head at the master's feet. Nyoshul Lungtok has just recited the scriptural verse: "Plant well the victory banner of the Dharma," which indicated that the young tertön would serve an important role in spreading the Buddhist doctrine. That Tertön Sogyal was wearing white and had long hair was taken as a sign that not only would he remain a lay yogi, he would in fact become a precious jewel within that lay tantric community.

If Tertön Sogyal's earlier training from Nyala Pema Dündul and Lama Sonam Thaye had been like daybreak, meeting Nyoshul Lungtok was like the sun actually rising. The teacher wasted no time in imparting instructions from *The Heart Essence of the*

*Vast Expanse.* Nyoshul Lungtok, a pure monk whose vows were unsullied by the slightest impairment, first gave Tertön Sogyal teachings on the four thoughts that turn the mind away from mundane concerns and toward spiritual practice.

> *First, contemplate the preciousness of being free and well*
>   *favored.*
> *This is difficult to gain, easy to lose; now I must do*
>   *something meaningful.*
>
> *Second, the whole world and its inhabitants are imper-*
>   *manent;*
> *In particular, the life of beings is like a bubble.*
> *Death comes without warning; this body will be a corpse.*
> *At that time, the Dharma will be my only help;*
> *I must practice it with exertion.*
>
> *Third, when death comes, I will be helpless.*
> *Because actions bear their inevitable effect,*
> *I must abandon evil deeds*
> *And always devote myself to virtuous actions.*
> *Thinking this every day, I will examine myself.*
>
> *Fourth, attachment to home, friends, wealth, and the*
>   *comforts of samsara*
> *Are the constant torments of the three sufferings,*
> *Just like a feast before the executioner leads you to your*
>   *death.*
> *I must cut desire and attachment and attain enlighten-*
>   *ment through exertion.*

Though Tertön Sogyal had already contemplated these four thoughts for years, he realized even more profoundly how fortunate it was that he had met teachers who could transmit the precious Dzogchen teachings. Inspired by this realization, Tertön Sogyal never lay down but rather meditated throughout the night, contemplating repeatedly the preciousness of his human birth and accepting the inexorability of death, the nature of cause and effect, and that there is no lasting happiness to be found in samsara. Tertön Sogyal's practice during this period was known as "when the day and night continuously meet," for he was never separate from the most profound states of meditation. Just as he had done with the instruction of Nyala Pema Dündul and Lama Sonam Thaye, he did not leave the teachings as words on the page, but rather progressively applied each and every instruction so that it became part of his being.

Tertön Sogyal proceeded through the foundational practices of the Dzogchen training. During this period, he had only one robe and nothing on which to sleep. He lived among the forest animals, sleeping on the ground or flat rocks just as they did. He had no pans with which to cook, so his daily sustenance consisted of roasted barley porridge mixed with crystal water from a nearby spring. He endured these austerities without saying a word to his teacher. When Nyoshul Lungtok became aware of Tertön Sogyal's asceticism, the teacher ordered him to take up residence next to the tent-kitchen.

After Tertön Sogyal completed the foundational practices, he began his uncommon yogic training. Nyoshul Lungtok imparted instructions, section by section, sending Tertön Sogyal away to meditate after each teaching. Nyoshul Lungtok looked for signs when his student returned to report his meditative experiences and dreams, and then he gave the next section attuned to Tertön Sogyal's experience and deepening realization. This experiential-oriented instruction responds to the predisposition of the student in an immediate and character-altering way, just as a wish-fulfilling jewel grants whatever is desired. Nyoshul Lungtok's teaching was not in written form, but rather transmitted by whispering the pith instructions into the student's ear so that it remained uniquely private and profound. Like many of the doctrines taught in Tibet, the transmission that Tertön Sogyal received from Nyoshul Lungtok, who had received it from Patrul Rinpoche, can be traced in an unbroken verbal conveyance of enlightened beings such as

Padmasambhava, the saints of India and Tibet, and indeed back to the time of the Buddha.

Nyoshul Lungtok continued to grant the uncommon Dzogchen teachings to Tertön Sogyal, whereby a yogi develops the spontaneous ability to distinguish precisely between reality and delusion. Through this practice, Tertön Sogyal became intimately conscious of the root cause of his own and others' suffering, which fundamentally is the lack of awareness of the nature of mind. Radical practices are then employed to cut through the ignorance brought on by perpetual clouds of thinking and habitual patterns, to expose vividly the ever-present and all-pervading nature of mind.

Nyoshul Lungtok sent Tertön Sogyal into uninhabited forests where the calls of wild animals echoed throughout the night, and to charnel grounds to meditate where the stench of death was palpable. Sometimes Tertön Sogyal dug a shallow pit into the hillside, creating a low-angle lean-to where he stayed for months, his gaze fixed in the vast sky, merging his awareness with space. With unshakable confidence in the master's instructions, Tertön Sogyal meditated and engaged in yogic practices until exhaustion overwhelmed both body and mind and he collapsed. Then, lying like a corpse, Tertön Sogyal rested in thought-free wakefulness, allowing the clarity of his lucid awareness to meet face-to-face what is present when thinking is not.

Returning to Nyoshul Lungtok to further clarify specific meditational experiences, Tertön Sogyal received even more refined pith instructions. Applying the instruction to his meditation, Tertön Sogyal continued to purify his body and mind, releasing his inner wisdom from the bonds of subtle ignorance of reality. In solitary retreats, he would assume yogic postures and repeat a mantra while visualizing luminous syllables entering into and dissolving all inner and outer phenomena, including his own body. Then, letting go of all recitations and visualizations, he rested in that which remained present, the spacious and luminous primordial nature of mind.

At night Tertön Sogyal did not drift in mindless dreams but rather remained unaltered in pristine awareness, even as his body went to sleep. As images and emotions from his dreams arose in his mind, he was not led astray like an ox with a nose ring, nor did he fear them like a nightmare. The images and feelings in his dreams flowed by as if in a mirage, where Tertön Sogyal was not attached or averse to them but simply vividly aware of the appearances. After practicing this form of dream yoga, the mental repository from where Tertön Sogyal's dreams arose was soon emptied. His awareness was freed from his thoughts, which made no more impression on the mind than the writing in a pool of water with a finger. And what remained when his conceptual mind completely collapsed was a constant flow of pure awareness itself—this was the practice of Dzogchen.

Dzogchen is not only an ancient teaching; it is the state of total awakening, buddhahood itself. To practice Dzogchen is to abide in the recognition of one's primordial nature—and that which recognizes the primordial state is the nature of mind. Though meditation techniques are taught and insights cultivated along the spiritual path, Dzogchen takes the goal of the path as the path itself. Enlightenment is the path, and the path is nothing other than abiding in the natural state. Dzogchen meditation is the recognition, in the present moment, of one's indwelling perfect buddhahood. Buddhahood, or awakening, is not to be sought in any other place than in the nature of one's own mind. Tertön Sogyal recognized through his training with Lungtok, again and again, that he was never actually separate from the primordial state of buddhahood.

In order to recognize one's inherent buddha potential, the student depends upon a realized master's introduction to the nature of mind. When Lungtok introduced Tertön Sogyal to the nature of mind, it was not as if the master gave the disciple anything he did not already possess. Rather, Lungtok simply pointed out nakedly and vividly what had always been present but had not yet been recognized. It is as if the master holds up a mirror of wisdom and says to the student, "Look, this is your true nature. This is who you really are."

Donning the yogic mantle of Padmasambhava under Nyoshul Lungtok, Tertön Sogyal embodied the essence of the yogi's

Dzogchen practice. Padmasambhava was once asked how yogis in the future should behave, and he responded:

> *Listen here, Tibetan yogis endowed with the confidence of view and meditation. The real yogi is your unfabricated innate nature.*
> *"Yogi" means to realize the wisdom of pure awareness. That is how you truly obtain the name yogi.*
> *Be free from ambition in the view; do not indulge in partiality.*
> *Be free from reference point in the meditation; do not indulge in fixating your mind.*
> *Be free from accepting and rejecting in the conduct; do not indulge in clinging to a self.*
> *Be free from abandonment and attainment in the fruition; do not indulge in grasping to things as real.*
> *Be free from limitation in keeping samaya; do not indulge in fraud and pretense.*
> *Be free from bias toward the Buddha Dharma; do not indulge in scholastic sectarianism.*
> *Appearances are delusion; do not indulge in ordinariness.*
> *Food is merely to sustain your life-force; do not grovel for food.*
> *Wealth is illusory; do not indulge in craving.*
> *Clothes are to protect you from cold; do not indulge in opulent fashions.*
> *Equality is nondual; do not indulge in intimate companions.*
> *Be free from preference to country; do not indulge in a homeland.*
> *Make your dwelling an empty cave; do not indulge in monastic life.*
> *Do your practice in solitude; do not indulge in social gatherings.*
> *Be detached and free from clinging; do not indulge in attachment.*
> *Be a self-liberated yogi; do not indulge in charlatanism.*

*I, Padmasambhava, am now taking leave. Whether you live in the present or will appear in the future, Tibetan yogis of future generations, keep this in your hearts.*

Though Tertön Sogyal was engaging in profound Dzogchen practices, he still had to maintain his usual chores, including chopping wood for the fire and hauling pails of water to his teacher's kitchen. One day, Tertön Sogyal returned from the mountainside after a week's retreat on the *Hum*-syllable recitation—a yogic practice that releases the mind of grasping at the external environment, and at thoughts and emotions, as real and independently existing. When Tertön Sogyal attempted to fill the wood-slat pails at the riverside, they could not hold water. The pails appeared perfectly intact upon examination, but still the water would flow right through the sides. Tertön Sogyal was anxious, seeing the smoke from Nyoshul Lungtok's kitchen rising and knowing the cook was waiting to boil water for the master's tea. Nothing that Tertön Sogyal could do kept any water in the pails. Finally, he left, despondent.

Tertön Sogyal walked directly to his teacher's residence and, bowing down, apologized.

"If I can't even carry out a menial task like fetching water for tea, how can I realize the highest Dzogchen teachings?"

"Sogyal, my son, do not be ashamed. This is what happens when one accomplishes the Dzogchen *rushen* practice of the syllable *Hum*," Nyoshul Lungtok said with a broad grin. "It is the sign that you are not investing objects with a false sense of reality."

Later, when Tertön Sogyal reported to Nyoshul Lungtok that he actually shattered a clay pot in the kitchen with the power of his mantra recitation, the teacher replied, "When Mingyur Namkhai Dorje was in training using the *Hum*-syllable, none of the containers in all of Dzogchen Monastery would hold water!"

Tertön Sogyal was purifying his psychophysical constituents through his meditation practice. The knots in the body's subtle channels that tend to become constricted were opening so that the inner prana energy flowed smoothly. Signs of this purification manifested in his ability to see through solid objects and prescience.

One morning, Tertön Sogyal saw in his mind a horseman riding toward the encampment. The horseman was a few hours away and, at one point, dismounted to relieve himself. When he got off his horse, the wooden cup inside his overcoat fell to the ground. The man jumped back onto his horse without seeing the cup and continued riding. When he arrived at Nyoshul Lungtok's tent to pay traditional respects, Tertön Sogyal offered him tea, chuckling, "You'll have to use one of our bowls, as you won't find yours inside your coat!"

"Go on, Sogyal, tell him where he lost it," Nyoshul Lungtok said.

When the nomad returned to where Tertön Sogyal told him, he found the wooden cup.

Studying alongside Tertön Sogyal was Lama Ngakchen. Of Nyoshul Lungtok's many disciples, they became known as his sun and moon students. They first met while studying together with Lama Sonam Thaye and continued their friendship under Nyoshul Lungtok. One of the similar qualities they developed was a mastery over philosophical and scholarly treatises with little or no study. When wise scholars from the surrounding monasteries such as Katok and Palyul met Tertön Sogyal or Lama Ngakchen, they were immediately struck with the erudition of these men who had not engaged in extended academic training. For Dzogchen yogis, who spend their time in retreat and devoutly serving their master, their meditative experience allows wisdom to unfold from within, awakening the luminous clarity of the mind. This incisive clarity can know all aspects of reality, so even yogis who have studied very little can become omniscient because they see reality as it is.

Privately, these cordial yogi brothers would challenge each other by seeing how far they could move their teacup with telekinesis, or how long they could remain suspended in levitation. Though highly accomplished spiritually, Tertön Sogyal and Ngakchen were not beyond mischief. Once, when Nyoshul Lungtok was away at a local monastery, Tertön Sogyal and Ngakchen skipped a meditation session, led their horses down a secluded tree-lined gulch, and rode into town. They heard from a kitchen hand that a group of Chinese travelers was passing through the area. When the two yogis passed by the Chinese camp, there were two girls in the fields picking flowers.

Tertön Sogyal asked his Dharma brother, "If I can magnetize those girls to come here, what will you give me?"

"Whatever you want."

"Well, you know that copper Padmasambhava statue in your tent that you meditate on? How about that?"

"I challenge you," Ngakchen said with a slap on the shoulder.

In a captivating gaze, Tertön Sogyal enticed the Chinese girls to them, hooking them with silent magnetizing mantras emanating from his heart and a majestically slow hand movement. The women walked joyfully toward the two yogis. After flirting briefly with the girls, Tertön Sogyal and Ngakchen were back at the hermitage before Nyoshul Lungtok returned from his ritual duties.

One day Nyoshul Lungtok decided to send Tertön Sogyal on a mission close to Derge in the Tinlung Valley. In this valley there had once lived a wealthy family with large herds that grazed in the meadows above their terraced barley fields, and they had been tormented by a series of severe natural disasters and disease. The family's yaks and sheep were decimated and their crops were ruined. The family members died one by one. One of the daughters had been reborn in the Tinlung Valley as a vicious and harsh witch. The witch was wreaking havoc in the surrounding valleys with her curses, causing even more death and destruction. Villagers had employed a local shaman to duel the witch. This only encouraged her malevolent deeds. Finally, the village leaders went to Nyoshul Lungtok to ask what should be done.

Nyoshul Lungtok summoned Tertön Sogyal. He knew this was an assignment for the confident, and sometimes rowdy, mantra practitioner.

"The people in that valley need someone who can cut through the many dangers, both apparent and unseen. Go there to sort the problem out."

Tertön Sogyal convinced his friend Gyawo to accompany him. They rode until they came upon a large black nomad tent with no signs of habitation, where not even a guard dog barked. Pulling back the entry flap, they found the tent ransacked, with kitchen utensils, sleeping blankets, and a broken stove strewn about. Nine corpses lay amid the destruction. Tertön Sogyal surveyed the massacre and looked into the eyes of one dead girl, whose fear at the time of death was frozen on her young face. It was as if the terror on her face screamed a warning to steer clear of the horrific scene.

"This is precisely why Nyoshul Lungtok sent us here," Tertön Sogyal said quietly to Gyawo. "We must not lose our compassion. Conquer your fear, my friend, and power will rise from within."

They set up camp and boiled water for tea as the sun set. In hushed voices, they spoke about how the violent deaths inside the tent were certainly caused by the witch's curse. The dead would not be left in peace but would be continually tormented, lost in the in-between *bardo* state before their next rebirth. Tertön Sogyal and Gyawo recited prayers into the night's darkness for these nine dead individuals.

A rush of air and a swirling of dust near the tent indicated the arrival of malicious spirits that eat corpses. Gyawo heard his own name being called by the spirits, as if a hundred owls were whispering in his ears.

"Gyawo, Gyawo, you will be next."

Gyawo's heart pounded. A ghostly corpse-eater dressed in rags carrying a hatchet entered the tent. Fearing for his life, Gyawo sped off on his horse without even a saddle.

Tertön Sogyal's equipoise was as stable as a mountain during a storm. He knew that all fear and anxiety come from an untamed mind. Neither the threats of the corpse-eating spirits nor the risk of a witch's curse could shake his stability. The task at hand required him to wrathfully subjugate and destroy fear and its many guises. More spirits loitered around the tent as Tertön Sogyal took refuge in Padmasambhava's teachings, visualized offerings to the Great Guru and lineage masters, and then invoked Vajrakilaya, merging his mind with the wisdom deity: *Om Vajra Kila Kilaya Hum Phat.*

Tertön Sogyal approached one crazed ghoul that was chewing on a bloated corpse and stabbed the spirit with his phurba dagger, dissolving the phantom in an instant, sending its consciousness to a pure realm. The tertön then took a seat on another corpse's bloated belly that was an arm's length from the girl with the fearful expression. Of all the family who died in the tent, only the consciousness of the fearful girl had not departed from her body.

Tertön Sogyal took out his ritual instruments. He remained in thought-free awareness for a few minutes and then from the meditative space that recognizes the dream-like quality of phenomena, Tertön Sogyal manifested himself as Vajrakilaya. He summoned Dharma protectors by blowing an eerie drone from a thighbone trumpet and playing a small hand drum. Visualizing himself with bone ornamentation and clothing made of flesh symbolically reminded Tertön Sogyal of the wrath needed to subjugate demonic forces. *Om Vajra Kila Kilaya Hum Phat.* Using a human thighbone and skull drums in rituals not only gave Tertön Sogyal a tactile connection to mortality but served as an esoteric offering to wrathful deities while scaring away worldly ghosts.

Maintaining the inseparability of primordial awareness and the wrath of Vajrakilaya, Tertön Sogyal recited, "*Hum, Hum, Hum . . .*" while forcing threatening spirits outside the tent. Bansheelike spirits from around the valley had gathered around the perimeter of the tent, shrieking in the night's darkness that the long-haired yogi Tertön Sogyal was the next to die. Then, the witch who had originally set the curse upon the family appeared as nine female spirits with matted hair. These vengeful spirits tried to distract and entice Tertön Sogyal through sexual entrapment. When unsuccessful, they turned into horrific bitches, yapping loudly and tearing at Tertön Sogyal's arms and legs. The commotion raised by the witch and her manifestations only made Tertön Sogyal's flames of compassion blaze higher. Unable to move his attention away from the task at hand, the bitches slowly shrank to the size of thumbnails and then disappeared, bringing to an end the witch and her curses.

Tertön Sogyal continued to recite "*Hum, Hum, Hum . . .*" while visualizing a protective light dome around the girl. Then, he let out an earth-shattering "*Phat!*" that forcibly ejected the girl's consciousness from the corpse, out the fontanel and into a rebirth in a pure celestial realm.

Tertön Sogyal prayed throughout the night, and by the time the morning light stretched across the valley floor, all that remained in the tent were skeletons. Tertön Sogyal dissolved the visualization at the conclusion of the ritual, reminding himself that deity yoga is only a skillful means to accomplish enlightened action. Vajrakilaya is nothing other than a name and form given to the Buddha's activity, enlightened troubleshooting.

> *Now, all forms that appear are the wisdom deities,*
> *All sounds are mantra, all thoughts the wisdom mind of*
>     *Vajrakilaya;*
> *This whole existence is the perfect play of interdependence.*
> *In the confidence of this recognition,*
> *I vow to work always for the benefit of beings.*

After nearly two years, Tertön Sogyal was ready to leave the care of Nyoshul Lungtok. The master called his disciple into his tent. Nyoshul Lungtok was holding an eight-inch phurba dagger. The phurba, made of meteorite, had previously danced on its sharp point in the middle of the shrine while Nyoshul Lungtok was performing a Vajrakilaya ceremony.

"You will reveal profound cycles of Vajrakilaya treasure teachings in the future. Now take this activity phurba; wield it in the world, but do not be of the world," he said, empowering Tertön Sogyal with the blessing of his wisdom mind.

"Use the phurba to destroy the self-cherishing ego and its many guises."

By the time Tertön Sogyal perfected his skill in meditation with Nyoshul Lungtok, he had arrived at a place of deep conviction for his life's mission as a treasure revealer. Tertön Sogyal said, "To revive the Dharma and inspire beings in these degenerate times, Guru Padmasambhava concealed various terma treasures.

Padmasambhava gave prophecies about whom he had blessed to retrieve the treasures. Padmasambhava advised tertöns like me to never, even for a moment, delay in accomplishing the task of revealing the treasures—even at the cost of our life!"

The depth and quality of realizations that emerged from Tertön Sogyal's years of retreat were like those of past masters of India and Tibet. He had recognized that all the Buddhist teachings were ultimately free from contradiction; that the instructions of the guru are the path by which one purifies the mind from the veils of ignorance. He understood that all of the guru's instructions were to be actively applied to one's mind and habits and were not merely for philosophical or intellectual speculation. And because he diligently applied his teacher's pith instructions and swiftly realized the mind of the Buddha, he naturally refrained from deviations on the spiritual path.

Tertön Sogyal's life continued to be led not by his own volition but by Padmasambhava's prophecies and the direction of the Dharma protectors and treasure guardians. He had spent nearly a decade in retreat under his masters—Khyentse Wangpo, Jamgön Kongtrul, Nyoshul Lungtok, Lama Sonam Thaye, and Dza Choktrul—who understood well these prophecies for Tertön Sogyal's life. Padmasambhava had laid out the plans for his life long ago; every move, from whom he should receive teachings, the places where he should practice, the people he should meet, what rituals to conduct, and the eventual treasure discoveries—these were all given in prophecies. One of the principal goals of a Dharma practitioner is to stop yearning for anything in this life; yet that does not imply letting go of diligence, a necessary quality if one is going to strive to accomplish great virtue. Just so, with every terma treasure and prophecy, hidden statue and sacred substance, Tertön Sogyal strove with great effort to reveal them successfully. His days and nights were now spent either finding prophecies and treasures or enacting the prophecies and practicing the treasure teachings themselves.

# CHAPTER 6

# A TREASURE REVEALER'S CAREER UNFOLDS

DERGE REGION, EASTERN TIBET

*Year of the Wood Monkey to the Fire Dog, 1884–1886*

As Tertön Sogyal stayed in the Derge region, spending long stretches of time in retreat and studying with his main teachers Khyentse, Kongtrul, and Nyoshul Lungtok, he began receiving frequent predictions about the future of Tibet and its Dharma practitioners. The ominous messages spoke of an age of degeneration, or *kaliyuga,* when the dark force of harmful emotions such as anger, pride, and jealousy would overcome the minds of Tibetans, leading them to fight among themselves and invite conflict from beyond their borders. And the welfare of Tibet would be especially endangered, Padmasambhava warned, if monks and lay tantric practitioners transgressed their vows and precepts and did not adhere to their gurus' instructions.

Padmasambhava told Tertön Sogyal in one vision that, "those who have achieved the name of 'scholar' will do exactly what is prohibited by the Dharma; there will be sectarianism and this will destroy the Buddha Dharma. Those who have practiced little will call themselves a yogi; they will denigrate others and speak harshly to those who are actually authentic practitioners."

Padmasambhava frequently spoke to Tertön Sogyal about the corruption of *samaya*. Samaya is a set of precepts taken during a tantric initiation—in essence, commitments to live in accordance with the truth, with the Dharma. Samaya is articulated in vows between a guru and disciples, toward the doctrine of the teachings, and among the community of practitioners with whom they have been initiated. Samaya is the spiritual thread woven through a community that secures pure intentions and harmony and propels one's Dharma brothers and sisters toward enlightenment in a single mandala. Tertön Sogyal was acutely aware of the extreme importance of maintaining samaya and the dire consequences when it was broken.

"Beings with perverted aspirations who appear in the community will actually be demons," Padmasambhava said in a vision to Tertön Sogyal. "There will be those who do not hold samaya but will still sit in the empowerments among the community of practitioners. They will continue to carry out ill will."

Jamgön Kongtrul once told Tertön Sogyal, "Various ghosts and in particular the *damsi*, the samaya-breaking demon from the dark side, will possess people. People who have been touched by damsi demons will have some power, some clairvoyance, and will be able to speak partial truths; but theirs is an evil path. Many in the populace will hold them in high regard and even take refuge in those who have been touched by the damsi. These poor Tibetans! They are being deceived!"

Padmasambhava warned that internal strife among Tibetans would render them vulnerable to sickness, famine, and attacks from beyond Tibet's borders "with an arsenal never witnessed before."

But, there was a remedy.

"In order to reverse this trend and to restore positive virtue to Tibet, the termas I have hidden for Tertön Sogyal can be a medicine for this particular degenerate time."

Tertön Sogyal knew that if the tantric practitioners, monks and lamas, and religious benefactors of the Dharma in Tibet lived harmoniously and avoided waging interdenominational battles, then the Dharma would be sustained.

One evening, by candlelight, Tertön Sogyal wrote, "Even someone such as myself, who is such a lowly being—who has been born in last place at the end of the queue of supreme Dharma holders who have had the fortune of being granted the power to reveal the termas of Guru Padmasambhava—if there is any virtue in my accomplishments of the past, present, or future, may this contribute to the longevity of all the traditions' lineage holders, may it cause the Dharma to flourish, and in all my future lives may I be blessed by the gurus and dakinis. With the profound activity of these treasure revelations, I pray I fulfill my own and others' aspirations. *Mangalam.*"

In the eighth month of the Fire Dog year (1886), when Tertön Sogyal was 31 years old, he stayed with Khyentse Wangpo at Dzongsar.

"You have really reached a level where you know all the teachings, sutras, and tantras. There seems to be nothing that is not within the scope of your knowledge. Tell me, how did you come to know all this?" Khyentse asked, knowing that Tertön Sogyal had not studied formally at any of the great monastic universities.

"All I have done was to complete the training in the *nyongtri*—the experiential-oriented instructions of Nyoshul Lungtok. That's all."

When Khyentse heard this, he praised the lineage masters, saying, "That extraordinary nyongtri method can awaken a student's inner wisdom in such a manner that they can become a master of all teachings without even having to study them."

One morning Khyentse called for Tertön Sogyal, and as soon as he walked into the presence of the lama, Khyentse handed him a piece of paper and said, "Write, just write what I'm saying!"

Khyentse then said, "*Mahasukha jnana kaya ya!* Extremely pure, the one of great bliss, immovable throughout the past, present, and future, the ever-enduring body, supreme wrathful lord, I will bestow upon you the method of protection from the fear of birth and death. Samaya!"

Tertön Sogyal wrote quickly as Khyentse continued to speak in the form of prophecy about sacred medicinal pills that Padmasambhava had concealed as a terma substance. He narrated where they were hidden and how, if certain rituals and mantras were accomplished, the sacred pills could be discovered and then multiplied.

When Khyentse finished speaking, Tertön Sogyal asked, "What is this? Did someone else tell you this, or did you just reveal a prophetic guide from your mind?"

"Oh, why try to say this or that about what you just wrote down?" Khyentse responded. "I have just spoken whatever came to mind. But yes, the meaning is flawless. You see, I know where the treasure substances are located. The medicinal pills are a share of treasure that Padmasambhava hid for me to reveal, but I have not been able to find them. The pills, which are named the *Boiling Dew of Nectar* and the *Essential Drop of Immortality,* are substances that, when combined with pith instructions and mantras, can grant liberation to yogis and yoginis."

"What has to be done to retrieve these treasures?"

"Go tomorrow to the Crystal Lotus Cave and try to extract the pills from the cave wall!"

Tertön Sogyal left just after midnight so that he could arrive at the cave by sunrise. He climbed a dozen steps up the side of a rock wall to access the cave entrance. In a space large enough to fit a dozen monks, Tertön Sogyal lit a butter lamp and took a seat on the cold granite floor. After meditating for a short time to gain clarity about where the treasure was placed, Tertön Sogyal withdrew his phurba dagger. As he pointed it toward the wall, a small door opened by itself in the rock; therein lay a square bronze casket. Tertön Sogyal took the casket, replacing it with a small statue he drew from the fold of his gown, and closed the door. He descended from the cave and rushed with the casket to present it to Khyentse. They found the *Essential Drop of Immortality* medicinal pills in the container as well as a yellow dakini scroll about six finger-widths long and two finger-widths wide.

Khyentse handed the scroll to Tertön Sogyal and told him to return to the room where he was staying at the monastery and to decipher the meaning. Later that morning, as Tertön Sogyal was deciphering the dakini script from the scroll, an old monk suddenly appeared in his room and declared, "Sogyal, Khyentse Rinpoche said that you should go and retrieve a terma from White Ah Cave." Then the monk walked out the door. Tertön Sogyal thought the intruder was joking and ignored the directive. The next day, as Tertön Sogyal was reciting morning prayers in his room, the same monk appeared. As Tertön Sogyal thought, *Who might this be again, and where did he come from?* the monk walked out the door in the way that a rainbow fades and disappears.

*Ahh, this is just a spirit trying to trick me,* he thought, and he recited the mantra of Vajrakilaya, *Om Vajra Kila Kilaya Hum Phat . . .* and cast a gaze of a wrathful deity.

Two days later, the same monk appeared.

"Who are you?" Tertön Sogyal yelled.

"I am an attendant of Khyentse Rinpoche."

"No, you are not! I have never seen you around here."

"I normally stay inside. You wouldn't know."

As the monk disappeared through the door, grayish clouds formed in his wake. Tertön Sogyal got up and looked out the window and saw the monk transform into Rahula, the nine-headed protector of the Dzogchen teachings. With his serpent-like lower body, Rahula slid down the steps from Tertön Sogyal's room and across the courtyard. Tertön Sogyal smelled something burning, and a small earthquake shook the buildings at the monastery. One of the monastery's abbots came running down from Khyentse's residence to Tertön Sogyal's room and, out of breath, said, "Now! Now is the time to go to the White Ah Cave!" Tertön Sogyal grabbed his phurba and rushed from the room, jumped on a horse, and rode straight to the cave in a side valley northwest of the monastery. No sooner had he dismounted at the cave's entrance than Rahula slid toward him and handed him a treasure *vajra*, a phurba, and the *Boiling Dew of Nectar* medicinal pills.

Such was the relationship that Tertön Sogyal had with the great Khyentse. It was as if the master were ensuring that the young tertön acquired the necessary esoteric skills and confidence, so that he would be ready when the time arose for his most significant revelations that could protect Tibet and the Dalai Lama.

Some months later, after Khyentse had bestowed a series of empowerments and teachings with Kongtrul and other eminent masters present, Khyentse told Tertön Sogyal to go back once more to the Crystal Cave of Padma to reveal a lock of Yeshe Tsogyal's hair that had been hidden as a treasure. When Tertön Sogyal returned to Khyentse with a small rock casket, it opened spontaneously to reveal a curl of hair and a scroll with dakini writing. Khyentse immediately understood the meaning contained in the scroll, and he bestowed the empowerment and instructions upon Tertön Sogyal.

Tertön Sogyal asked, "When you see dakini script on the scrolls, how do the instructions appear to you? Does each syllable progressively become other words, or do you comprehend all of the dakini syllables together at once?"

Khyentse responded, "How do you think this dakini script represents such vast teachings? In reality, the true meaning in these few syllables arises unmistakably through the power of the tertön's memory, and that elaborates by itself."

Tertön Sogyal could only bow in silent reverence, for it was not only the words that his guru spoke, but it was his presence that was the teaching. In Tertön Sogyal's mind, Khyentse was inseparable from Padmasambhava.

Nearing the end of the Fire Dog year, in Tertön Sogyal's 32nd year, Khyentse bestowed a long series of ripening empowerments and liberating teachings to a gathering of students. After Khyentse had given a commentary on the *Heart Essence of Chetsun* to only a few close disciples, he asked them what other teachings they wished to receive. The group unanimously requested him to give

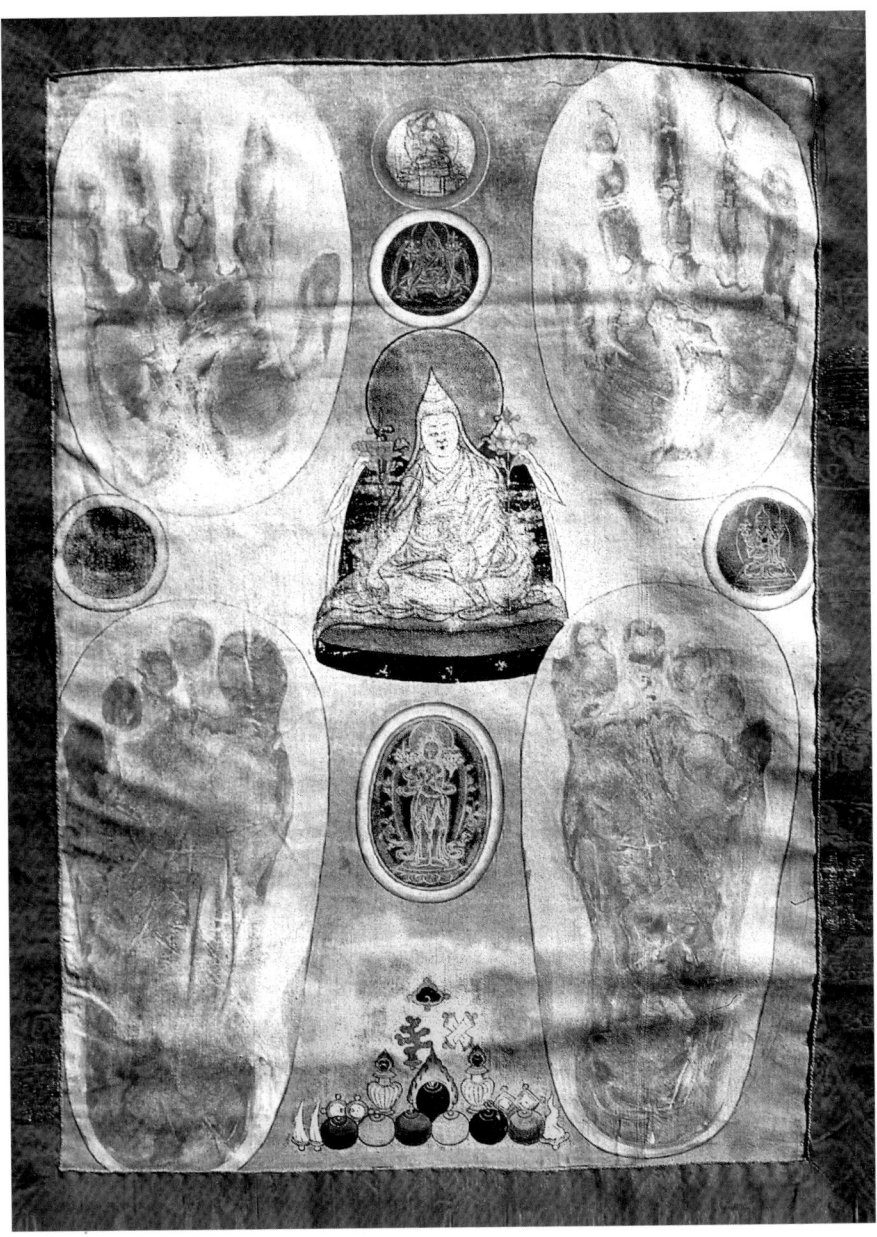

A scroll painting of Jamyang Khyentse Wangpo with his hand- and footprints.

once again the very same teaching they had just received on the *Heart Essence of Chetsun*. Khyentse agreed. After every session, Tertön Sogyal wrote down from memory what had been taught.

At the end of the many days of teachings, Tertön Sogyal presented his notes to Khyentse, who looked at them and commented, "This is exactly what I said, without anything missing or added.

"To this commentary, from time to time you yourself do a consecration ceremony upon the text," Khyentse told Tertön Sogyal. "Then make a final proofreading. In the future, nobody should make any changes."

At the conclusion of the empowerments and transmission, Khyentse told Tertön Sogyal that in order to increase his treasure revelations, the tertön from Nyarong needed to have a long life. Khyentse decided to bestow a longevity ritual upon Tertön Sogyal. Tertön Sogyal was placed on a high throne in front of the congregation of monks and yogis at Dzongsar, and offered symbols of the enlightened body, speech, mind, qualities, and activities. Monks dressed as dakinis, summoning longevity and vitality and banishing obstacles to his life, performed ritual dances around Tertön Sogyal. At the end of the joyful ceremony, a life-size effigy of Tertön Sogyal, which was attired in the tertön's shirt that he had worn for six months, was taken out from the congregation and ritually offered to the harmful spirits as a ransom payment against meddling with the tertön in the future.

"I have spent many months throughout the last years with Tertön Sogyal Lerab Lingpa. Our connection is not a mundane one; rather, it is in the realm of the revelation of treasure teachings. We have understood together how to accomplish all of the outer, inner, and innermost activity," Khyentse said.

"Sogyal has never wavered in his diligence of hearing, contemplating, and meditating upon the long Oral Transmission lineage and the shorter Treasure Transmission lineage of the Nyingma school. There is a saying that when you are near a great being, everything around you will be well and pacified. Just like that, while I was bestowing the innermost cycle of empowerments, and Sogyal was my ritual attendant, it was not as though he did it with half-understanding or pretense; rather, without a trace of fault, he carried out everything to perfection. Not only that, but he also looked after me by making the fire, pouring me tea, cleaning, and doing all kinds of activities. For this

I am immensely grateful. To an old lama like myself, Sogyal has looked upon me as if viewing dust as gold. For me to have had Sogyal as my attendant was like using the finest precious sandalwood staff to stir a fire."

As the great master concluded his speech during the ceremony, Tertön Sogyal remembered that from the first time he met and received teachings from Khyentse to the present moment, he had never, not even for an instant, had a single thought of competition nor felt anything but unconditional love for him.

# CHAPTER 7

# FINDING HIS SPIRITUAL CONSORT

Derge and Gonjo Regions, Eastern Tibet

*Year of the Fire Pig, 1887*

The ripple of Tertön Sogyal's activity was widening as his treasure revelation career unfolded. Each revelation and subsequent practice endowed Tertön Sogyal with additional power to benefit others. As his power increased, so did antagonistic views toward him, including a sense of resentment over the termas he revealed. The ill will that some people directed, like the umbrage of a poisonous tree's shadow, caused Tertön Sogyal to become very sick in the Fire Pig year (1887). Chinese and Tibetan herbs were given to restore his vital energy, which had been disturbed. Esoteric rituals were also employed to avert the harmful situation, attempting to ricochet the negativity back to destroy the malicious attitude that sent it. One of Tertön Sogyal's teachers, Dza Choktrul from Katok, and his elder Dharma brother from northern Nyarong, Tertön Rangrik Dorje of Lumorap, visited him at a village in the Garje region. They came to perform long-life empowerments and ablution rituals and administer medicine to ward off the cause of his sickness. Stricken with illness as he was, Tertön Sogyal took the occasion to meditate deeply on the practice of giving away his own happiness and taking upon himself others' negativities. He contemplated repeatedly the verse, "I offer my joy and happiness to all mother-like sentient beings, and secretly take upon myself all of their harm and suffering." He meditated like this for many days in an attempt to actually remove the suffering of others.

The great Khyentse told Tertön Sogyal two years prior, "When you are about to achieve great accomplishments, intense obstacles will rise up in the Pig year [1887]." Khyentse's long-life ceremony at that time was an antidote to such obstacles. And he had reminded Tertön Sogyal to be aware of others' ill will and jealousy, even among so-called disciples. As Jamgön Kongtrul stated, "These days the merit of disciples is too low for auspices to occur spontaneously, wrong views are rampant, doubts are manifold, disciples treat their guru like a normal friend, and their samaya commitments are ruined. In these times when those who follow and place trust in a guru find fault in everything he does, the arrangement of good auspices is difficult."

With the combination of Khyentse's blessing, the averting rituals from the lamas, and Tertön Sogyal's own purification meditations, his health eventually improved. Villagers were relieved of their worries that the young treasure revealer might die, and it was said that "the moon has escaped Rahula."

When Tertön Sogyal recovered, he went to see Khyentse. Tertön Sogyal told him he had received signs that the time was right to search out his prophesied dakini consort, Pumo of Gonjo. The time had come. If Tertön Sogyal could find that consort, Padmasambhava said, "Your activities will increase, but if you do not meet her or even if you delayed, then your life will be shortened." A prophecy that Tertön Sogyal found at the granite arête known as White Rock Sword stated that there would be a consort who is known as "the one bestowing great bliss," and if he could find her, "You will have power over wealth and prosperity, your life will be prolonged, and you will have power to retrieve many termas." The same prophecy warned that if Tertön Sogyal failed to find her, "You will be poor, decrepit quickly, be unsuccessful, and you won't retrieve your share of treasures."

Khyentse confirmed the signs were correct.

Tertön Sogyal explained to Khyentse a vision he had experienced when he was told, "In the place of Gonjo, born in the Wood Ox year [1865], there will be a daughter from the Khangsar house who will have strong renunciation toward samsara, will be interested only in the Dharma, and will be quick to learn, to read, and to write." In the vision, Tertön Sogyal saw the daughter's parents had secretly attempted to arrange a marriage for her at the age of 16 with a district official.

"I do not want to get married to that old man," the girl said, and withdrew a knife and handed it to her parents, telling them to cut her hair off. "I'll be a nun instead!"

In the vision, Tertön Sogyal saw the girl's parents pleading with her to marry the high-ranking official, but she became like an uncontrollable yak, running throughout the house and around the estate.

"Your clairvoyance is correct. She holds all the auspicious signs of the prophesied consort," Khyentse said. "My root guru's name is Minling Jetsuma Trinley Chödrön. You should give your consort part of her name—Trinley Chödrön." Tertön Sogyal bowed in gratitude for the blessing he would carry to Pumo of Gonjo.

Tertön Sogyal returned to Drikok encampment to speak with Lama Sonam Thaye and Nyoshul Lungtok about the prophecy and to seek their blessing before he ventured off to Gonjo. They gave him protection for the journey and assured him that he was acting in accordance with the wishes of Padmasambhava.

Tertön Sogyal left for Gonjo with a few of his yogi friends on their stout Tibetan ponies. They were traveling southwest across the heart of the "Four Rivers, Six Ranges" where the headwaters of the Salween, Mekong, Yangtze, and Yalong cut between six parallel mountain ranges. Brown bears, wild boar, wolves, and marmots scurried away as the group descended into the deep valleys. They moved with ease on horseback through fields of spiked blue poppies, edelweiss, and golden cobra lilies, and through forests of oak, birch, and scarlet rhododendron. Riding before dawn after consuming a bowl of roasted barley porridge, butter tea, and hardened cheese, they stopped several times a day to brew tea, and while the others were gathering wood, Tertön Sogyal set up a three-rock tripod upon which he balanced his blackened and dented kettle. As the fire was boiling the tea, Tertön Sogyal would sometimes poke one of the rocks with his phurba dagger, whereupon an aperture would appear from which he extracted small treasures—sometimes a small statue of Padmasambhava, or simply a blessed dzi onyx stone. These treasures were not connected to a specific teaching as such, but rather were objects to inspire devoted practitioners. As the yogis passed through mountain hamlets and tent encampments, Tertön Sogyal blessed the locals with these objects, sometimes leaving a treasure relic behind to increase the vitality of the sacred landscape.

The One-Eyed Protectress led Tertön Sogyal and the group across the Drichu River, around the limestone escarpments, and through the densely fir-spruce forested region of Gonjo. She guided them to avoid the fortified *dzongs,* or fortresses, of the local rulers towering above the terraced barley fields. When the group arrived to the Khangsar estate after a week of travel, smelling of oiled leather saddles and campfire smoke, they were feared to be nothing more than a group of bandits.

"How could you possibly ask for our daughter?" the matriarch of the aristocratic Khangsar household asked incredulously on beholding the dust-covered tertön. Tertön Sogyal handed over the letter from Khyentse.

"We can see this letter comes from Master Khyentse, and we have heard stories that you may be a treasure revealer. But, if you are a charlatan with long hair and white robes, you certainly won't be the first!"

"For my daughter's hand," Pumo's father bellowed, "you must prove yourself."

Tertön Sogyal was up for the chllenge. The group from Nyarong erected yak-hair tents in one of the estate's fields. The Khangsar family was generous with butter, jerky, and roasted barley flour, sending large portions to the yogis. Servants from the household carried pails of water from the river and tended to other needs. Before the sun rose, and in the dying hours of the day, the beautiful Pumo could hear Tertön Sogyal's drum and bell as he practiced rituals invoking Vajrakilaya's wisdom mind and convening local protectors. Pumo held back her yearning to meet with Tertön Sogyal. In the afternoon, when local spirits roam in search of sustenance, a burnt *sur*-offering of roasted barley flour, butter, and dried cheese smoldered outside of Tertön Sogyal's tent. Days turned into weeks in Gonjo as Tertön Sogyal waited for the auspicious conditions to ripen and for positive omens to signal that it was time to prove himself to Pumo's parents. During this period, Tertön Sogyal's dreams indicated an imminent treasure revelation associated with Avalokiteshvara, the Buddha of Compassion.

On the morning following a prophetic dream, Tertön Sogyal told his attendant to get Pumo and meet him at a granite cliff by the river. She was to carry a ritual long-life arrow decorated with five-colored silken tassels. Word spread around the village quickly that the Khangsar daughter might soon take the hand of the Nyarong treasure revealer. By the time Pumo went to meet Tertön Sogyal, most of the village had assembled at the cliff, including her mother and father and the household staff.

Tertön Sogyal told the local villagers to make a juniper smoke offering and asked for everyone to begin reciting the supplication prayer to Padmasambhava:

> *Hum. In the northwest of the land of Oddiyana,*
> *In the heart of a lotus flower,*
> *Endowed with the most marvelous attainments,*
> *You are renowned as the "Lotus Born,"*
> *Surrounded by hosts of dakinis.*
> *Following in your footsteps,*
> *I pray, come, inspire me with your blessing.*
> *Vajra Guru Padma Siddhi Hum.*

As everyone recited the prayer, Tertön Sogyal's attendant, Atrin, set a small chalice on a flat boulder and poured rice wine until it overflowed—an offering to telluric spirits. Tertön Sogyal threw blessed barley seeds into the water and against the rock wall as a pre-payment for the treasure he was going to reveal.

As he made his way through the crowd, Tertön Sogyal stopped to gaze into Pumo's auburn eyes. The arm-length tassels from the long-life arrow she held upright waved with the flowing tresses of her black hair. In that moment, the perceptions of both of them were transformed. She saw Tertön Sogyal as none other than Padmasambhava, and for him, she was Yeshe Tsogyal in the flesh. Still, they had never spoken a single word to each other.

Tertön Sogyal continued to the rock wall and took his seat on the ground. Pumo followed, and before kneeling close behind him, she blew a conch shell three times. Everyone placed their palms together in supplication to Padmasambhava while Tertön Sogyal chanted. Tertön Sogyal prayed that, if marrying Pumo was the proper course of action to benefit beings, may he be able to prove his worth to the family. Upon raising his eyes at the end of the prayer, Tertön Sogyal saw an aperture slowly being stretched open in the granite cliff. Villagers held their breath in awe.

He reached into the opening and retrieved several treasures, including a ritual phurba and a small statue and a scripture of the Buddha of Compassion. Tertön Sogyal handed the blessed objects to Atrin, who wrapped them in silk scarves. Reaching into his wool overcoat, Tertön Sogyal took his own teacup and placed it where the treasures had been so as not to leave the land empty of blessing. He nodded his head toward the rock wall, thanking the local earth and water spirits whom he had befriended with his nightly offerings, and the rock-portal sealed closed in response.

"Padmasambhava is still before us," some in the crowd gasped. "Treasure revelations in public are as rare as a white yak."

Handing over the phurba dagger, Tertön Sogyal told Pumo's father to place the treasure in the Khangsar family's main shrine. The 23-year-old Pumo approached Tertön Sogyal and offered him the long-life arrow, symbolizing their spiritual union, and thereafter was known as Khandro Pumo. Before sunrise the next day, Tertön Sogyal, Khandro Pumo, and the Nyarong congregation had broken camp and were heading back to Drikok.

# CHAPTER 8

# OFFICIAL SUMMONS
## *from the* DALAI LAMA

DRIKOK ENCAMPMENT, EASTERN TIBET

*Year of the Earth Rat to the Earth Ox, 1888–1889*

Accounts of Tertön Sogyal's spiritual power spread throughout eastern Tibet to the marketplace and teahouses of Lhasa. Devout pilgrims arriving in central Tibet from Kham told of the emerging treasure revealer from Nyarong who was pulling termas out of granite and appearing in different villages at the same time. Traders brought stories of Tertön Sogyal's blessed talismans that safeguarded them from the dangers of robbers and the punishing hailstorms. Even the monks and teachers in Lhasa at the great monastic universities of Sera, Drepung, and Ganden began hearing about Tertön Sogyal.

At the beginning of the Earth Rat year (1888), a messenger on horseback was dispatched from the Dalai Lama's Potala Palace in Lhasa to eastern Tibet with a message for Tertön Sogyal. The horseman found Tertön Sogyal at Drikok encampment where he was staying with Nyoshul Lungtok.

"You must come immediately," Tertön Sogyal read from the communiqué from the Thirteenth Dalai Lama. "Without delay!" He showed the letter to Nyoshul Lungtok and Khandro Pumo.

Soon thereafter, Tertön Sogyal received another summons from the Dalai Lama saying that his presence in Lhasa would benefit Tibet and the Buddhist teachings in general, and, specifically, that he needed to meet with the Tibetan leader. Khandro Pumo began arranging Tertön Sogyal's belongings for the five-week overland journey to Lhasa, and she told others in their encampment to prepare the saddles and tack.

Tertön Sogyal was being called to Lhasa to perform tantric rituals capable of turning back the British army that was deploying on Tibet's southern border. Mantras recited by Tertön Sogyal were believed to provide protection from the threat of foreign invasion. The State Oracle had told the young Dalai Lama that Tertön Sogyal must serve the nation. This was Tertön Sogyal's effective appointment as chaplain to the Dalai Lama. Becoming Tibet's tantric defense minister, Tertön Sogyal was charged with the special responsibility of using his mastery of the Vajrayana for the protection of the Dalai Lama and Tibet. Within the short arc of Tertön Sogyal's life, he had gone from being a yak herder to a bandit to a mountain yogi, and was soon to become the teacher to the Dalai Lama and defender of the realm.

Tertön Sogyal's meeting with the Dalai Lama would reenact the spiritual dynamism between the Great Guru Padmasambhava and the imperial kings, a period in history thought of as a golden age of Tibet. The Dalai Lamas are the embodiment of the Buddha's compassion, and just like previous kings, they were responsible for maintaining the political and spiritual vitality of the nation-state. And Tertön Sogyal, as Padmasambhava's emissary, was charged with protecting Tibet, repulsing threats to the nation so that its Dharma practitioners would find there the most conducive conditions for the spiritual path. This was the time for Padmasambhava's concealed treasure teachings that specified exact rituals for Tibet in times of crisis. Extremely fierce practices were vital, such as phurba dagger rites and other rituals, and the erecting of

The Thirteenth Dalai Lama, Thubten Gyatso was the spiritual and political ruler of Tibet and a disciple of Tertön Sogyal.

strategically placed temples and stupas that can ward off or even destroy invaders.

When Tertön Sogyal arrived in Lhasa to meet the Dalai Lama, it appeared to some as though this was their first encounter. But both the tertön and the Dalai Lama knew that this was but a continuation of the bodhisattva promise they had made together many lifetimes ago.

The Dalai Lamas are both the protectors and patron saints of Tibet. Like many other gurus in Tibet, they receive their devotees' most sincere prayers and highest aspirations. But it is to the Dalai Lama that the hopes of the nation are directed. In no other lama or lineage of incarnations in the recent history of Tibet have the Tibetan people so fully invested their aspirations and prayers.

The institution of the Dalai Lama rose to religious and political prominence after the reformist Gelug school, one of the four major schools in Tibetan Buddhism, came to power in the middle of the 17th century. In the previous four centuries, the Sakya, Karma Kagyu, and Gelug schools competed for rule in Tibet by gaining the patronage of the Mongol Yuan (1271–1368) and Chinese Ming (1368–1644) dynasties. These foreign patrons of Tibetan Buddhism, to varying degrees, provided monetary support and military backing. The Tibetan lamas in turn provided spiritual legitimacy to their rule. This "lama-patron" relationship was reciprocal where the lay community supported the ordained community and the spiritual body endorsed the political rulers. Tibet used this lama-patron bond as the foundation of their international relations with eastern neighbors.

Tibetan Buddhism has never treated politics and religion separately. Tibetan nationalism, as understood during Tertön Sogyal's life, had commenced in the 8th century when King Trisong Detsen gained rule of the Tibetan Plateau through the esoteric achievements of Padmasambhava. From the Tibetan nation's inception, politics and religion have been inseparable, and any notion that rule of the country should not flow from Buddhist principles is thought to be foolish. Buddha's teachings on impermanence, causality and karma, and compassion are the very foundation upon which Tibet's leaders are meant to govern, whether ordained monks or lay officials. It is from these fundamental Buddhist principles that leaders glean the needed wisdom to rule effectively. And the embodiment of the merging of politics and spirituality is found in the institution of the Dalai Lama.

The incarnation lineage of the Dalai Lama began in the 15th century. The first four Dalai Lamas were scholar-meditators who did not exercise significant political power. However, in the 17th century, the Great Fifth Dalai Lama rose to consolidate secular and religious power over the nation—he was the first Tibetan ruler to do so since the imperial period of the 7th and 8th centuries. Tibetans nostalgically heralded the Fifth's rule as a return to the grand era when King Trisong Detsen ruled through Buddhist decree and his control extended throughout China and central Asia.

The Great Fifth is remembered for his mysticism, poetry, and prose; his architectural aptitude, of which the Potala Palace was the result; and his statesmanship. It is no coincidence that the Great Fifth achieved political and religious dominion because of his strong devotion to Padmasambhava and his spiritual relationship with the Dzogchen master Chöying Rangdrol and the white-bearded tertön of Mindroling, Terdak Lingpa, who, like all tertöns, were envoys of Padmasambhava. As the successive incarnations of the Dalai Lamas are spiritual descendants of the imperial kings of Tibet, when a bond is made with the representatives of Padmasambhava, the treasure revealers, then the Dalai Lama's success is considered secured. The First, Second, and Sixth through the Twelfth Dalai Lamas' spiritual and political activities were limited, and indeed the lives of some of them were shortened because they were not protected by, nor did they receive teachings and empowerments from, tertöns. It was now the Thirteenth Dalai Lama's turn to connect with his karmically connected treasure revealer—Tertön Sogyal.

Government representatives in full regalia and the Medium of the Nechung Oracle formally greeted Tertön Sogyal a few hours outside of Lhasa and escorted him toward the Potala Palace. As they rode on horseback, Tertön Sogyal could see the towering white and red Potala Palace in the far distance. With more than a thousand rooms of living quarters, chanting halls, reliquaries, shrines, libraries, ceremonial reception areas, and government chambers, this was the most spectacular of all structures in Tibet. It was home to all the Dalai Lamas since the time of the Great Fifth, more than 300 years before.

As the small procession with honor guard escorted Tertön Sogyal into Lhasa, residents of the Shol neighborhood below the Potala Palace stopped chitchatting and bartering to take notice. It was infrequent that the Dalai Lama summoned a lay tantric yogi to the Potala, and even more unusual that monastic prelates of the Tibetan government received a layman en route. Necks stretched through the window frames of whitewashed buildings to watch as Tertön Sogyal rode tall in the mount that the government provided—a ceremonial stallion instead of the sure-footed mountain ponies to which he was accustomed. His confidence as a treasure revealer was apparent, not because of arrogance but because, as Padmasambhava's emissary, he rejoiced that he was reestablishing a spiritual bond with the ruler of Tibet.

Tertön Sogyal, Atrin, and others in the small group were ushered up the hundreds of stone-carved steps to the Potala and into an ornate reception room where they were served fine tea and sweet rice unlike anything they had ever tasted. Golden statues and exquisite murals were in every room they passed, as if proceeding through different Buddha realms. Tertön Sogyal was then shown to his quarters in the palace, and Atrin and the others went to stay in the neighborhood below. Tertön Sogyal had hardly dusted himself off when he was called to meet the refined and regal Ngawang Lobsang Trinley Rabgye, the Demo incarnation from Tengyeling Monastery. Demo was the powerful regent of Tibet.

The Thirteenth Dalai Lama was nearly 20 years Tertön Sogyal's junior and had yet to assume political rule of Tibet. With succession by reincarnation, there was always an interim period when the Dalai Lamas were not of age to rule. The Dalai Lama's political duties were carried out by his regent until he attained a majority. The regents came from prominent and historically influential aristocratic households in central Tibet—Tengyeling, Reting, Tshomoling, and Kundeling—and they were selected by Tibetan government ministers and senior monastic hierarchs. Though charged with overseeing the nation with the same Buddhist principles that the Dalai Lamas embodied, some of the regents of the past were the cause of religious sectarianism, corrupt cronyism, and in some cases, it is believed, the premature death of the Dalai Lama.

Demo, the ninth incarnation of his lineage and head of the prominent and wealthy Tengyeling Monastery in Lhasa, was the Dalai Lama's regent when Tertön Sogyal arrived in Lhasa. He was competent in directing the young Dalai Lama's early studies so that he simultaneously developed his spiritual and political acumen. Demo took the State Oracle's pronouncements very seriously, including how critical it was that the Dalai Lama establish a deep relationship with his karmically connected tertön. For the regent, the State Oracle, and the tertön, the highest priorities were to prevent obstacles to the Dalai Lama's long life and secure the nation's borders so that the teachings of the Buddha in Tibet would flourish into the 20th century.

Regent Demo welcomed Tertön Sogyal on behalf of the Tibetan government, offered him a new set of woolen robes, and told him that he would meet with the Dalai Lama the next day. Tertön Sogyal shared with the regent one of Padmasambhava's prophecies from the Avalokiteshvara treasure cycle that he had just discovered in eastern Tibet.

"The holder of the lotus, manifestation of all Buddha's compassion and wisdom, the emanation of the previous Dharma Kings, incarnation of the Great Fifth, the unsurpassable Lord of Refuge of the present and future for the Land of Snows and the Dharma, is the one known as Thubten Gyatso, the Thirteenth Dalai Lama, born in the Fire Rat year," Tertön Sogyal read the prophecy to Regent Demo. "If the auspicious conditions ripen, in his thirteenth year, Thubten Gyatso will meet the tertön and become the holder of Padmasambhava's treasure teachings, and the doors to the Dharma will effortlessly open, and from then onward their wisdom minds will be inseparable."

Tertön Sogyal awoke early on his first morning in Lhasa. He prepared his offerings to present to the Dalai Lama—a treasure statue, holy substances that he had discovered, and a number of treasure texts he had written from his revelations. After he wrapped them in silk, he sat alone in his room.

> *Meditate by means of the recognition of the inseparability of space and awareness, which is self-luminous and immutable, the primordial mode of being. Keep only this as the heart of the practice.*

When the knock on his door sounded, he took the meditative equipoise with him into the world just as a warrior would secure his armor.

Tertön Sogyal was escorted in the predawn hours through cold stone hallways illuminated by torches. Weaving through this maze of endless hallways in the Potala Palace, they passed small niches where single butter lamps illuminated the wide-eyed gaze of figures in ancient statues and scroll paintings. Deep chanting resounded from various chapels where monks paid daily obeisance to the array of Tibet's Dharma protectors. They walked past larger halls with tall stupas housing bone relics of yogis and masters from the past millennium. Monks passed them walking in the opposite direction, holding torma offerings to place on the hundreds of shrines throughout the Potala. Here the walls were permeated with blessings, resonant with prayers.

When they arrived at the reception hall, brocaded woolen hangings were pulled back from the door and Tertön Sogyal entered to see the Dalai Lama, Avalokiteshvara, the Buddha of Compassion in person, sitting on a high throne. Regent Demo and the Dalai Lama's Lord Chamberlain were standing on either side of the throne. The monk who served as the Medium of the State Oracle, Nechung—with whom Tertön Sogyal would soon work closely—was also present to complete the mandala gathering. Tertön Sogyal prostrated on the floor three times, unrolled a white silken offering scarf, and approached the Dalai Lama. The young monk accepted the offering scarf and touched his forehead to Tertön Sogyal's in an act of mutual benediction.

Demo stepped forth and, speaking in a soft tone, requested that Tertön Sogyal explain the circumstances of the treasure revelations and related prophecies. Attendants unwrapped the silk from the statues and manuscripts, and Tertön Sogyal spoke of each item's significance. A translator was sometimes needed because the Dalai Lama was not familiar with Tertön Sogyal's Nyarong dialect, nor did the tertön use the customary formal and refined parlance of Lhasa. Linguistic limitations mattered little. The Dalai Lama and Tertön Sogyal connected at the deepest and most profound level.

The Dalai Lama took great interest with the recounting of terma revelations, in particular the Avalokiteshvara treasure from Gonjo and other prophecies Tertön Sogyal had received. Guru Padmasambhava's prophecies concerning Tertön Sogyal, given in two different treasure revelations, stated, "I [Padmasambhava] have limitless profound treasure and they are all the essence of the Dharma. Of those beings who will reveal them in the future, there will be one from eastern Tibet who is the emanation of Dorje Dudjom, who was born in the Fire Dragon year, whose body will be short and he will have a bold character, who is wise with few attachments to worldly possessions, and who will have great devotion to me. Although he will comport himself with an unconventional character, his heart carries my blessings. If he is not overpowered by the demon of obstacles, he will live beyond seventy years." The prophecy went on to identify Thubten Gyatso as the principal upholder and guardian of Tertön Sogyal's terma revelations.

"The emanation of the King, born in the Fire Rat year in the land of Dakpo; if he [Thubten Gyatso] and the emanation of Dorje Dudjom [Tertön Sogyal] meet and have pure samaya heart connection that is never corrupted, then the treasure teachings of Padmasambhava will flow effortlessly. Specifically, the treasure teachings of the three inner cycles, treasure statues and substances, and in particular the life-force stone will reach the hands [of Thubten Gyatso]. If the auspiciousness is well connected for the accomplishment of this and the spreading of the terma teachings, then he [Thubten Gyatso], Tibet, and living beings will live in happiness."

The Dalai Lama was overjoyed. There and then he requested that Tertön Sogyal become his guru and asked for tantric empowerments and oral transmissions for Padmasambhava's treasure teachings. Tertön Sogyal wasted no time in bestowing them upon the Dalai Lama, and, as if water were being poured into water, the wisdom minds of these two great masters merged as one.

The reconnection of the Dalai Lama with Padmasambhava's emissary in Tertön Sogyal was significant not only for the Tibetan leader's spiritual advancement, but also for Tibet's defense. Geopolitical tensions in the 1800s were squeezing Tibet. And with the specter of armed conflict hovering on the eve of Tertön Sogyal's arrival, his presence could not have been more opportune.

Since the early 1800s, Tibet watched British India progressively gain control over Nepal, Kashmir, Ladakh, and Sikkim, and now in 1888, the British had their sights set not only on Bhutan but the entire Tibetan Plateau. The British had previously sent spies disguised as pilgrims to Tibet to map the region, hiding cartography instruments, sketches, and notes in amulet boxes and handspun prayer wheels. They wanted to control the lucrative trade route between China and India through Tibet. Britain had already signed various trade compacts with China and was treating Tibet as a soon-to-be colonial spoil. Additionally, the Qing's representative in Lhasa was a constant thorn in the side of the Tibetan government because Peking saw their representative as an extension of their dynastic rule. Farther away, but significant to this geopolitical tension, Tsarist Russia had notions of incorporating Tibet as a protectorate, just as they had done in Mongolia. While the British and Russians were vying for clandestine information about each other's intentions in Tibet, and at the same time trying to influence the Tibetan government and the Dalai Lama, Tibet maintained its long-held isolationist policy.

By 1883, the Tibetan government's Council of Ministers had banned all foreigners from central Tibet. Four years later, in 1887, when the Tibetan army sent a small detachment to inspect the British trading outpost near the Sikkim border, the British threatened retaliation. The threat prompted the Tibetan government to conscript able-bodied men into the military, and the Dalai Lama and Regent Demo called for prayers at the three monastic universities of Lhasa. Additionally, yogis like Tertön Sogyal and a group from Rebkong in the far northeastern region of Tibet, who were in Lhasa, were called upon to conduct tantric rituals to defend Tibet's borders. Tertön Sogyal started his own rituals and directed his mantras to the battle just as military skirmishes were beginning with the British.

While staying a few weeks in the Potala Palace, working in the Great Fifth Dalai Lama's sleeping chambers called Blissful Abode of Amitabha, Tertön Sogyal deciphered terma teachings and wrote them on the finest handmade paper he had ever used. Then he moved to a room on the roof of the Jokhang Temple in the center of town. With its population of 50,000 and a constant stream of pilgrims and nomads, Nepali craftsmen, Chinese and Indian merchants, and Silk Road wanderers from as far away as Iran and Russia, Lhasa was the most cosmopolitan city Tertön Sogyal had ever seen. The bazaar was full of tools, ceramics and pans, and silk and tea, all from China. From India, tobacco, saffron, sugar candy, dates, shells, coral, and amber stocked the market. Wool, felt, hides, medicinal herbs, musk, and salt were being sorted and packed to take eastward to China by camel and horse caravans.

Tertön Sogyal had little interest in the marketplace or in the ways of the aristocrats; instead, he immediately embarked on religious activity to strengthen the Tibetan nation. Monks from the Dalai Lama's personal chapel of Namgyal were dispatched to support the tertön. With the monks seated in facing rows and Tertön Sogyal presiding on a throne, thunderous chants rolled out of the temples that Padmasambhava had himself first consecrated, and offerings and incense were presented in abundance. The phurba dagger was brandished in rituals to destroy evil in whatever form it manifested. The Medium of the State Oracle also joined in, at times becoming possessed and thrashing about, issuing prophecies and directives to protect the Dalai Lama's life. These rituals lasted for weeks.

The Tibetan forces suffered losses during the six-month battle, though the British were still unable to march on Lhasa because of the yogis' protective shield and the Tibetans' collective storehouse of positive merit. But, if Tibet's reservoir of positive karma had somehow held back the British during this siege, it was being quickly evaporated back in Lhasa, where sectarian rivalries proliferated among the various schools of Tibetan Buddhism.

Padmasambhava told Tertön Sogyal in a vision, "In these degenerate times, when evil forces are strong, obstacles will come like unending waves. In actuality, the negative forces will come from within your own ranks and seek to destroy you. There will be a time when students receive teachings, even placing their guru's feet upon their crown, and then backbite their teacher straightaway." Another prophecy told Tertön Sogyal, "The evil beings whose minds have been tormented by the damsi demon will have smiling faces but a black heart and skill in double-speak. Toward the Dharma they have small minds, but they are clever in doing wrong. They have no wisdom but are quick in pointing out the faults of others. They always have negative thoughts. Whoever is more refined, they want to belittle; and toward whomever they are equal, they have strong jealousy. And the less fortunate, they will disparage. The samaya commitments between gurus and disciples will not be maintained. And, no matter how strong the power of prayer is, the results will be slow to come."

Tertön Sogyal saw these kinds of prophecies playing out in the overarching conservative attitude pervasive among the influential Gelug lamas and government officials in the Potala Palace and large monasteries. The conservative elements had strong misgivings about the Dalai Lama's personal relationship with an idiosyncratic, mystical tantric yogi like Tertön Sogyal and others from the Nyingma tradition. While many Lhasa lamas bowed before the Dalai Lama, they whispered to one another that the Tibetan leader was wrong to associate with Tertön Sogyal. Given that Tertön Sogyal and other yogis like him had no direct connection with any particular monastery in Lhasa, and that they questioned the status quo, their presence in Lhasa was perceived by many as a challenge to the monastic hierarchy.

The Dalai Lama and Regent Demo became aware that there were some in the Tibetan government and aristocracy who objected to Tertön Sogyal. Regent Demo knew that some monks had even employed the dark arts—filling yak horns with cursed black mustard seeds, small pebbles, and the name of Tertön Sogyal and his astrological sign written on parchment, which, when mixed together and shaken, caused debilitating migraines—in an effort to drive Tertön Sogyal away from Lhasa. Not wanting even the vapor of black magic anywhere near the Dalai Lama, Regent Demo sought to apply the antidote of positive public opinion. Demo requested that the Dalai Lama command Tertön Sogyal to display his spiritual accomplishments by revealing a treasure in public from within Jokhang Temple. The Dalai Lama agreed that such a rare event as a public treasure revelation would help correct the mistaken view of the misguided officials and sectarian monks, and increase public confidence and devotion for Padmasambhava and Tertön Sogyal.

A date was set when the stars, planets, and elements were propitiously aligned. The time of day when the treasure discovery should take place was announced, and invitations were delivered. Lhasa residents knew a momentous event was being planned, as lamas and dignitaries began filing into the temple. Broad-shouldered disciplinarian monks of Jokhang Temple and Demo's private security force kept the order. The Dalai Lama rode in a silk-curtained palanquin from the Potala Palace to the Jokhang Temple. An elaborate throne was set up for the young leader, and cushion seats were arranged for the ranking lamas, the Medium of the Nechung Oracle, and monastic and government officials, as well as the foreign representatives from Nepal, Bhutan, and China. Thousands of devoted city folk circumambulated the outer boundary of the temple, reciting prayers and mantras.

The scene was set. The Dalai Lama presided over the congregation of lamas and monks. Brocade-clad Tibetan monk officals with their long, single turquoise earrings and hair tied in oiled topknots, and aristocrats in richly attired silks, took their seats according to rank. Tertön Sogyal sat in a deep state of meditation, his carpeted seat to the right of the Dalai Lama's throne. A deep, sonorous chant began. Invocation prayers were accompanied by rolling drum beats and long trumpet drones followed by the liturgical recitations in guttural multitones. With hundreds of monks chanting in unison, it was as if the earth were rumbling below Lhasa. Shrine attendants passed with smoking urns of incense to purify the environment, and when the myrrh-like resin *guggul* and mustard seeds were spread atop the embers, any troublesome spirits who may have been attracted to the scene were chased away.

After an hour of chanting, no extraordinary signs had occurred. Some of the monk officals began to scoff to one another that Tertön Sogyal was a fraud. Whispers spread outside the temple among the shopkeepers that Tertön Sogyal was an impostor. Tertön Sogyal read what was on the weak minds of the cynics in the crowd, but he did not react. Just the day before, Tertön Sogyal had confronted a handful of monk officials in the Potala and told them that they had better follow to the letter all of Padmasambhava's prophesies to avert danger from outside Tibet.

"You must build the requisite reliquaries and temples that Padmasambhava presaged, sponsor the specified rituals, and desist from using the monastery's finances for personal gain," Tertön Sogyal said, wagging his finger at the lavishly attired monks.

"Ah, you smelly so-called treasure revealers from eastern Tibet are a scourge to the Buddha's teachings," the portly monk-official responded. "Move out of the way. My assembly of two thousand monks needs me to guide them in prayer."

"If you don't follow the Great Guru Padmasambhava's prophecies," Tertön Sogyal shot back, "I will hold you and those with similar views responsible for the death of our nation."

When there was a lull in the chanting, Tertön Sogyal rose to his feet, bowed to the Dalai Lama, and approached the central altar. Elaborate butter sculptures, copper bowls filled with scented water, and ritual offerings were arranged on wide tables in front of the shrine. The tertön took a cone-shaped torma, made of barley dough, in his right hand and a skull cup overflowing with barley beer in his left. He stepped toward a wall painting of Palden Lhamo, the wrathful Dharma protectress of Lhasa and the Dalai Lamas; she rides a mule and carries in her two hands a club and a skull cup of blood. With a tiger skin tied around her waist and human skin over her shoulder, Palden Lhamo moves with an ever-present storm of flames. Her mule's panniers contain a skull, poison, and two divination dice.

Tertön Sogyal communicated to Palden Lhamo, circling the skull cup in front of the image on the wall. One of the ministers jabbed his fat colleague, chuckling that Tertön Sogyal was sure to fail. Tertön Sogyal stared widely. He dropped the torma below the image on the wall and grabbed the phurba dagger from his belt, holding it with a threatening gesture. Eye to eye with the protectress, he reminded her of her oath to protect the nation and the Dalai Lama. Immediately, the painted mule on which Palden Lhamo rode came to life, brayed, and kicked its right leg toward the open space of the courtyard. In the space where the hoof had passed, suspended in midair, seethed a vicious blue-black serpent coiled 21 times, holding a small treasure casket.

"Cover your eyes, nose, and mouth," the Dalai Lama shouted from his throne. As the snake hissed, a wave of commotion spread about the congregation as monks covered themselves with their burgundy shawls. Two of the cynical ministers bolted out of the temple, shaking with panic.

"If you ingest any of the poisonous vapors of this serpent, you will certainly meet your death!" the Dalai Lama warned.

Tertön Sogyal presented the skull cup to the snake, barley beer dripping over the edge. The phurba in his right hand pointed in a threatening gesture. There was a pregnant silence. Steam rose from silvery venom that dripped from the snake's fangs. Tertön Sogyal moved slowly closer, and closer. Atrin draped a silk scarf between Tertön Sogyal's outstretched wrists.

The assembly began to peer over one another again, keeping their shoulders hunched and heads lowered as if the snake were going to spit at them. Tertön Sogyal continued to stand firm. Hissing and writhing, the serpent swelled in size and, snapping its body, pitched an emerald-colored treasure casket toward Tertön Sogyal, which landed in the middle of the open silk scarf. He quickly wrapped the treasure with the scarf and stepped backward. He nodded to the treasure-protecting serpent for its service, and the snake dissolved into light.

Tertön Sogyal presented the treasure casket to the Dalai Lama at the throne. It was marked with the personal seals of the ruler and treasure revealer and was placed in the inner sanctum of Jokhang Temple. The stunned monks began reciting auspicious prayers to Padmasambhava as Tertön Sogyal returned to his seat.

"He has done it!" Word spread quickly from inside the temple to the public outside. "Tertön Sogyal is Guru Padmasambhava's representative!"

Devotion welled from the hearts of the faithful, causing the treasure casket to open by itself. Shrine attendants held the casket for the Dalai Lama, who removed an exquisite statue of Guru Padmasambhava known as *Blazing with the Glory of Auspiciousness*, as well as five small golden treasure scrolls and a crystal capsule of spiritual medicine, with which he blessed the congregation.

Tertön Sogyal stayed in Lhasa more than a year and continued to perform rituals to protect Tibet. His connection to the young Dalai Lama deepened, while his position in the inner court was firmly established, even though some resentment of his influence on the Dalai Lama still remained within orthodox elements in the Tibetan government. Tertön Sogyal was exposed to the opulent lifestyle in Lhasa, with the lavish dress, rigid seating arrangements, honorifics of speech, and use of aristocratic ranks and titles for the enrichment of a select few. Tertön Sogyal observed Lhasa residents spending the lion's share of their time immersed in worry about relative prestige and status, and thought them to be like children building sand castles.

When Tertön Sogyal was not bound to duties in Lhasa for the Dalai Lama, he went on pilgrimage to sites where Guru Padmasambhava had lived and taught. Coming to central Tibet for the first time was of great consequence for Tertön Sogyal, as he could make a physical connection to the sacred topography, remembering his time as Dorje Dudjom in the 8th century. Visiting the tombs of Tibet's imperial kings, as well as many sacred stupas, pilgrimage places, and other monuments, and walking on the hallowed ground of Padmasambhava were catalysts in his mind. He remembered having been there in his past lives. After he discovered treasure scrolls that were written in the hand of Yeshe Tsogyal in a place to the south of Lhasa near the Crystal Cave of Yarlung Valley, he returned to Lhasa and offered these scrolls to the Dalai Lama at the Summer Palace. The Dalai Lama deciphered the teaching. Inspired by the connection to Tertön Sogyal, the young Tibetan leader instructed the Dagchen throne holder of Sakya Monastery, who was present at the time, to decode the meaning of another treasure scroll Tertön Sogyal presented. The scroll contained only one line of script, though the meaning of the syllables when decoded filled 50 pages of meditation instructions associated with Vajrakilaya. After both the Dalai Lama and Sakya Dagchen decoded the dakini script and put the instruction in writing, Tertön Sogyal gave them the empowerments for the meditation practices. Soon the Dalai Lama began to have pure visions that resulted in his own treasure revelations, which later he wrote under the secret name of Dratang Lingpa. Undoubtedly, the Dalai Lama looked to the tertön for guidance on treasure revelation and the esoteric process of decoding dakini script, just as Tertön Sogyal had been guided by the great Khyentse Wangpo.

Nearing the end of Tertön Sogyal's first sojourn in Lhasa, Padmasambhava and the One-Eyed Protectress appeared to the tertön in visions and dreams, telling him of additional treasures he needed to reveal in eastern Tibet. Before his departure audience with the Dalai Lama to request leave, Tertön Sogyal met with Regent Demo to tell him about one special treasure, a powerful statue of Padmasambhava still hidden in eastern Tibet. Tertön Sogyal first became aware of this statue in an associated prophecy in his own Vajrakilaya revelation. If this *Wish-Fulfilling Jewel Guru Statue That Liberates Upon Seeing* could be revealed and strategically placed in Lhasa's Jokhang Temple, Tertön Sogyal said, it would serve as an exceptional means to prevent invaders from entering the Land of Snows.

Before Padmasambhava left Tibet, he hid a number of statues to serve as his representatives. In the future when afflictive emotions will be strong, Tertön Sogyal told Demo, and when respect for the Dharma and lineage holders is waning, at that time, this very statue should be revealed to counteract the corrupted views.

"This statue is inseparable from me," Padmasambhava said to Tertön Sogyal in a vision identifying the exact location. "It must be placed at the right side of Jowo Shakyamuni Buddha statue in the Jokhang Temple in Lhasa."

Regent Demo presented Tertön Sogyal with beads of turquoise and coral, and a bag of silver coins, and said, "Endeavor with all your efforts to find this statue!"

# CHAPTER 9

# DISCOVERING *the* WISH-FULFILLING JEWEL GURU STATUE

DRIKOK ENCAMPMENT, EASTERN TIBET

*Year of the Earth Ox to the Iron Hare, 1889–1891*

Tertön Sogyal and his cohorts returned to eastern Tibet by the southern tea-trade route in the first month of the Earth Ox year (1889). The terma protectors accompanied him along the mountain trails eastward. They passed caravans of mules carrying puer tea toward Lhasa, while Tibetan traders brought salt and medicinal herbs off the Tibetan Plateau to China. When they camped at the Secret Cave of the Living Dakinis near Barkham's most sacred mountain, the protectors delivered to Tertön Sogyal a golden parchment in which he was given further clues to finding the *Wish-Fulfilling Jewel Guru Statue That Liberates Upon Seeing.*

After six weeks of travel, Tertön Sogyal arrived at Drikok at Nyoshul Lungtok's encampment. There he was reunited with his teacher Nyoshul Lungtok, Khandro Pumo, and disciples. The snowy peak of Mount Lotus Hermitage towered in the northeast with the expansive Trom plains to the south. In front of the encampment ran the Yile River, and a few miles below, the water flowed so gently that it made no sound. Locals said that even the water that came from Nyoshul Lungtok's encampment flowed with a meditative silence.

Tertön Sogyal presented Nyoshul Lungtok with all the jewels, silver, and gold that he had been offered to him in central Tibet. It was clear that Tertön Sogyal was perfecting the three gatherings: people during the day, dakinis during the night, and material offerings throughout. The teacher accepted Tertön Sogyal's gifts and the next day sent them all away to various monasteries, not keeping a single coin for himself.

Tertön Sogyal stayed for some months with Nyoshul Lungtok and received teachings and empowerments that the master rarely bestowed. During this time, Tertön Sogyal told his teacher about the *Wish-Fulfilling Jewel Guru Statue*. When Tertön Sogyal went to visit his other teachers, including Jamgön Kongtrul, Lama Sonam Thaye, and Dza Choktrul, they were unanimous in their encouragement not to delay in the treasure revelation. "Do whatever is necessary in order to reveal the *Wish-Fulfilling Jewel Guru Statue!*"

In Tertön Sogyal's 35th year, he revealed a guidebook to the *Wish-Fulfilling Jewel Guru Statue,* which stated, "Just as the veins of the body converge at the heart, go to the auspicious cave in the remote area of Derge where there are seven stone steps. You will see unmistakably, on the rock wall, an eight-spoked wheel. In the middle of the wheel there will be dakini script. There, behind, look for the extraordinarily blessed statue that liberates any individual who is fortunate to lay eyes upon it."

The guide also instructed Tertön Sogyal about the astrologically appropriate date for revelation, the number of disciples who should accompany him, and the purification rituals to conduct, all of which needed to come together perfectly for the treasure revelation. The guidebook concluded, "When Guru Padmasambhava hid this statue, he entrusted it to Rahula and the naga treasure guardian named Jeweled Goddess. These two guardians will watch over the *Wish-Fulfilling Jewel Guru Statue* for many centuries. The person who will reveal this terma is an emanation of me, is empowered by me, and remains inseparable from me. His character may be unconventional and unpredictable as he subdues unruly disciples. He, who is an emanation of Nanam [Dorje Dudjom], is known as the great treasure revealer Sogyal."

Rahula, the nine-headed Dharma protector, led Tertön Sogyal to the sacred mountain in the Derge region. Tertön Sogyal took with him 25 yogis and yoginis with whom he had a pure heart connection. As they walked through the rocky terrain and deep ravines, the entire group began having visions of Padmasambhava, who to some appeared in various forms such as a pandita and an ascetic yogi, and to others the guru rode a fearsome tigress. Clouds formed in the azure sky into mantra syllables—*Om Ah Hum Vajra Guru Padma Siddhi Hum*—while others saw *Hum,* the seed syllable of the enlightened mind of all the buddhas, reflected off mountain lakes and in the rivers.

When they arrived at a campsite at the base of a snow-covered mountain, Tertön Sogyal immediately took his seat and recited the syllable *Ah* in a yogic manner 100 times. He remained seated in meditation as others pounded the pegs to erect yak-hair tents while a few monks collected firewood, hauled water, and established a kitchen area. Nobody except the tertön knew how long they might stay.

After weeks of prepatory rituals, Tertön Sogyal and the monk assistant Dorje ascended the mountain one morning to search for the door to the treasure. When they found the seven steps that led to the eight-spoked wheel, Tertön Sogyal withdrew his phurba dagger and struck the rock in four places. He told Dorje to bore out holes, and therein Tertön Sogyal placed ten precious stones of coral, turquoise, amber, and crystal beads to symbolize seizing the power to accomplish the four kinds of tantric activity—magnetizing, enriching, subjugating, and pacifying. Tertön Sogyal carved a larger hole in the rock and placed ten dzi onyx beads and a conch shell to represent the all-encompassing accomplishment of enlightenment itself. Before returning to camp, Tertön Sogyal concealed the holes, and he told Dorje to maintain great secrecy about what he had hidden.

The disciples continued to conduct extensive ceremonies during the waxing August moon. On the 14th day of the lunar month, Tertön Sogyal told them to prepare a ritual feast in anticipation of the pending revelation. Ritual feasts not only accumulate positive karma, but they also serve to purify the disciples' hearts and minds. By subsuming all objects of the senses—from the aroma of incense and food, to the taste of spiritual medicine and beer, to the sounds of ritual music and the mountain wind, to the very movements of thought and emotions in the mind—in the nondual state of unbound awareness, vast merit is accumulated and any corruptions in the yogis' samaya are purified.

The next morning, Tertön Sogyal and Dorje walked up the mountain with a few others, including Atrin. When Tertön Sogyal climbed the rock staircase, the treasure door to a vault opened by itself, and Dorje helped Tertön Sogyal remove a large treasure casket two arm-lengths long. Tertön Sogyal put a treasure replacement of ten golden coins in the crypt and closed the stone door. The ease with which the treasure discovery happened, Tertön Sogyal knew, was a sign that all the necessary interdependent circumstances had coalesced precisely at the right time, in the right location, with pure devotees around him.

The casket was extremely heavy and the other yogis approached to help take it down from the rock perch. Dorje and Atrin put the treasure casket on the backs of two helpers, but they could barely take a step without losing their balance because of the sheer weight.

"If you can't manage, then set it down," Tertön Sogyal said.

Tertön Sogyal hoisted the load onto his own back and hiked down the mountain with granite scree rolling off cliffs on either side of him. One of the yoginis met Tertön Sogyal on the trail and ceremonially led him back to camp, holding incense and singing melodic mantras. Tertön Sogyal saw clouds of incense rising from the campsite where fresh juniper branches smoldered atop hot coals for a smoke offering. The other yogis and yoginis had cleaned the campsite and prepared another ritual feast of barley cakes, yogurt, sweet potatoes, and barley wine. They had dusted off their red and white shawls and washed themselves as if the Great Guru Padmasambhava himself were soon arriving at their camp.

Atrin and Dorje assisted Tertön Sogyal to set the heavy stone casket next to the mandala and feast offerings. They immediately offered devotional prayers to Padmasambhava, and made offerings to Rahula and the treasure guardians living in the underworld, including pouring pails of blessed milk into the nearby stream for the naga Jeweled Goddess. As the offerings were being made, Tertön Sogyal mixed a sacramental brew and had the congregation drink it while he distributed palm-size ritual mirrors that the yogis and yoginis affixed to their belts as a protection against any deleterious fumes or sorcery with which they may have recently come into contact.

As the disciples continued to chant and abide in the sublime Dzogchen view, Tertön Sogyal approached the stone casket. He washed it with saffron-infused water and purified it with incense. Birds gathered in the trees and sang soft melodies as deer walked by the encampment unafraid. With the help of the treasure guardian invisible to all except him, Tertön Sogyal lifted the lid to the casket, wherein sat the *Wish-Fulfilling Jewel Guru Statue*. The congregation prostrated with tears of devotion, offered sacred substances, and made aspirational prayers.

> *To the Lotus-born Guru of Oddiyana, we pray!*
> *Grant your blessing, so all our wishes be spontaneously fulfilled!*
> *When beings of all six realms are tormented by immense pain,*
> *And especially when our leaders and people are engulfed in suffering,*
> *With intense longing and devotion, from the depths of our hearts,*
> *With no trace of doubt or hesitation we pray:*
> *O Guru Rinpoche, Padmasambhava, with your unchanging, unwavering compassion—watch over us!*
> *To the Lotus-Born Guru of Oddiyana, we pray!*
> *Grant your blessing, so all our wishes be spontaneously fulfilled!*

The height of the statue of Guru Padmasambhava was just longer than an arm's length. He sat in a cross-legged posture and wore a maroon pandita's hat with elongated ear flaps; his right hand at his heart was in a gesture of offering and his left hand held a skull cup filled with the nectar of immortality.

Tertön Sogyal explained that such sacred treasure statues were meant specifically for the degenerative times because they have the very warm breath of the dakinis on them. Because the statues and teachings were hidden with Padmasambhava's direct blessing, the essence and power found within that blessing had not been lost nor corrupted over time by coming into contact with negative attitudes. These holy objects, whose potency has not declined, are meant to reinspire spiritual practitioners whose diligence has wavered, to reconsecrate lands that have been desecrated, and to repair corrupted samaya commitments.

"The potency of Padmasambhava's wisdom intent has not diminished over time, even as the negative actions of beings have increased in this degenerate age. In order to revive Padmasambhava's blessing, to increase the activity of the Dharma, to guide politics, this statue is a wise method demonstrating enlightened activity."

After a few days of offering ceremonies and celebratory feasts, the *Wish-Fulfilling Jewel Guru Statue* was taken to Drikok encampment and for six weeks rituals were accomplished at its feet. Leaving the statue at Drikok, Tertön Sogyal went to see Khyentse Wangpo to inform him of the revelation, and while in Dzongsar, he redacted *The Guru Yoga of the Profound Path*, a powerful treasure liturgy associated with the revelation of the statue. As with all guru yoga practices, the intention is to lead the mind of the yogi or yogini to merge with the wisdom mind of the master, to gain supreme confidence that is not dependent upon anything other than recognizing one's inherent perfection, which is the ultimate guru. *The Guru Yoga of the Profound Path* in part reads:

> *Hum Hum Hum*
> *Lamas, please inspire me with your blessings!*
> *On my body, bestow the supreme empowerment of enlightened form!*

*On my voice, bestow the supreme empowerment of en-*
  *lightened speech!*
*On my mind, bestow the supreme empowerment of en-*
  *lightened wisdom!*
*Grant me the supreme empowerment of inseparability.*
*Perfect the strength of my realization,*
*And cause me to accomplish the four kinds of activity!*
*The guru dissolves into me and we merge inseparably.*
*My mind blends with his wisdom mind in the all-encom-*
  *passing space.*
*In that space, the ongoing experience of the absolute lama,*
*Do not alter, but simply settle and rest at ease.*
*A A Ah!*

Although the treasure liturgy was now on paper, Tertön Sog-yal knew the time to spread it had not yet arrived, so he rolled the scroll, and when Khyentse was not looking, hid it in a golden ritual container on his altar, and then returned to Drikok encampment.

At the beginning of the Iron Hare year, the Nechung Oracle informed the Dalai Lama that Tertön Sogyal had revealed the *Wish-Fulfilling Jewel Guru Statue That Liberates Upon Seeing* in eastern Tibet and that it should be housed in Lhasa. The Tibetan leader followed the Oracle's command and wrote a letter to Tertön Sogyal:

> In the year of the Iron Tiger [1890], I beseeched you, Rinpoche, to reveal treasures. Now, you have brought forth the *Wish-Fulfilling Jewel Guru Statue That Liberates Upon Seeing*. This must be due to the blessing and power of the gurus, devas, and dakinis, the Dharma protectors and the host of enlightened deities. In particular, this has been accomplished because of your own aspirations and prayers made in your past lives, and from the power of the Truth. Now, so this great object of blessing may benefit the Dharma and beings throughout the realm, you should bring it to central Tibet to rest in the Jokhang Temple. In order to avert any and all hindrances on its journey to

Lhasa, please do obstacle-removing rituals and prayers. In addition to the statue, please bring its prophetic guide that you revealed so that it can also be present during the consecration ceremony in Lhasa. With my prayers, I am sending you fifteen silver coins, sacred substances for you to offer along the way as incense, and five-colored offering scarves; please accept them. Regarding the palanquin upon which to transport the Guru Statue and other matters of security and logistics for the statue en route to the capital, please acquire the assistance of the Tibetan government representative in Kham. If you have any questions or concerns, please tell me openly. I send my deepest prayers.

# CHAPTER 10

# *The* GURU RETURNS *to* LHASA

LHASA, CENTRAL TIBET

*Year of the Iron Hare, 1891*

While Tertön Sogyal prepared his return to Lhasa with the *Wish-Fulfilling Jewel Guru Statue That Liberates Upon Seeing*, Khandro Pumo gave birth to their first child. They named him Rigdzin Namgyal. Khandro Pumo knew that Tertön Sogyal had to fulfill his karmic duty for Tibet and the Dalai Lama, and she could not ask him to stay with them. Difficult though it would be to leave his family right after the birth of his son, the tertön directed his disciples to attend to his wife at Drikok encampment, and in the sixth month, Tertön Sogyal, Atrin, and others began the journey, taking the statue westward.

The Nechung Oracle had spurred the Dalai Lama's first meeting with Tertön Sogyal in 1888. With the revelation of the *Wish-Fulfilling Jewel Guru Statue,* the Nechung's insistence grew stronger that Tertön Sogyal meet with the Dalai Lama for a second time and bring the statue to Lhasa. The tertön's upcoming visit would strengthen the triumvirate work of the Dalai Lama, Tertön Sogyal, and the Nechung Oracle, which lasted throughout the rest of their lives.

The Dharma protector Nechung has a unique role in service to the Dalai Lamas, Tibet, and Buddhism in general. When Padmasambhava came to Tibet and subdued local spirits in the earth and water, he assigned various spirits to protect locales, monasteries and temples, and specific Dharma activities. But to protect the entire realm of Tibet and the teachings of the Buddha, Padmasambhava knew he needed a very powerful spirit. The 25 disciples discussed the matter and asked Padmasambhava where the spirit who could fulfill such a task lived.

"Ahh, there is Pehar in the monastery in Bantahor," Padmasambhava said.

Bantahor was a region in current-day western Mongolia. Pehar resided there in a small temple. But he was not keen to go elsewhere. When Padmasambhava magically projected his own body to Bantahor, Pehar threw a rock at the Great Guru and hit him in the head. Pehar was almost as obstinate as the Tibetans themselves; Padmasambhava thought this was not going to be easy. Padmasambhava told his disciples to organize an army to go to Bantahor, but they need not raise arms.

"Just find Pehar's temple. Take the turquoise Buddha statue, his throne made of conch shells, and Pehar's purple-brown leather three-eyed mask. Pehar is so attached to those objects that he will follow them all the way back here to Samye."

Indeed, Pehar pursued his stolen objects to central Tibet. Padmasambhava met Pehar with astonishing splendor and brought him directly into his service by capturing his life-force. Imprinting the crown of Pehar's head with a ritual dorje and anointing his tongue with immortality nectar, Padmasambhava bound the protector by oath to guard Tibet and the spiritual practitioners in Tibet. Pehar relocated during the time of the Great Fifth Dalai Lama to the small temple of Nechung near Lhasa, and since that time the two names, Pehar and Nechung, have been synonymous. Nechung's special skill in communicating through possessing a human medium was greatly utilized, and in time Nechung became Tibet's State Oracle, though not without competition from other oracles and spirits.

Cavalry from the Tibetan government in Lhasa arrived to meet Tertön Sogyal and to guarantee the *Wish-Fulfilling Jewel Guru Statue*'s safe journey. Shortly thereafter, an escort party of monks from Nechung Monastery met Tertön Sogyal and together they performed consecration ceremonies upon the statue. One of the monks from Nechung Monastery did not accompany the group west to Lhasa; he continued eastward to Dzongsar after having met Tertön Sogyal. The monk had a different mission. Before leaving Lhasa, the Nechung Oracle had told the monk to find the guru yoga liturgy that Tertön Sogyal had hidden in Khyentse's room.

When the monk arrived in Dzongsar to see Khyentse, he bowed before the master and humbly requested a copy of *The Guru Yoga of the Profound Path* liturgy that Tertön Sogyal had written. Khyentse, taken aback, told the monk he did not know of such a liturgy.

"Lama, before I left Lhasa, the Nechung Oracle told me that if there are any obstacles to my returning with the liturgy, I should ask you, the great Khyentse, to bless me with the barley grains from your golden container on your prayer table."

Khyentse opened the golden container to sprinkle blessed grains upon the monk, and said, "Ah, that Nechung and Sogyal work in stealthy ways!"

Khyentse found the liturgy that Tertön Sogyal had hidden.

"Many people in Kham think that the *Wish-Fulfilling Jewel Guru Statue* should remain here to protect us," Khyentse said. "But as we have this guru yoga text now, it will provide what we need. Make a copy of it to leave behind in Kham before you return to Lhasa."

The monk left Dzongsar and caught up with Tertön Sogyal and the large party from Nechung Monastery as they traveled slowly west. It took nearly twice as long to journey to Lhasa with the statue because the caravan of yogis was required to regularly stop and perform ceremonies as ordered by the Dalai Lama. When they arrived on the outskirts of Lhasa, they remained for more than a week to clean the statue of dust, adorn it with jewels, paint the face with gold, and perform ablution rituals.

Finally, in the ninth lunar month during the religious festival commemorating the Buddha's descent to earth from the Joyous Tushita Heaven, the *Wish-Fulfilling Jewel Guru Statue That Liberates Upon Seeing* entered Lhasa. The city waited in anticipation. Thousands of nomads lined the road to Jokhang Temple as shop owners locked their doors to come out on the street, shoving one another aside to get a glimpse of the sacred image. Monk security guards with wooden staffs cleared the way, pushing back devotees, while government officials made their way to the temple. As the statue and Tertön Sogyal proceeded toward the Jokhang, led by monks twirling parasols, beating drums, and playing the *gyaling*, a high-pitched short oboe, plumes of juniper incense rose from kilns to fill the sky above the Barkhor neighborhood. Other monks carried long poles with victory banners flapping in the wind. From the temple's rooftop boomed the drone of long horns and the crash of cymbals, and monks blew the conch shells in the ten directions to invoke the blessings of enlightened beings. It was as if Padmasambhava, in the flesh, had returned to Lhasa. The Dalai Lama and other throne holders stood as the Guru Statue was taken into the inner sanctum of the Jokhang and offered a throne to the right side of the most sacred statue in all of Tibet, the Jowo Shakyamuni Buddha. A massive ritual feast and prayers were offered that continued for ten days, and the Dalai Lama thereafter used the statue as an object of devotion in the Potala. After a month, the statue was returned to its throne in the Jokhang Temple.

The *Wish-Fulfilling Jewel Guru Statue That Liberates Upon Seeing* of Padmasambhava that was discovered as a terma by Tertön Sogyal and resides in the Jokhang Temple in Lhasa.

Tertön Sogyal did not stay long in Lhasa on his second visit—delivering the Guru Statue was his main purpose. But while in central Tibet, he was sure to connect with his close Dharma brother, Tertön Rangrik, who stayed just south of Lhasa at Mindroling Monastery. They were similar in some ways: both hailed from

Nyarong, were disciples of Nyala Pema Dündul, and were revealing many of Padmasambhava's termas. The disposition and demeanor of the two tertöns, however, could not have contrasted more. Tertön Rangrik preferred the hermit's life and shunned contact with government officials and Lhasa's socialites. Tertön Sogyal, on the other hand, did not mind being in the public eye and even took it upon himself to command Lhasa residents to follow the teachings of Padmasambhava and not squabble about whose worldly spirits were more powerful. Tertön Rangrik, echoing Nyoshul Lungtok's warnings, once cautioned Tertön Sogyal not to become fond of his influential connections in Lhasa.

At one point, Tertön Rangrik and Tertön Sogyal were summoned by the Tibetan government to perform a ceremony together in the Jokhang. As Tertön Sogyal was the recognized teacher of the Dalai Lama, the monks of the temple arranged Tertön Sogyal's throne a hand-span higher than the senior Tertön Rangrik's carpeted seat. While Tertön Rangrik did not care if he was on a throne or on the muddy slab in the courtyard, the seating of the two lamas upset one of central Tibet's mountain protector deities, Nyenchen Tanglha. Tanglha presided over the entire Himalayan range, was charged by Padmasambhava to protect authentic Dharma practitioners, and had a connection to Tertön Rangrik.

Tanglha was dismayed to find that Tertön Rangrik sat at a deferential height across from Tertön Sogyal's throne. The mountain protector asked Tertön Rangrik if he could teach the younger tertön and the Jokhang monks a lesson in humility. The elderly lama, in a rare show of emotional delight, slightly grinned at Tanglha's mischievous request.

Tanglha magically manifested himself into a large group of nomads from the northern plains of Tibet, with thick wool overcoats lined with wolf and fox fur. The illusory nomads were laden with huge sacks of offerings of dried cheese and wooden buckets of curd and butter. They rambled into the courtyard of the Jokhang and began to prostrate en masse before Tertön Rangrik, their backs to Tertön Sogyal. It surprised the monk assembly and other pilgrims and onlookers that Tertön Sogyal was being completely ignored. The nomads approached Tertön Rangrik to present the offerings and receive a blessing by touching their heads to his throne. After the first few nomads made offerings to Tertön Rangrik, they turned around to depart, without even looking at Tertön Sogyal.

The attending monks and curious onlookers encouraged the nomads to bow down to Tertön Sogyal. The monks, attendants, and pilgrims attempted to help but began bumping into one another in the confusion, with people walking in all directions. Tertön Rangrik watched the pandemonium as if it were child's play.

Tertön Sogyal observed Tanglha's magical display and how it played with the minds of the monks and pilgrims. Reclined into meditation, Tertön Sogyal slowly chanted the syllable *"Hum, Hum, Hum . . ."* and directed the syllable to weave an impenetrable dome of protection around the temple chamber. Gripping his phurba dagger, Tertön Sogyal directed the point at the nomads, freezing them in their footsteps. The temple monks, baffled by what was happening, sat in awe. Others tried to continue to push the unmoving nomads to receive a blessing.

Observing the protection dome that Tertön Sogyal had created, Tertön Rangrik felt sympathy for the immobile Tanglha and the confused people. He sat up and boldly yelled to Tertön Sogyal, *"Ta tong, ta tong*—right now, right now—let them go!"

Tertön Sogyal bowed his head toward his elder Dharma brother. With a snap of his fingers, Tertön Sogyal dissolved the dome, and at that moment Tanglha stood down from the contest and disappeared.

That evening during tea, Tertön Sogyal told Tertön Rangrik that he would soon return home. The elder tertön had cautionary words. He told Tertön Sogyal that the mother of a gifted young boy in Nyarong was trying to pass her son off as the incarnation of Nyala Pema Dündul, their teacher who had attained the rainbow body.

"As we say in Nyarong, a mother with a skilled tongue can turn any child into an incarnate lama," said Tertön Rangrik.

Tertön Rangrik explained that a special boy had been born in Shayul village in Nyarong, not far from Tertön Sogyal's birthplace. The boy displayed unique characteristics, and a local shaman predicted the boy's future power and influence. However, there was caution with the prediction; the boy could acquire occult powers—and it was uncertain if he would use these powers to benefit beings or harm others.

Tertön Rangrik was certain that the boy was not the reincarnation of Pema Dündul. Before Pema Dündul dissolved into light, he had told Tertön Rangrik and other close disciples that if anyone claimed to be his reincarnation after his passing, that claimant must be buried nine body-lengths underground and a black stone monument placed on top. Tertön Rangrik certainly did not want to have to vanquish a fellow Nyarong villager, and building such a black monument would take so much effort and be a distraction from his meditation—but he would have to do so if the boy claimed to be Nyala Pema Dündul's reincarnation.

The boy's mother had tried to place the teenager under the tutelage and care of Tertön Rangrik a few years before. Tertön Rangrik refused because he foresaw involvement in the politics of recognizing reincarnations. The mother persisted in her attempts to gain favor for her son among other Nyarong lamas.

"When you return home, look into that young boy from Shayul," Tertön Rangrik commanded. "We don't want any black magicians coming from Nyarong."

# CHAPTER 11

# *The* RAZOR *of the*
# INNERMOST ESSENCE

DERGE REGION, EASTERN TIBET

**Year of the Water Dragon to the Wood Sheep, 1892–1895**

Tertön Sogyal returned to eastern Tibet and passed the next two years with his wife and child in Drikok, spent time in retreat at holy caves in the Derge and Tromthar regions, and practiced the treasure teachings he had already revealed. He was also discovering more treasures, coded maps, and prophecies.

Tertön Sogyal learned in the second month of the Water Dragon year (1892) that his teacher, the great Khyentse Wangpo, had passed away at the age of 73 at Dzongsar. Khyentse had been Tertön Sogyal's spiritual father, and nearly everything he accomplished in his life had been influenced by the advice, guidance, and blessing of the great lama. Their bond throughout their many lifetimes together had been strengthened by their pure heart connection in their present lives, and it would continue into their future incarnations.

Now that Khyentse had passed away, Tertön Sogyal turned to the remaining spiritual luminary in eastern Tibet, Jamgön Kongtrul, as his touchstone. Tertön Sogyal had already received many teachings and empowerments from Kongtrul. As their relationship deepened, Kongtrul acknowledged that Tertön Sogyal was unique among his disciples, and that he placed great trust in the tertön and relied on his divinations to extend his life. In 1895, while Tertön Sogyal stayed with Kongtrul at Dzongshö, the two collaborated to reveal a Vajrakilaya treasure that was destined to become part of Tibet's national defense—the treasure teaching was known as *The Razor of the Innermost Essence*.

When Padmasambhava began teaching the Vajrayana in Tibet, his first instructions to his heart-disciples had been the practice of the phurba-wielding deity, Vajrakilaya. The reason he taught Vajrakilaya practices first was to enable his students to remove obstacles on their spiritual path and to vanquish impediments to the flourishing of Buddhism in Tibet. Some of Padmasambhava's Vajrakilaya liturgies were practiced straightaway in the 8th and 9th centuries, while others were hidden as treasure texts to be revealed in the future by tertöns when the instructions would be more effective against the prevailing spiritual malaise.

One cycle of the Vajrakilaya teachings that was hidden was known as *The Razor of the Innermost Essence*. Padmasambhava uncharacteristically entrusted *The Razor* to five of his disciple's reincarnations, rather than to just one tertön. Padmasambhava wanted to ensure its revelation. Tertön Sogyal had discovered the coded map to *The Razor* more than eight years before in Katok, but it was only now that the right circumstances—principally Kongtrul's blessed guidance—were coalescing that would bring it forth.

In the autumn of the Wood Sheep year (1895), Kongtrul assembled Tertön Sogyal, Lama Trime, Dza Choktrul, and others who were emanations of Padmasambhava's heart-disciples and who were karmically connected to *The Razor*, to perform preparatory ceremonies. They conducted the rituals for a week at his hermitage at Dzongshö, set among the craggy limestone precipices. For yogic practitioners who have mastered the energies in their own bodies, an outer journey to sacred sites like Dzongshö is a

A scroll painting of Jamgön Kongtrul with his hand- and footprints.

catalyst to evoke their enlightened nature. Perched on a mountain ledge, the gathering of yogis saw the landscape with its forests, rivers, and mountains as a sacred mandala—the outer mirroring the inner. Every place in the sacred topography related to the yogis' energy and vital essence. The peak above them was in the form of the Buddha of Wisdom, Manjushri; when the wind blew over the pine- and birch-covered hills, Padmasambhava's enlightened speech could be heard. The limestone crag to the west was a jewel offering to wrathful deities, and to the east was the site of *The Razor of the Innermost Essence* treasure, concealed below the Jeweled Cliff inside a secret cave.

Kongtrul had gone to that secret location at the Jeweled Cliff, known as the Cave That Delights the Awesome Heruka, a year before to find the treasure door. While Kongtrul was there making preparations, Tertön Sogyal was in central Tibet to conduct specified preparative rituals at the caves of Sheldrak, Drak Yerpa, and Samye Chimpu. Distance mattered little, as their enlightened intent bound their mission.

After Kongtrul and the group of yogis completed the week-long preparatory rites whereby they cleansed the external landscape of pollutants and purified their inner channels, Tertön Sogyal assisted the 82-year-old Kongtrul to the cave. Tertön Sogyal helped his mentor in the steep terrain and negotiated shallow but icy rivers. As they approached the cave, vermilion dust began to flow profusely from the edges of the treasure door. Tertön Sogyal's mind was drawn like a magnet to the circular portal. He raised his phurba dagger in a threatening gesture and reminded the treasure guardian that he was a representative of Padmasambhava. He then hurled a stone at the red-dusted door. The earth shook with a thunderous crash. A small aperture where the rock had hit opened and a fragrant smell burst forth like rain of rose water. Tertön Sogyal plunged his hand into the opening of the granite, pulled it wider, and withdrew a statue of Padmasambhava in a striding posture holding a phurba dagger and vajra scepter. With the treasure door open, Kongtrul stepped forward and from an already opened casket withdrew a golden scroll from which the Vajrakilaya practices of *The Razor of the Innermost Essence* would be decoded.

Scroll painting of the Varjakilaya terma revelation by
Tertön Sogyal known as *The Razor of the Innermost Essence*.

"This treasure is the one and only revival of the Buddha Dharma for this degenerate time; it is the armor to protect us for all negative times; it is the weapon to avert all negative conditions."

The trove in the rock was also full of medicinal nectar that liberates when tasted, but Tertön Sogyal said it was meant for another tertön. A dakini in the group pleaded with Tertön Sogyal for a small portion, and to avoid disappointing her, he took some and gave it to her. Tertön Sogyal set a replacement offering inside and closed the treasure door. The group performed feast offerings to the terma guardians and recited verses of dedication and prayers of auspiciousness.

> *Ho! Through the power of generation and completion*
>     *phases, mantra recitation and samadhi meditation,*
> *Within the state of the wisdom body, speech and mind of*
>     *Vajrakilaya,*
> *May we and others all accomplish the accumulation of*
>     *merit and wisdom, and so*
> *Swiftly and directly realize the perfect state of omni-*
>     *science.*

During the ceremony, Kongtrul presented the key—the golden scroll—to Tertön Sogyal with a mandate to decipher its meaning.

Padmasambhava prophesied two holders for *The Razor* treasure: Khyentse Wangpo and Thubten Gyatso, the Thirteenth Dalai Lama.

> *The principal holders will be one of two Great Beings;*
> *One will appear in Kham and one in central Tibet.*
> *The first is Jamyang Khyentse Wangpo, born in a male*
>     *Iron Dragon year,*
> *The second is the sovereign master named Thubten, born*
>     *in a male Fire Rat year.*
> *There is no difference whichever of these two is found.*

*The phurba dagger, the manifest symbol of the teaching,*
*Should be placed before the Jowo Shakyamuni Buddha*
*statue;*
*The emissary statue of the Guru will also subsequently*
*Come into the Jowo's presence.*

By the time Jamgön Kongtrul and Tertön Sogyal discovered the key to *The Razor*, Khyentse Wangpo had already passed away; therefore the responsibilities to disseminate the Vajrakilaya treasure rested with the Dalai Lama.

The significance of *The Razor* treasure discovery for the Dalai Lama and the Tibetan nation cannot be overstated. The majority of the treasure revelations, visions, and prophetic dreams that came to Tertön Sogyal throughout his life were tailored by Padmasambhava to remove obstacles to the Dalai Lama's life and to protect the nation of Tibet, and *The Razor* was supreme among them. In addition to guaranteeing the health and longevity of the Thirteenth Dalai Lama, its practice promised to quell the internal strife in the Dalai Lama's court, as well as to subdue the damsi demons within the influential monasteries in Lhasa. If *The Razor* rituals were carried out in the specified manner, including strategic protection of Lhasa by placing a phurba before the sacred Jowo Shakyamuni Buddha statue in Jokhang Temple, then, as a prophecy within *The Razor* states:

> The Gelug teachings will be strengthened and not wane, and in particular, the successive Dharma masters [the Dalai Lamas] will henceforth be assured uninterrupted life spans. The sovereign master named Thubten [Gyatso, the Thirteenth Dalai Lama] will surely live beyond his sixtieth year. The hostile elemental spirits promoting conflicts at Sera and Drepung [monasteries in Lhasa], and encouraging foreign armies, will be subdued. The ruler will not face opposition from his subjects [and] Tibet will be at peace, and the ruler's command will be strengthened. Of this there should not be the slightest doubt!

As with all treasure revelations, the tertön himself must practice it for a period of time to reignite the blessing and power within himself before it is taught to others. It would still be three years before Tertön Sogyal would offer *The Razor* to the principal individual whom it was meant to protect, the Thirteenth Dalai Lama.

# CHAPTER 12

# The DARK FORCES COALESCE

LHASA, CENTRAL TIBET

*Year of the Fire Monkey to the Earth Dog, 1896–1898*

The Nechung Oracle issued a prophecy in the Fire Monkey year (1896) that Tertön Sogyal must return to Lhasa and deliver recent treasure revelations to their owners. Official summons were issued from the Potala Palace, and Tertön Sogyal was soon riding west on horseback to central Tibet on his third trip to Lhasa.

Before Tertön Sogyal was summoned to Lhasa, he spent some months with his wife, Khandro Pumo, and son. Theirs was a relationship founded on the practice of the Dharma and on creating auspicious conditions for each other's swift awakening.

When Khandro Pumo left her life in Gonjo, she quickly adjusted to the meditative space around Tertön Sogyal. She had a natural disposition for spiritual practice and devotedly assisted Tertön Sogyal, as she had not only taken him as her spiritual partner but also as her Dzogchen teacher. For Khandro Pumo, Atrin, and others who assisted Tertön Sogyal, the opportunity to work closely with the tertön provided them continual glimpses into a meditator's mind that did not separate from a state of nondistraction. Discursive thoughts seemed to be swallowed into the enormity of Tertön Sogyal's presence. Serving a cup of tea or adjusting the treasure revealer's shawl was as much a part of their spiritual practice as prostrating and making offerings before images of Padmasambhava in a temple. To see their lama immediately sparked the recognition in themselves of their own enlightened nature. When Tertön Sogyal traveled without them, Khandro Pumo and others did not relax but rather diligently remained in meditation retreats.

Before his trip to Lhasa, the astrologically appropriate day had arrived for Tertön Sogyal to replace the sacred substances he held within his braids of hair tied atop his head. His yogic braids reached well below his chest when let down. Khandro Pumo rolled and cleaned the locks. Few words were exchanged. Tertön Sogyal was not one for banter. Winding a lock around a cloth sachet of medicinal powder and relics, Khandro Pumo placed it upon Tertön Sogyal's crown aperture. Taking each matted dread to hold the sachet in position, she layered them into the finished crown-like arrangement.

Lay tantric yogis on the high plateau, like the wandering *sadhu* mendicants in India, often let their hair grow long. The mass of hair tied in a bundle of a lay yogi in Tibet reminds the community at large that the yogi had dedicated his life to spiritual practice, not unlike one of the external purposes of the shaved head of a monk or nun. Internally, the lay yogi's hair reminds him to be free of convention and mundane concerns, while the shaved head of a monastic constantly reminds him that his path to liberation is through discipline. Ultimately, however, the outer form—red or white robes, tonsured head or long hair—serves only as support for the essential point of Dharma practice, which is to release spontaneously all appearances and rising thoughts into the space of unborn awareness.

Tertön Sogyal relied on Khandro Pumo's advice, for she had the uncommon ability to see into the future. Looking into a doorway or a cave entrance, or even her thumbnail, she received

An image of Khandro Pumo, the spiritual wife
of Tertön Sogyal, from her stupa at Kalzang Temple in Nyarong.

predictions that were luminously written in the empty space. Because her inner winds and energies flowed smoothly in the channels of her subtle body, the ability to peer into the future came almost effortlessly. Though aware of her power, she never offered counsel unless she was asked. When Atrin and others around Khandro Pumo asked her advice, she shied away from the attention and said her only ability was to recite mantras. Later in her life, villagers and farmers continually sought her advice for the best time to plant their crops or the most favorable day to begin a long journey, or to find out whether an illness was going to be fatal. Her predictions were accurate.

Khandro Pumo gathered Tertön Sogyal's personal and religious items for his impending journey, including his prayer beads and a large silver amulet that contained blessing substances and relics of past masters. She presented Tertön Sogyal with a copper tube that had been fashioned by a metalsmith in Derge. She suggested that Tertön Sogyal place his ritual phurba in the container, as it had an eyelet through which a leather tie could thread. Khandro Pumo had premonitions that Tertön Sogyal's phurba dagger might be lost during the long journey ahead of him. She also wanted to ensure that no hand other than Tertön Sogyal's ever touched the sacred object. Like all treasure revealers, Tertön Sogyal was never separated from his phurba, which he concealed in his waist belt—it was a physical reminder of his duty as Padmasambhava's representative.

Tertön Sogyal took his phurba dagger out of his belt. This was the phurba given to him by Nyoshul Lungtok. Tertön Sogyal employed the phurba as a support for his Vajrakilaya meditation, placing it before him and visualizing the wrathful deity emerging from and dissolving into it. The phurba was made of meteorite. Meteorite's ability to slice effortlessly through sky and earth is a metaphor for the Vajrakilaya adept who cuts through confusion and obstacles with the force of his meditation. Tertön Sogyal had such a profound connection with this particular phurba that when he was feeling unwell, or if any of his disciples developed an impure view of the teachings or of their teacher, the blades would secrete rusty-colored oil. At other times, when prophetic visions of Padmasambhava unfolded in Tertön Sogyal's mind or when the auspicious time approached to reveal a treasure, the phurba would vibrate and a whitish substance would trickle from the edges. Holding the phurba in the air, Tertön Sogyal recited an auspicious prayer and lightly touch Khandro Pumo's crown as a blessing, and then placed it in the protective container.

When Tertön Sogyal arrived in Lhasa after five weeks of travel, he went straight to see the Dalai Lama. He wasted no time in showing the Dalai Lama the golden scroll for a Vajrakilaya practice known as *The Deepest Heart Essence of Vajrakilaya.* As Tertön Sogyal had not practiced and matured the blessing in his own mind with *The Razor of the Innermost Essence,* it was not the time to expose it, even to the Dalai Lama. When the Medium of the Nechung Oracle saw the scroll for *The Deepest Heart Essence,* he grabbed it and said, "I must have this!"

"Before you decipher this text, the precious tertön himself must make grand offerings in the Jokhang Temple in front of the Jowo Shakyamuni Buddha statue and the *Wish-Fulfilling Jewel Guru Statue That Liberates Upon Seeing.*"

Tertön Sogyal took up residence in a small room at the Norbulingka Palace of the Dalai Lama, and after he accomplished the rituals Nechung had ordered, he completely deciphered *The Deepest Heart Essence* liturgies into 13 chapters. During this time at the summer palace, monks from the Dalai Lama's personal monastery, Namgyal, performed phurba dagger rites in the temple adjacent to Tertön Sogyal's residence.

Before his arrival in Lhasa in 1896, Tertön Sogyal had gone to Nyarong to check on the young man from the village of Shayul that Tertön Rangrik had mentioned. The boy's mother was indeed pushy in her manner, but Tertön Sogyal simply deflected her insistence to recognize her son, Nyagtrül, as Nyala Pema Dündul's reincarnation. Still, Tertön Sogyal thought the 20-year-old Nyagtrül could use some tutoring, especially since he had displayed some minor meditative accomplishments, such as summoning thunderstorms. After the mother's persistent requests over tea and dumplings, it was agreed that Nyagtrül could travel with Tertön Sogyal's large entourage to Lhasa.

Upon their arrival in Lhasa, Tertön Sogyal found himself too busy to look after Nyagtrül. Tertön Sogyal was bestowing Vajrakilaya empowerments and meditation instructions on the Dalai Lama, and performing rituals for the Tibetan government, which took all of his time and energy. Nyagtrül stayed with a tea-trading Nyarong family residing in Lhasa. They helped the young lama with the language barrier between the Lhasa and Nyarong dialects. But Nyagtrül was precocious enough to navigate his way around Lhasa alone. While he found entertainment in the bazaar and sweet teahouses in the market area, Nyagtrül maintained a strict regimen of meditation and ritual. But a dark force was shrouding Nyagtrül's heart, and his actions began to be taken over by the demon of self-cherishing.

Given that Nyagtrül had arrived in Lhasa with Tertön Sogyal, some believed the young Nyarong lama was his close disciple. Nyagtrül took advantage of this impression and claimed that Tertön Sogyal had taught him how to perform prosperity rituals. Nyagtrül's ability to read people's thoughts led some aristocratic families to bring him to their homes to preside over elaborate rituals to increase wealth in the family.

After some time, however, the Nyarong merchants in Lhasa conveyed messages to Tertön Sogyal that they felt Nyagtrül had turned to the dark side. Their messages to the tertön did not state their reasoning exactly, but they sensed Nyagtrül was up to sorcery because of the dreadful odors, akin to burning flesh, and ominous cries coming from his room, which he never allowed anyone to enter.

"What rituals or black magic is Nyagtrül up to?" they questioned Tertön Sogyal.

Aware that yogis, if they have not steeped their minds in the ethos of the bodhisattva—that deep longing to benefit all sentient beings—can become overwhelmed by their own self-cherishing thoughts, Tertön Sogyal sent a message to Nyagtrül to leave Lhasa immediately and enter a long-term retreat at the holy caves near Samye Temple, southeast of Lhasa. Tertön Sogyal would arrange for a retreat attendant and food. Nyagtrül ignored the directive.

Tertön Sogyal's activities in Lhasa in 1896 included finding and deciphering treasures texts, teaching them to the Dalai Lama, and conducting rituals for the benefit of the nation, and he also visited holy places associated with Padmasambhava.

The Dalai Lama had ascended to power in 1895. It was a critical time, with increasing political pressure on Tibet from its neighbors, and he began to pay even closer attention to Padmasambhava's prophecies, which came to him from those lamas who were tasked with the protection of Tibet. Tertön Sogyal was the foremost of these tantric practitioners. The need for the Dalai Lama to follow in the footsteps of his imperial predecessors by following Padmasambhava's advice can be seen in official sources about the Dalai Lama's temple-building activities:

> Just as the Abbot [Shantarakshita], the Guru [Padma-sambhava], and the Dharma King [Trisong Detsen] had joined forces to establish the glorious Samye Temple and carry out inconceivable benefit to advance the Buddha Dharma, so now this esteemed ruler [the Thirteenth Dalai Lama], endowed with skillful means and great compassion, together with Tertön Padma Lingpa Hutuktu and Tertön Sogyal and other venerated masters of the Old and New schools have joined together in accordance with the timely prophecies intended to expand beneficial activity for the teachings and all sentient beings.

In Tertön Sogyal's tantric worldview, the ability of enemy forces to attack was because Tibet had become a spiritually diminished nation. The weakness of Tibet in the 19th and 20th centuries was not so much due to an ill-equipped army, but because Tibetans had amassed negative deeds in the name of religion. As Padmasambhava repeatedly warned, the nation's power was damaged by sectarian rivalries between monasteries, the illicit use of money donated to monks and nuns, and the practice of praying to enlightened beings for prestige and wealth. But the most pernicious deed that weakened both individuals and the nation was the failure to obey the instructions of their spiritual guides. Because Padmasambhava was the father of Buddhism in Tibet, when the Tibetan government did nothing to enact his instructions that treasure revealers had provided, and when sectarian abbots and monks publicly opposed Padmasambhava, the foundation of the Tibetan nation began to crumble.

The treasures that Padmasambhava concealed and that Tertön Sogyal and others discovered were a medicine, an antidote for the spiritual sickness. The Nechung Oracle continually urged the Dalai Lama to seek teachings, empowerments, and direction from Tertön Sogyal and other representatives of Padmasambhava because the threat to the Tibetan nation was as much from internal spiritual pollution as it was from external military aggression. The Nechung Oracle declared that Tertön Sogyal must continue to reveal treasures that would remove obstacles from the Dalai Lama's life and pacify conflict with forces from India and China and beyond. The need for the Nechung Oracle to continually direct Tertön Sogyal's activity was in fact a sign that the Tibetan nation was deeply polluted; no sooner had one ritual or revelation been accomplished than another was needed. Even during Tertön Sogyal's third visit, conflict broke out near his home area with the invasion by Qing troops from Dartsedo in 1897, and the British were eyeing an invasion of Lhasa from the south, which came about seven years later.

Tertön Sogyal stayed only six months in Lhasa before returning to Kham in the Fire Bird year (1897). Before he left, the Nechung Oracle told him not to be away from Lhasa for too long. Tertön Sogyal exchanged teachings and empowerments with Jamgön Kongtrul upon his return to eastern Tibet and also discovered a number of treasures in the summer, including a phurba dagger known as the Life-Force Phurba of the Dharma King of Tibet. The Life-Force Phurba belonged to the reigning Dharma King, the Dalai Lama. Its associated prophecy told Tertön Sogyal to deliver it to its owner by the autumn so that its full effectiveness in pacifying conflict could be utilized.

Tertön Sogyal came back to Lhasa on the less-traveled route on horses provided by the Office of the Tibetan High Commissioner in Nyarong. Tertön Sogyal's wife and son traveled as far as Kongpo and remained there while he continued to the capital.

At one campsite in the lush forests of Kongpo, Tertön Sogyal took time to decode additional liturgies of *The Razor* and wrote them down in his own hand or dictated to Kongtrul's scribe, who traveled with the group. Along the banks of the Three Cliff Lake, as smoke rose from the smoldering juniper reflected in the deep green waters, Tertön Sogyal called upon the One-Eyed Protectress of Mantras and the local treasure guardians to assist him.

> *You, protectors, by the power of this offering and commanding you to act,*
> *Make the teachings and holders of the teachings flourish,*
> *Make auspicious signs, of help and happiness, increase like the waxing moon,*
> *And make all our aspirations according to the Buddhist teachings be fulfilled!*

Local guardians delivered a treasure to Tertön Sogyal's hands, which included a prophecy entitled the *Luminous Garland of Sunlight* that Padmasambhava had originally given to King Trisong Detsen. The prophecy told of methods to repel harmful demon spirits in Lhasa who were intent on causing divisions among Dharma practitioners. Part of the prophecy called for the construction of various temples and stupas throughout Tibet, including at the historically significant royal chapels in Lhasa, Samye, and Tandruk, new border-protecting structures near Kalzang in Nyarong, among others. These temples, chapels, and stupas, empowered through mantras and filled with sacred substances, could ward off demons that invite military incursions bent on destroying the Buddhist teachings in Tibet. The prophecy warned that if the chapels and temples were not built at the specified time, "the Tibetan ruler and bodhisattva incarnation [the Dalai Lama] would be killed by the Chinese and the life spans of kings and ministers, both Chinese and Tibetan, will become short." If, on the other hand, the temples were built, "law would be established and invaders repulsed, and the sun of happiness will shine in Tibet for a long time to come." Tertön Sogyal arrived in Lhasa in 1898 for his penultimate visit. He offered the Life-Force Phurba, as well as the *Luminous Garland of Sunlight* prophecy, to which the Dalai Lama listened intently; he then ordered that every detail be attended to straightaway, including construction of the strategically placed temples. Preparations were also made for Tertön Sogyal to bestow upon the Dalai Lama *The Razor* phurba teachings. The empowerment ceremonies and complex explanations lasted weeks. Because *The Razor* protected Tibet and the Tibetan leader, both the Dalai Lama's personal chapel of Namgyal and the temple of the State Oracle incorporated the practice into their calendar of rituals, and woodblocks were carved so that texts could be distributed to the initiated. *The Razor* had effectively become part of Tibet's national defense policy.

The morning after *The Razor* empowerments, the Dalai Lama experienced a vivid dream in which he found himself before the palace of Padmasambhava where two dakinis met him and sang prophetic verses that referred to the empowerment that Tertön Sogyal had just bestowed. The celestial dakinis told the Dalai Lama that if he performed apposite ritual offerings according to *The Razor*, the three poisons—desire, anger, and ignorance—would be eradicated and profound spiritual realizations would unfold. They said:

> *Kyema!*
> *Profound, peaceful, and free from elaboration is the blissful power of mind,*
> *Its changeless compassion is the space of the four kayas, spontaneously perfect.*
> *From where, let the deity of wrath pacify the enemies and obstructers, and remove the three poisons—*
> *They will be pacified; this is guaranteed!*
>
> *May the magical form of the deity, wrathful and passionate, arise from the Dharmadhatu*

*To split apart the hearts of all hostile forces and impairers of samaya,*
*Who are like beings bewitched by delusion,*
*And destroy them. They will be overcome. This is guaranteed!*

*Within the charnel ground of the vast display of wrath,*
*By entering the mandala of the supreme secret of*
*The great awesome Vajrakilaya, and by keeping the samaya and vows,*
*Siddhis will be swiftly attained. This is guaranteed!*

*All aspects of this—past, present, and future—*
*Are shown clearly in the symbols of the dakinis;*
*While reciting the numbers required in this Vajrakilaya practice,*
*The holder of this teaching himself must definitely accomplish one thousand fulfillments of tsok offering.*

*But should you delay, the meaning of this prophecy will expire,*
*The guardians of the terma will transgress their vajra oath, and*
*This immutable prediction will become untrue;*
*So be diligent and take great care in how you act!*

The Dalai Lama awoke, remembering the words very clearly, and wrote them down. When he told Tertön Sogyal about the dream, they discussed its meaning. The Tibetan leader wasted no time in accomplishing the 1,000 feast offerings to Vajrakilaya as he was told to do in his dream.

Even though constant rituals and a host of other protective measures were carried out to avert external threats to the Tibetan nation, dangers to the Dalai Lama's life persisted. Indeed, the foreign menaces were coalescing and gathering strength. But Tibet's internal dark forces would strike first.

# CHAPTER 13

# SORCERER'S ASSASSINATION ATTEMPT *on the* DALAI LAMA

LHASA, CENTRAL TIBET

*Year of the Earth Pig, 1899*

In 1886, when the Thirteenth Dalai Lama was 11 years old, Demo became Tibet's regent. Demo was the head of the Tengyeling Monastery, and its estate was the largest and most powerful in Lhasa at the time. Demo served the young Dalai Lama well, and thanks to his position, his monastery increased its already substantial wealth. In the Wood Sheep year (1895), Demo stepped aside and the Dalai Lama was enthroned as the spiritual and political ruler of Tibet. Many in Demo's court were not pleased with their loss of power. In particular, Norbu Tsering, Demo's nephew and manager of the Tengyeling estate, was distressed at the sudden reduction in Tengyeling's political clout after the Dalai Lama ascended to the throne.

The wealth of Tengyeling in the late 1800s was a testament to Norbu Tsering's proficiency in worldly ways. He not only employed financial skills and real estate management, but he also relied heavily on tantric practitioners to perform wealth rituals. But now Tengyeling's influence was waning.

Increasingly discontent with Tengyeling's lot, Norbu Tsering believed the regency would be returned to his uncle Demo if something suddenly caused the Dalai Lama's life to end. So he began to conspire against the Tibetan leader. Unable to gain access to anyone who worked with and served the Dalai Lama's food, Norbu Tsering felt that poisoning, a common method used in China and Tibet at that time to eliminate enemies, was not an option. Then, on the occasion of hosting a ritual in their family home in the west part of Lhasa, presided over by Nyagtrül, the young tantric practitioner from Nyarong, Norbu Tsering hatched a plot to assassinate the Dalai Lama.

Nyagtrül's rise to prominence in Lhasa had been quick. He had chosen to ignore Tertön Sogyal's directive to leave Lhasa for an extended meditation retreat. He had not studied under a teacher since arriving in Lhasa and had not seen Tertön Sogyal or Tertön Rangrik. Nonetheless, his occult powers had increased greatly.

Before coming to Lhasa, Nyagtrül had been taught sorcery. A combination of the shamanism of Tibet's past and Indian tantra, certain spells were the source of his magical powers to influence others, make matter invisible, or control the weather. The efficacy of this sorcery is ignited when a prescribed ritual is performed by a yogi who has mastered, among other talents, undistracted visualizations and mantra recitation. Such practices were taught rarely, for fear they would be misused.

Without a constant spiritual guide to look over Nyagtrül's progress, the original pure motivation behind his spiritual practices became obscured by a sinister urge to acquire many disciples, wealth, and temples. Nyagtrül began to picture himself ruling over a monastic estate similar to Tengyeling, where thousands of students would bow at his feet. As his motivation to benefit others was overshadowed by an egoistic longing for material abundance, he began to rely solely on magic and worldly spells. He used them not to help others but rather for prosperity and influence for himself and for his patrons.

Just after dusk one evening, Nyagtrül agreed to assist Norbu Tsering in his conspiracy. Norbu Tsering did not mention the name of the Dalai Lama to Nyagtrül, however, saying only that a person needed to be eliminated in order for Tengyeling's power to return. Nyagtrül set about the task straightaway.

On thin rice paper, Nyagtrül sketched the body of a naked man, around which he drew a mantra wheel; bound with chains at the neck, the man was pinned down by two large scorpions that held his head and feet in their mouths. Then he inscribed a spell on the paper, slowly enunciating aloud each syllable—a specific spell used to deplete an individual's vital life-force. He recited the spell again and again, infusing the diagram with its injurious power. He strengthened the spell by visualizing scorpions and snakes dispensing the essence of their venom into the sketch. Burning poisonous herbs on a small ember, Nyagtrül held the diagram over the bluish smoke to saturate the paper with noxious fumes. After he folded the paper into a square smaller than the palm of his hand, he drew a smaller diagram on the outside, with flames around the edge, and inscribed more wrathful and violent spells. As he wrapped the paper square with black and red thread, Nyagtrül knew that the black magic he had employed was the strongest possible, and he was confident in its efficacy.

At the conclusion of the ritual, Nyagtrül called Norbu Tsering into the dark room where the wicked diagram lay on the table. "Give me the name and birth year of the person," Nyagtrül said. "I will write it on the paper."

"Thubten. Thubten Gyatso. Born in the year of the Fire Rat."

Nyagtrül paused. The bamboo pen in his hand hovered above the paper as the butter lamp fizzled out.

"You want to kill the Dalai Lama?" Nyagtrül questioned.

"Do it. I've backed you this whole time in Lhasa and provided you with whatever you wanted. Now just write what I have told you!"

Nyagtrül knew that his incantations and sorcery were power-ful enough to take the life of any individual, no matter how holy that person may be. He stared at the diagram. The ring of flames sketched around the edge and the inward-coiling mantras left just enough space to write the name of the intended victim.

"You write it. I am not writing his name," Nyagtrül said, thrusting the pen at Norbu Tsering.

"I don't care who is the scribe or the sorcerer. I just want what is due to me." Norbu Tsering grabbed the pen and wrote, *"SUP-PRESS THUBTEN GYATSO, BORN IN THE FIRE RAT YEAR."*

Nyagtrül hung his head between his shoulders as the Dalai Lama's name in ink dried on the agent of death.

When the Dalai Lama was 24 years old, he began having re-curring ominous dreams. He consulted Tertön Sogyal, who inter-preted the dreams as life threatening and suggested antidotes and rituals to drive away the source of the aggression. The Nechung Oracle began to warn of similar dangers to the Dalai Lama's life. A new menace had emerged. While the Oracle often gave cryptic allegories in his counsel, on this occasion he stated plainly that measures needed to be taken to protect the Dalai Lama.

The Nechung Oracle most often delivered his prophecies and advice to the Dalai Lama and government ministers in formal ceremonies. With the Dalai Lama presiding on a throne and the officials arranged by rank, the Oracle's medium would enter the temple in a meditative state, waiting to become possessed. As the assembly chanted invocation verses, the medium's ritual brocade robes and circular chest plate, weighing more than 100 pounds, were securely fastened. When Nechung entered the medium's body, the monk stomped and jerked in wrathful dances as a massive helmet-crown that weighed more than 30 pounds was tied to his head. As he hissed and jumped, bowed and twirled, attendants scrambled to listen to the Oracle's prophecies uttered through the medium. Helpful attendants supported the possessed monk and hoped his limbs and neck would not snap from the weight.

Before the Great Prayer Festival in 1899, although the Nechung Oracle strongly warned of threats to the Dalai Lama and cautioned him against being in any public space, the ruler still took part in ceremonies at the Jokhang Temple with Lhasa residents. Days after the ceremonies were complete, the Dalai Lama suffered from dizziness and nausea. Potala Palace doctors were summoned to assess the Dalai Lama's weakened condition. That evening, the Medium of the Nechung Oracle went into a trance at his small temple on the outskirts of Lhasa. The medium's attending monks knew something was very serious because Nechung rarely entered the medium when not summoned during a formal ceremony. But the message was indecipherable. The puzzling message mentioned death, the Dalai Lama, and a pair of boots.

A messenger was immediately dispatched on horseback to the Potala with the dire warning in writing for the Dalai Lama. As soon as Nechung had departed the monk's body, the exhausted medium put on his monk's habit and dashed to the Potala. A separate runner was sent in the dead of night to fetch Tertön Sogyal, for the Oracle had also said, "Ask the one with the title of Tertön."

By the time Tertön Sogyal arrived at the Potala, the Dalai Lama's attendants and advisors were trying to decipher the meaning of the Nechung Oracle's enigmatic warning, which spoke of perilous spells, ill will, jealousy, and footwear. The group made no headway in deciphering the Oracle's message. As they spoke in hushed voices, confused by the inclusion of footwear in the warning, a disturbed and tired Dalai Lama walked into the room. All present bowed their heads and bent at the waist.

"What then is this about?" the Dalai Lama questioned bluntly. "Sogyal, tell me!"

Tertön Sogyal asked the chamber attendants if a pair of boots had recently been gifted to the Dalai Lama. One of the attendants nodded affirmatively, grabbed a torch to illuminate the dark hallways, and ran to retrieve the footwear.

Some weeks before, Tertön Sogyal had visited Demo at Tengyeling Monastery. While there, Norbu Tsering had asked

Tertön Sogyal to put on a pair of boots that, he was told, had recently been delivered from an expert boot maker. Tertön Sogyal did not know that Norbu Tsering had sewn the black magic diagram into the heel of one of the boots. Norbu Tsering wanted Tertön Sogyal to wear the boots because if a powerful tantric practitioner like Tertön Sogyal stomps on such a heinous diagram, the curse is kick-started. As soon as Tertön Sogyal pulled on the knee-high boots, however, blood dripped from his nose. He took this as an extremely inauspicious sign and removed the boots immediately and departed from Tengyeling. Failing to get Tertön Sogyal to wear the boots, Norbu Tsering decided to try to have the Dalai Lama effect the spell himself by wearing the boots. Norbu Tsering arranged for the cursed boots to be offered to the Dalai Lama by Tengyeling Monastery during an offering ceremony that took place during the Great Prayer Festival two weeks before the Dalai Lama fell ill—precisely when the Oracle had warned of dangers.

The Dalai Lama looked on sternly at his most trusted attendants, the medium, and his teacher Tertön Sogyal, as they waited for the attendant to return with the boots. The echo of the scurrying steps of the chamber attendant grew louder in the hallway. Two separate pairs of boots had been given to the Dalai Lama during the offering ceremony, and the attendant held both pairs. Tertön Sogyal recognized the pair he had tried on a fortnight earlier. Upon seeing the boots, the Dalai Lama almost vomited, while the Medium of the Nechung Oracle began to sway back and forth as if he were going to be possessed.

"Give me those," Tertön Sogyal said as he seized a single boot with both hands.

Tertön Sogyal's body surged with wrath. He tore at the boot's leather and brocade and slammed the sole to the floor until the dense insulation in the heel broke open. The cursed talisman was ejected from the boot's heel and fell to the cold stone floor. The medium reached forward to grab it, but Tertön Sogyal pushed him away. Dark shadows slid around the room as wind pushed at the flames of the torches set in the walls. Holding the sorcerer's black magic diagram in the air, Tertön Sogyal did not dare voice what he read inscribed.

"Show it to me," the Dalai Lama commanded.

Tertön Sogyal dutifully walked toward the ruler and held the diagram in the torchlight.

### SUPPRESS THUBTEN GYATSO, BORN IN THE FIRE RAT YEAR

Dizzy and nauseated, the Dalai Lama squinted in anger, now realizing the gravity of the Oracle's pronouncement.

"There may be more than one person in Lhasa with the name Thubten Gyatso," the Dalai Lama said. "But only one Thubten Gyatso was born in the Fire Rat year. Find out who is trying to kill me."

The Dalai Lama's orders to find his would-be assassins were completed swiftly. Tibetan government documents show that ministers oversaw a brief investigation and judicial proceeding. Tengyeling was immediately suspected. As the former regent was ultimately responsible for the activities of Tengyeling Monastery, Demo was implicated in the assassination plot. He was summoned to the Potala on the pretext of an important ceremony. Upon his arrival, he was placed in shackles and thrown into the Shol prison below the Potala Palace. His nephew, Norbu Tsering, was also tricked into coming to the Potala on the fake summons that he was to be honored for his exemplary service to the Tibetan government. Nyagtrül was taken from the Barkhor neighborhood and dragged into a prison cell.

The black magician Nyagtrül was identified as the sorcerer assassin, and Norbu Tsering admitted being the ringleader of the plot, not only because of the deadly spell in the boot, but he had also buried four ceramic vases around the Potala Palace, empowered with different black magic substances. Demo and other family members at Tengyeling were not spared. More than two dozen individuals at Tengyeling sat in the dungeon below the Potala Palace within a week. News spread quickly around Lhasa of the assassination attempt on the Dalai Lama.

The Nechung Oracle continued to warn of other sorcery. The Oracle directed the Tibetan government officials to unearth additional buried spells. Another oracle was also consulted, and discovered a hand-size scorpion from under a willow tree in the courtyard of the Ramoche Temple. When attendants examined the scorpion, they found shreds of the Dalai Lama's monastic robe in its belly, which was seen as particularly harmful and inauspicious, and evidence of further black magic.

Punishment for crimes in 19th-century Tibet was severe; corporal and capital punishment were regularly employed. After a brief trial for treason, all the accused were found guilty and sentenced to death. Even though the Council of Ministers called for the conspirators from Tengyeling to pay with their lives, the Dalai Lama intervened and forbade any capital punishment in his domain.

Norbu Tsering and others at Tengyeling were sentenced to life in prison. Demo was never seen again in Lhasa. Perhaps he was held under house arrest in Lhasa for the rest of his life. But it is more likely that Demo was exiled to Ngari in western Tibet. The Demo incarnation line was banned, and much of the record of his previous incarnations' activities was scrubbed from the history books. The Tibetan government confiscated Tengyeling's vast estates, and statues and gold from its grand shrines were distributed to temples across the Tibetan Plateau. One hundred statues were offered to Tertön Sogyal to take on his return journey to Nyarong to be housed in newly constructed chapels at Kalzang.

As for Nyagtrül, despite the Dalai Lama's commutation of the death penalty upon Tertön Sogyal's urging, as well as the Nechung Oracle's strong and repeated urgings not to kill the Nyarong sorcerer, he was dead soon after imprisonment. Some say Nyagtrül was treated so badly by guards that he stabbed himself and died in a toilet; others say he was bound in a leather bag and beaten to death. Nyagtrül's body was buried at a location named the Black Mouth at Nyen, and a black stupa the size of a small house was built over the top in an attempt to suppress any further negative energy. If the revenge that the spirit of Nyagtrül soon sought for his treatment in prison was any indication, his death had certainly been horrific.

Escaping from beneath the black stupa, Nyagtrül's spirit haunted Lhasa and meddled in the Dalai Lama's affairs. The stupa built above Nyagtrül's corpse inauspiciously cracked whenever the Dalai Lama traveled the two miles between the Potala and the gardens of the Norbulingka estate, and the spirit stirred up dust and windstorms at the same time. The spirit became even more audacious and on a number of occasions tried to enter the Medium of the Nechung Oracle to confuse the government with misguided prophecies. The Dalai Lama finally summoned the individuals whom he thought capable of suppressing Nyagtrül's spirit—Tertön Rangrik and Tertön Sogyal.

Tertön Rangrik was preparing to return to his monastery in Nyarong and was not keen on becoming embroiled in an esoteric battle with the spirit in Lhasa—a duel that could go on for many months and would take a considerable toll on his physical constitution. Still, he went to Lhasa to attend an emergency meeting of the Council of Ministers. The Dalai Lama presided over the gathering of his council and the two tertöns in the Potala Palace. The dire situation was fully explained to the tertöns; both remained as austere as anyone had ever seen. The Dalai Lama commanded Tertön Sogyal and Tertön Rangrik to subjugate Nyagtrül's spirit. Though the Dalai Lama directed the tantric adepts to carry out rituals, the elderly Nyarong lama was having none of it. Frustrated that he had been dragged into the tumultuous political situation, Tertön Rangrik stood to end the meeting on his own terms. He bowed to the Dalai Lama and then turned to Tertön Sogyal.

"You brought him here," Tertön Rangrik said, referring to Nyagtrül. "You put him in the ground."

Immediately, Tertön Sogyal began trying to stop Nyagtrül's spirit from inflicting any more harm. During elaborate ceremonies with Namgyal Monastery monks, and in solitary retreat, images of Nyagtrül's spirit were fashioned from barley dough and summoned to enter the effigy. Tertön Sogyal stabbed and sliced the spirit with his ritual phurba dagger in an attempt to liberate the spirit from his harmful obsessions. Other lamas became involved; one of the Thirteenth Dalai Lama's tutors died of exhaustion from his own ritual efforts. It was not until early in 1902, after Tertön Sogyal had returned to eastern Tibet, nearly three years after Nyagtrül's spirit had roamed, that signs indicated that the subjugation of Nyagtrül was complete. However, this was only the beginning of the Dalai Lama's troubles and battle for survival.

# CHAPTER 14

# OVERCOMING OBSTACLES

KALZANG TEMPLE, NYARONG, EASTERN TIBET

*Year of the Earth Pig to the Iron Rat, 1899–1900*

Tertön Sogyal returned to eastern Tibet at the end of 1899. His prominence as a religious figure stretched from Lhasa to Dartsedo and indeed into China. Not only was Tertön Sogyal the Thirteenth Dalai Lama's teacher, but it was now widely known that he had saved the life of the Tibetan ruler. Tibetan government officials escorted Tertön Sogyal to his homeland of Nyarong from Lhasa with specific instructions to assist the tertön in the construction of the geomantic chapels at Kalzang, as the *Luminous Garland of Sunlight* prophecy had indicated.

Tertön Sogyal's wife, Khandro Pumo, and son, Rigdzin Namgyal, could see from their perch at Kalzang Temple the procession of horses and government cavalrymen approaching. Rigdzin Namgyal would follow in the tradition of his father as a lay tantric practitioner and later became known for his long meditation retreats, often while completely naked in his one-room cabin on the mountainside. Attendants would bring tea in the morning and, upon returning in the afternoon, find that the tea had not been consumed nor had Rigdzin Namgyal even moved from his meditation posture. Later in his life, it was said that dust would collect on Rigdzin Namgyal's shoulders and thighs while he sat in meditation for days on end.

Construction commenced on the border-protecting temple below Kalzang, the place where Tertön Sogyal had first met Nyala Pema Dündul. The Dalai Lama gave the name to the new temple—Glorious Palace of Joy and Total Victory Blazing Like Dzi Onyx—which was a small temple with four surrounding protector chapels, including one honoring the Nechung Oracle. Most of the statues housed in the new temple were offered by the Tibetan government, which had seized them from Tengyeling Monastery after the demise of ex-regent Demo. Concurrent with the construction, a 25-foot-high stupa, named Tamer of Demons and Subjugator of Haughty Spirits, was built at the confluence of two rivers at Deer Horn Junction. Tertön Sogyal told those at Kalzang, "Such strategically placed temples and stupas repel the kinds of demons who are inciting conflict, stirring up hatred, arrogance, and jealousy in people's minds."

After the new foundation was laid for the temple, Tertön Sogyal traveled with his wife and son to seek out Nyoshul Lungtok and Dza Choktrul in Thromthar for teachings and empowerments. Though Tertön Sogyal was in full command of the highest Dzogchen teachings and teacher to none other than the Dalai Lama himself, he still bowed before his own teachers and requested pith instructions for meditation and ritual activity. Tertön Sogyal's own teachers in turn would ask him to bestow upon them his many treasure revelations.

Nyoshul Lungtok was ill when Tertön Sogyal arrived, and he was asked to perform a ransoming ritual to extend the life of the elder master. An effigy of Nyoshul Lungtok made of barley dough was placed below a ten-foot-high intricate web of colorful threads that served as a temporary abode for the spirits. The effigy and structure were offered to local spirits, who were causing the ill health. At this time, Tertön Sogyal had a dream of a dakini

An earth treasure statue of Manjushri revealed
by Tertön Sogyal in Tromthar, eastern Tibet.

with glowing fair skin who warned him that if he did not bring auspicious conditions into line, then whatever he tried to do in the future would be in vain; yet he was not told the precise ritual activity to perform, so he became slightly frustrated. In the evening after the last day of rituals on behalf of Nyoshul Lungtok, Tertön Sogyal had a vision of Padmasambhava in the space before him, and then the Great Guru dissolved into a house in Lhasa. Tertön Sogyal awoke thinking it was a bad omen indicating Nyoshul Lungtok would soon pass away and that his reincarnation would be reborn in Lhasa. Then a voice came and said, "That is not it. Yet more will be clear soon."

Nyoshul Lungtok eventually recovered. Tertön Sogyal continued having many visions, intense dreams, and inconclusive signs, but little indication of the exact course of action to take. With threats to the Dalai Lama's life, trouble on Tibet's borders, and his increasing age, Tertön Sogyal was becoming impatient. A haze hovered over his ability to decipher the hidden meanings. When he returned to Kalzang Temple and went to meditate at dusk on the side of the hill named Meto Garuda Eagle, a rainbow appeared. Walking out of the five-colored lights was a man with reddish skin, holding a tiger-skin quiver of arrows, who said, "When the time comes, I will assist you. Not now." Tertön Sogyal prayed to Padmasambhava to gain clarity, saying:

> *Inspire us with your blessings in this life, the next, and*
> *the in-between state,*
> *Release us from samsara's ocean of suffering,*
> *Inspire us with your blessings to arrive at our unborn*
> *enlightened nature,*
> *And grant us the spiritual attainments, ordinary and*
> *supreme!*

As he was praying, Tertön Sogyal heard a voice say, "This will be very profound, therefore, the obstacles will be powerful. If you can counter the negative with the positive, then you yourself will be free from the demons." Still, Tertön Sogyal could not understand specifically what to do. Descending the mountainside, Tertön Sogyal walked back to Kalzang Temple, and that evening, the fair-skinned dakini again appeared to him and advised, "Just act according to the crucial points. And regarding the illusion-like appearances that will arise, be patient toward them." Then she vanished.

Tertön Sogyal's inability to understand the import of the visions and dreams was vexing him. Not only was he unclear about the visions, he was not receiving coded maps, or signs about treasure revelations. After one vision when he encountered a huge black snake that stood up straight like a pillar and would not budge, he became very upset. That evening, the fair-skinned dakini appeared and said, "If you allow conceptualization to proliferate in your mind—that is your demon that will usher forth obstacles! There is nowhere else that the obstacle rests apart from one's own mind's creation."

Tertön Sogyal believed that the unfolding of foreboding dreams, which lasted for some months, indicated that black magic was being directed against him. He also suspected that he was being slandered by some individuals with whom he had a personal connection and to whom he had given tantric empowerments—perhaps they were possessed by the damsi demon. He continued his stay at Kalzang Temple, where his wife and close companions became deeply worried. After three months of feeling the malicious intentions, insinuations, and sorcery, Tertön Sogyal completely lost his ability to speak.

One evening, the fair-skinned dakini returned in a vision and said, "There are those who are possessed by the demon; if you can seize their negativity as an array of powerful energy, the benefit can be vast!" Later that evening, Tertön Sogyal dreamed that his mother led him into a white tent. As she sewed the door closed, she said, "At the time of eight, you will be released because of your virtuous behavior." Tertön Sogyal awoke thinking it was a sign that he would be released from his muteness, but he did not know if it would be in eight days, or in the eighth month, or longer. Lama Trime, who was a fellow tertön and student of Tertön Sogyal, was consulted along with a doctor from Derge, but they were unable to identify the exact time Tertön Sogyal would be released from the spell of muteness. Again, the fair-skinned dakini appeared to Tertön Sogyal in a dream and told him, "Your main concern should be none other than what can be seen right here, right now," but she did not indicate which rituals to perform. For the next two months, Tertön Sogyal continued to have visionary encounters with Vajrakilaya, Padmasambhava, and Khyentse Wangpo, but no termas arose. It was the first time that Tertön Sogyal's prolific treasure revelations were blocked, and there was a fear that Tertön Sogyal's life-force was being sapped. His teachers and close disciples performed rituals to release him from his inability to speak, but nothing worked.

On the tenth day of the seventh month of the Iron Rat year (1900), Padmasambhava appeared to Tertön Sogyal in a dream and said, "You, my son, listen, many beings in these degenerate times will show you devotion, supplicate you, and request teachings from you. Even while praising you, they will be filled with doubts, wrong views, and belittling speech that does not recognize your greatness. Though their disregard will be like an unending wave that you cannot stop, cut your attachment to hope or fear. Confidently maintain the stronghold of your pure awareness. To dispel the negative circumstances, there is a profound and marvelous method that no one else has. It is known as *Tendrel Nyesel—Dispelling Flaws in Interdependence*. The guardians of this terma will hand it over to you."

In the vision, Padmasambhava, surrounded by many dakinis, bestowed upon Tertön Sogyal the complete empowerments and instructions of the teaching *Dispelling Flaws in Interdependence*. Various dakinis took turns delivering their own prophecy to Tertön Sogyal about future treasure teachings, the companions he should have around him, and associated prophecies. When the last dakini spoke, she told Tertön Sogyal of the need to practice the Vajrakilaya rites to avert military incursions by foreign armies, after which the dakini dissolved into his heart. Padmasambhava then told Tertön Sogyal that he needed to paint 1,000 Buddha statues and 1,000 Vajrakilaya images, and, most significantly, that he needed to maintain great secrecy about not only the *Dispelling Flaws* treasure and these prophecies, but all subsequent revelations.

Scroll painting of the terma revelation of *Dispelling Flaws in Interdependence (Tendrel Nyesel)* with Guru Padmasambhava in the center.

"If you diligently apply the act of secrecy, your realization will increase and you will be freed from the demons of conceptualization," Padmasambhava said. "There will be no hindrance to your accomplishment practices, and the door will be open to benefit beings, and the sickness of your body will stop."

Tertön Sogyal realized that *Dispelling Flaws in Interdependence* was a critical antidote needed for his own path to enlightenment, as well as a remedy for the Tibetan nation, because it could foster a unified Dharma approach for the religious and political leaders.

*Dispelling Flaws in Interdependence* is a tantric practice that deals directly with the fabric of existence, bringing about wholly auspicious circumstances conducive to spiritual realizations. In his original teaching of *Dispelling Flaws* to Yeshe Tsogyal, Padmasambhava taught that circumstances in life come about in various ways—some circumstances naturally appear, like the weather, and little can be done about them. There are other situations that can come about by someone deliberately assembling the causes and conditions. And there are those circumstances that, after they unfold, can be transformed. Padmasambhava explained that whether a circumstance unfolds auspiciously or inauspiciously has much to do with a person's attitude, which further fuels a situation. The operating principle of *Dispelling Flaws in Interdependence* is thus: Because the nature of reality is interdependent, spiritual practitioners can affect their universe by preventing inauspiciousness from arising, eliminating inauspiciousness when it does come about, and transforming inauspiciousness into auspiciousness. Through the combination of the visualization of deities and their activities, recitation of specific mantras, and resting in the sublime view of Dzogchen, the promise of *Dispelling Flaws* is that harm can be healed, future danger can be prevented, and positive circumstances among the population can be increased.

> *For us and those who need protection:*
> *May all harm and faults in outer, inner, and secret interdependent circumstances be pacified!*
> *May all goodness increase and spread!*

*May all favorable circumstances come under our power*
*and mastery!*
*May all negative circumstances cease to exist!*

On the 25th day of the lunar calendar, Tertön Sogyal gathered a group of yogis and yoginis who maintained pure samaya. The assembly included a prophesied dakini who sat next to the tertön. Tertön Sogyal was still unable to speak. While they offered a ritual feast, Tertön Sogyal understood that the *Dispelling Flaws in Interdependence* delivery was imminent. He wrote a note informing Dza Choktrul about the forthcoming revelation, which included a medicine that would cure his muteness. Tertön Sogyal prayed fervently that there would be no obstacles to the discovery of the treasure and that its revelation would bring a great wave of benefit.

Two days later, after Tertön Sogyal had made many aspirational prayers and was resting in the profound state of meditation, a treasure guardian handed him a terma casket that contained spiritual medicine that cured him of his muteness. He showed the casket to the dakini, who said, "The treasure must be deciphered now because it is like a medicine targeting a sickness." The next night, Padmasambhava, riding a tiger, appeared to Tertön Sogyal and made a prophecy about deciphering *Dispelling Flaws in Interdependence*. Tertön Sogyal felt more joy than when revealing any of his previous termas. With diligence and a newfound enthusiasm, Tertön Sogyal wrote out the elaborate practice text of *Dispelling Flaws in Interdependence,* which included instructions on repairing inauspicious circumstances by striking at the heart of ignorance itself.

*All these momentary thoughts, perceptions, and perceiving*
*Arise from interdependent circumstances,*
*And yet they are unborn,*
*For they are, by their very nature, empty.*

*So before them, be without grasping, be without effort or*
*striving.*

*The unaltered state of rigpa, natural condition of the*
    *unending innermost mind,*
*Is free of all conceptual thinking: indestructible and*
    *sky-like.*

*Rigpa is empty from the very beginning,*
*Radiant in and of itself,*
*An all-penetrating limitlessness:*
*Unmoving, beyond all knowledge or knowing.*

*Because rigpa illuminates itself,*
*It automatically resolves*
*All doubts and misconceptions.*
*Because it is not based on the intellectual mind,*
*It rests in its own natural condition, as it is.*

*Unbounded by time, unmoving and unchanging,*
*In this state, no inauspiciousness can ever exist;*
*Everything is self-liberated as the state of great bliss,*
*And right there buddhahood is accomplished, without*
    *any seeking.*

*Buddha is not to be sought anywhere else.*

# CHAPTER 15

# NEVER GIVE UP

LHASA, CENTRAL TIBET

*Year of the Iron Ox to the Wood Dragon, 1901–1904*

After two years in Kham, Tertön Sogyal returned to Lhasa in the Iron Ox year (1901) with the *Dispelling Flaws in Interdependence* terma and resumed his position in the court of the Dalai Lama. It would be his last trip to central Tibet. At this time, there was no disputing the Dalai Lama's reliance on Tertön Sogyal and the responsibilities he entrusted in him. Yet some in Lhasa, including prominent monastic leaders, continued to oppose the tertön. They resented him not only because of his unorthodox and rough character, but because of his influence on the Dalai Lama regarding religious matters. The central issue that some of the monks from Sera and Ganden monasteries raised questioned the authenticity of Padmasambhava's concealed treasures and prophecies—the very spiritual practices to which the Dalai Lama, the Nechung Oracle, and others were devoted. While sectarian monks' protestations persisted, the Dalai Lama still relied upon Tertön Sogyal for spiritual guidance, as well as advice on how to handle the growing political threat from British India and Tsarist Russia, as well as the Qing Manchus.

As soon as Tertön Sogyal arrived in Lhasa, he offered the empowerments and transmissions of *Dispelling Flaws in Interdependence* to the Dalai Lama, who composed a prayer of offering to the Dharma protectors of the teaching. Such treasure teachings as *Dispelling Flaws* and *The Razor* were specifically catering to Tibet's troubles at the end of the 19th and the early 20th centuries. The *Dispelling Flaws* revelation was meant to repair the disharmony of Tibet's political leaders and the sectarian monks through unification. One of the special qualities of treasure teachings is that revelation occurs at precisely the time when the instructions are most needed. As it says in the *Dispelling Flaws in Interdependence* liturgy:

> *Pacify all outer, inner and secret inauspicious circum-stances: Let the past ones cease to exist! Let future ones not arise! Let present ones never harm us! And, from within the space of wisdom, transform all harm and inauspiciousness into good.*

Yet the revelation of a treasure teaching and prophecy is not effective in and of itself. The instructions and meditations taught in the treasure need to be practiced in full, the rituals must be carried out to the letter, and the prophetic instructions must be heeded. Because of the many interdependent causes and conditions that make up a given threat, oftentimes a multifaceted antidote must be applied. For this reason, the Dalai Lama was following the spiritual advice of Tertön Sogyal and other highly accomplished meditation masters in his attempt to rule effectively, employing many remedies for the looming internal and external threats in Tibet.

Tertön Sogyal received news at this time that his teacher Nyoshul Lungtok had left his body at the age of 72 at his retreat in Tromthar in eastern Tibet, where he had lived for his last 12 years. Just before Nyoshul Lungtok's mind dissolved into the primordial state of basic awareness, he gave his last testament, which described his profound realization:

*To be immersed in genuine, unfettered being is to*
*    be like the sun rising at dawn.*
*This is the vision of the ultimate nature—how*
*    marvelous!*

Tertön Sogyal was indebted to Nyoshul Lungtok for the refinement of his yogic training and the lineage of whispered instructions that he had received. Tertön Sogyal practiced guru yoga to merge his mind with the wisdom mind of his guru.

*The knots of the eight worldly concerns have come un-*
*    tied in the state of equal taste.*
*The designs of ordinary consciousness have faded in the*
*    basic space of original purity.*
*You have directly experienced the way of abiding that is*
*    the Great Perfection.*
*[Nyoshul] Lungtok Tenpe Nyima, I pray to you.*

Tertön Sogyal continued to reveal termas in central Tibet and, as the dakinis had advised, he kept many of the revelations secret, even from those in the Potala Palace. However, when he was given a prophecy concerning the chapels at Kalzang, Tertön Sogyal knew he would need the assistance of the Dalai Lama. Tertön Sogyal told the Tibetan leader he needed to take back to Nyarong an exceptional statue that could serve as additional protection.

"As there are not many goldsmiths in eastern Tibet," Tertön Sogyal explained, "could Your Holiness provide me with a splendid image?"

"We have many Nyingma statues in Lhasa, but the most precious ones are in chapels in the Potala; those chapels were sealed with nails and molten bronze when we were protecting them from the Dzungar Mongol armies many centuries ago."

The Dalai Lama had his blacksmith unseal one of the temples, and therein he found a list of the ancient contents.

"There are five images blessed by Padmasambhava himself in this temple. Although it would be a disaster for Lhasa to be without them, nonetheless I will not let you down!"

The Dalai Lama commissioned an exact replica of the most magnificent statue in the previously sealed chapel and placed inside, at the heart, an ancient hand-size image blessed by Padmasambhava. On the day that the Dalai Lama offered Tertön Sogyal the statue and ordered the governor of Nyarong to look after its transport to Kalzang, Tertön Sogyal expressed his gratitude. The Dalai Lama responded, "Now, for your son and your lineage, I will bestow upon you this glass seal so that the next generation of your family will be in good standing, along with an estate."

"That you, a great sublime object of refuge, look upon me with compassion and bestow such kindness is truly incomparable. This is really too much," Tertön Sogyal said. "I accept your kindness and will fulfill the aspirations of my gurus. For me, Your Holiness, I am an aging yogi who prefers to dwell in the mountains and who has no use for seals of rank or tracts of land. But I will find a way to put it to good use."

At the beginning of the 20th century, the Russian and British empires competed for Central Asia supremacy, a rivalry known as the Great Game. Russia had steadily expanded its territory from the end of the 18th century under Peter the Great and the tsars from Alexander I to Alexander III, all of whom gained territory for Russia. By the time the trans-Siberian railway was complete, Britain was worried that Russia might extend its reach into Tibet, and farther into India. Britain, on the other hand, was consolidating control in the Indian foothills in Sikkim, and farther to the west near Ladakh. The British were intent on establishing secure trade routes with Tibet. During this period, Britain and China were negotiating trade and suzerainty agreements concerning Tibet, but without Tibetan representation. Tibetans viewed the various Anglo-Chinese and Russo-Chinese agreements as illegitimate.

In the summer of 1901, one of the assistant tutors of the Dalai Lama, a Buryatian scholar known as Dorjieff, went to Russia carrying a letter of greeting from the Dalai Lama to the Tsar. This raised considerable suspicion that the Dalai Lama was courting Russia to stand up against Britain and China. The possibility of Russia extending its sphere of influence into Tibet caused significant angst in Peking and London, for they believed Russia had goals of complete Pan-Asian dominance. The Japanese scholar-spy Ekai Kawaguchi erroneously reported seeing two waves of camel caravans from Russia entering Lhasa carrying gifts and weapons for the Dalai Lama from the Tsar. Britain's erroneous belief in 1902 that a large cache of Russian weapons was being delivered to Lhasa was enough evidence for them to begin planning an invasion into Tibet, though in the name of a "trade mission."

As the threats from British India continued to increase, the Dalai Lama felt it most appropriate for him to personally engage in esoteric means to avert the danger. In the fourth month of the Water Hare year (1903), the Dalai Lama decided to enter an extended meditation retreat. Tradition prescribed the Dalai Lama to enter retreat for three years. Along with the Dalai Lama's senior tutors, Tertön Sogyal offered him instructions for the retreat. Being certain that trouble was on his doorstep, the Dalai Lama intended to perform rituals and meditate upon the deity Yamantaka, as well as the Vajrakilaya treasure teachings that Tertön Sogyal had revealed. Both Yamantaka and Vajrakilaya—two extremely wrathful deities—are believed to be not only powerful antidotes to spiritual pollution, but especially swift.

As the Dalai Lama began his meditation retreat, Tertön Sogyal departed for a few months of pilgrimage throughout central Tibet, revealing more treasure teachings and practicing esoteric rites to strengthen the Tibetan nation and push back the invaders. A few months later, the British regiment led by Francis Younghusband crossed the Indo-Tibetan border and began to increase its troop numbers. Britain had been unable to communicate directly with the Dalai Lama, who, unbeknownst to them, was in meditation retreat. Even if the Dalai Lama had not been in retreat, due to Tibet's dismissive view of previous Anglo-Chinese trade agreements, it is unlikely that he would have responded to any communiqués. As Younghusband moved his army farther into the Land of Snows, Britain was unsure whether the Tibetans had already signed an agreement with Russia—which they had not.

With no direct contact with the Tibetan government, Younghusband marched his 8,000 troops northward and encountered the poorly equipped and trained Tibetan army at the town of Gyantse. Many of the Tibetan soldiers brandished lances and bows and arrows as weapons, and amulets believed to protect them from bullets. Fighting erupted and the Tibetans were massacred by the British. News of the carnage quickly made its way back to the Tibetan government. The Nechung Oracle was delivering regular pronouncements to the Dalai Lama's advisors that the Tibetan leader should break his multi-year retreat and flee. Tibet's Council of Ministers concurred with the Oracle's direction and advised the Dalai Lama to leave immediately for Urga, the capital of Mongolia.

In the first days of August 1904, British forces entered Lhasa just below the Potala Palace without resistance. Had the Dalai Lama been in the Potala, he would have had a bird's-eye view of the impressive legion of khaki-clad military units marching through the city's west gate. But to the dismay of Younghusband and the British, they still had no Tibetan leader with whom to negotiate. A few days prior, under the cover of night, the Dalai Lama had fled northeast to exile in Mongolia.

Less than a month before the British entered Lhasa, Tertön Sogyal had been summoned to meet with the Dalai Lama. They discussed whether the tertön should take up residence in eastern Tibet, because he had been moving about continually for so many years. They asked the Nechung Oracle at which base it would be better for Tertön Sogyal to stay: in Dzak, where the tertön had an encampment near Derge, or at the new temple in Nyarong below Lhangdrak Peak.

"Go to Lhangdrak, and there stay in a retreat house below the peak. Build a residence not too big but not too small," was the Oracle's instruction.

Both the Dalai Lama and Tertön Sogyal agreed this was best. Tertön Sogyal sent a messenger straightaway to Dzak instructing Khandro Pumo and their son to move back to Nyarong.

"According to your predictions about these unstable times, both within central Tibet and coming from outside forces," the Dalai Lama said to Tertön Sogyal, "I myself do not know if I can remain for long in Lhasa. But you leave first and safely return to Nyarong in eastern Tibet."

They touched foreheads in a sign of mutual devotion and reverence. Tertön Sogyal knew that despite all of Padmasambhava's prophecies and the ritual combat against foreign invaders, the collective negative karma of the Tibetans had weakened their national defense. There was nothing more for him to do. He knew that the battle for the spiritual life-force of his country was going to take him to the eastern regions of Tibet, and beyond. Tertön Sogyal and the Dalai Lama were never to meet face-to-face again, at least in their present incarnations.

# CHAPTER 16

# HIDDEN VALLEYS

NYARONG, EASTERN TIBET

*Year of the Water Hare to the Wood Snake, 1903–1905*

Tertön Sogyal returned to Nyarong and the Dalai Lama fled to Mongolia. Some say that the phurba dagger practices ensured that Younghusband's forces only stayed in Lhasa for a month and were unable to secure their commercial interests. Others assert Younghusband's late conversion to modern mysticism was a result of the ritual bombardment of phurbas directed upon him. Regardless, there is certainty that the invasion of Lhasa by British troops prompted the Qing government to consolidate its control in eastern Tibet to keep from losing ground to the British or Russians. This was a wake-up call for the Qing. Even before Younghusband's march into Lhasa, the Qing had positioned their troops in eastern Tibet with the intent to establish forceful rule over the tribal chiefs and monasteries, and then extend their control to Lhasa.

When Tertön Sogyal returned home, he walked directly into this emerging battlefront between the Qing military and the eastern Tibetan tribal warriors. Qing troops arrived in 1904 in Litang and Batang, south of Nyarong, and were poised to conquer and begin the first-ever planned transfer of Chinese migrants into Tibet, as well as the initial mining of the area's rich mineral deposits. By the spring of 1905, open rebellion against the Chinese troops and settlers broke out, and Han migrants and Qing government officials were killed. Reinforcements were sent from Chengdu to secure Litang and Batang and then turn north and move into Nyarong. Tertön Sogyal read with great concern ancient prophecies by earlier tertöns:

> The age of degeneration will come when the damsi demon enters the heart of the Tibetans, giving rise to all kinds of nonvirtuous thoughts and actions by the populace. Due to this nonvirtue, foreign forces will successfully invade Tibet. At this time of degeneration, charlatan practitioners of the Dharma will fool the populace and appear to be accomplished yogis, while the realization of the highest truth will only rest in space, not within them. The common people will disregard the Dharma and think only of their own importance, and will be more intent on accumulating wealth, food, clothing, and success instead of practicing the secret Tantra. The ordained sangha will merely appear, a hollow shell, and not be authentic.

Another prophecy from the 16th century stated:

> The formless demon will enter many of the ministers and those in position of power, and thereafter there will be disharmony and quarrel. Even some of the incarnate lamas will in fact be possessed by the demon and will create disharmony between the traditions, and by doing so, they will bring to disrepair the practice and intellectual lineages of the Buddha Dharma.

The prophecies were confirmed by what Tertön Sogyal saw in Lhasa, where, as it is said, drinking the wine of pride and wrong views makes one act like a crazy elephant. One particular Gelug teacher in Lhasa named Phabongka Dechen Nyingpo, who claimed he upheld the unsullied teachings of Je Tsongkhapa, the great 14th-century reformer and founder of the Gelug order, gained a large following of monks and laypeople; he preached widely that the teachings of Padmasambhava, and in particular the Dzogchen teachings, were not Buddhist, and that the treasure teachings were merely fabricated by charlatans. Phabongka and his followers claimed that the mantra of Padmasambhava was meaningless, and some of his disciples threw statues into rivers and burned copies of the Great Guru's biography.

Why were Phabongka and his disciples so fundamentalist in their sectarian view? When Phabongka was 37 years old, he became very ill. A conniving spirit named Dorje Shugden, or Dogyal, offered to help him to recover from his sickness and fulfill his wishes. But he had to strike a deal—Dogyal demanded that Phabongka practice only the Gelug teachings. He insisted that Phabongka seek out and destroy those practitioners who practiced the teachings from other schools of Buddhism, namely Padmasambhava's Nyingma school, alongside the practices of the Gelug order. The spirit promised worldly wealth along the way to enlightenment.

Phabongka asserted that Dogyal was enlightened, having transcended samsara's cycle of birth and death. Dogyal appeared to Phabongka as a monk wearing a gold riding hat, seated atop a lion, and presented himself as a Dharma protector of the teachings of Je Tsongkhapa. In fact, Dogyal was nothing more than a worldly spirit, though powerful, with a particular bent toward intolerance and not a Dharma protector of the Gelug. Some say Dogyal was the spirit of a 17th-century monk who had been a candidate for the Fifth Dalai Lama but ultimately passed over. Having cursed the Tibetan leader and worked against him during his lifetime, he vowed on his deathbed to take revenge on the Great Fifth. The spirit has remained a perfidious force ever since, even to this day.

The Fifth Dalai Lama called Dogyal a malicious spirit, a demon who causes sectarianism. This was not just a doctrinal difference, for Dogyal was known to incite violence toward those who bring other teachings into the Gelug curriculum of study and practice. Phabongka was reflecting a sectarian response to the ecumenical Rime lamas like Khyentse, Kongtrul, Tertön Sogyal, and indeed the Thirteenth Dalai Lama. The Dalai Lama reprimanded Phabongka in no uncertain terms and told him to desist from propitiating the demon spirit. Feigning allegiance to the Dalai Lama, Phabongka ignored the Tibetan leader and spread sectarian biases, causing harmful rifts among different monastic colleges in Lhasa. Phabongka wanted Dogyal to replace Nechung as the State Oracle of Tibet, and he told his Gelug followers that if they practiced any of Padmasambhava's teachings, Dogyal would crush them. Even the Thirteenth Dalai Lama himself practiced both the Gelug and Padmasambhava's teachings, but still, Phabongka prayed:

> *I bow down to you [Dogyal], who punish lamas and
>     disciples
> Who are not qualified because of lack of training on the
>     path,
> And who introduce corruption to the doctrine of the Yel-
>     low Hats [Gelugpas].*

Phabongka was not the first to promote Dogyal, but because of his charisma, the cult spread among Tibet's political aristocracy and Gelug elite, major monasteries, and the common people, especially because the spirit often delivered on his promise of increasing material wealth. Soon, Phabongka's Dogyal worship was taken eastward to challenge Rime masters. With such demon worship on the rise and Dogyal's influence gaining traction in Lhasa and beyond, the foundation of Tibet's strength—unity in the Dharma and devotion to Padmasambhava—was dissolving, making the country vulnerable to outside forces.

One of the foreign forces first to take advantage of Tibet's weakened position was the Qing—led by the wiry imperial general of Han descent, Zhao Erfeng. Zhao had already earned himself the nickname among fellow Sichuanese of Butcher Zhao because of his favored method of execution—beheading. The eastern Tibetan tribal chiefs and the monasteries in Litang and Batang that were fighting the Qing's advance came to lamas like Tertön Sogyal for counsel. They reported atrocities by Qing troops: looting the grain reserves of monasteries; plundering gold, silver, and rare bronze

Buddha statues and other relics; and casting bronze and copper offering vessels of worship into bullets and coins. The most sacrilegious of all was that Butcher Zhao had paper shoe soles made from pages of sacred Buddhist scriptures. Local Qing officials in 1904 attempted to limit the number of monks who could stay in the Tibetan monasteries and ordered most to leave their monasteries to work as farmers instead. Opposition by monastic leaders led to armed battles. The abbots from Tinglin Monastery attempting to negotiate with Butcher Zhao were beheaded on the spot. He would eventually behead hundreds of Tibetans from Litang to Lhasa, and his brutal efficiency was rewarded with the highest Manchu military decoration. Tertön Sogyal said, "If Tibet is overrun by China, there will be an ever-turning wheel of blood."

As Tertön Sogyal heard the reports from locals of Butcher Zhao's violent activities, he stayed in retreat and focused on Vajrakilaya and summoned the two main protector deities of Kalzang Temple—Karmo Nyida, the White Lady of the Sun and Moon, who peacefully holds a jewel in her right hand and crystal prayer beads in her left, and Düdgyal Tötreng, the Skull-Garlanded King of Illusion, a black, wrathful male protector who rides a horse and holds a necklace of human heads symbolizing overcoming mortality. Precisely for the same reason that the Dalai Lama entered retreat when the British military was advancing to Lhasa, Tertön Sogyal also employed tantric ritual, mantra, and prayer to avert negativity and aggression. In deep meditative states, Tertön Sogyal manifested himself as Vajrakilaya and wielded his ritual phurba dagger to combat and subjugate military aggression.

It was as if the demon spirit Dogyal and Butcher Zhao were unknowing partners. Because the nation of Tibet existed as a support for spiritual practice, Tertön Sogyal knew the worship of the likes of Dogyal and other demon spirits could deal a fatal blow to Buddhism in his homeland—inflicted by the opportunistic Zhao. For Tertön Sogyal, everything was becoming unstable and unreliable; even the land itself, upon which the Dharma had been carried out for thousands of years, was having blood spilled upon it. The terma guardians cautioned him that even those close to him might be deceitful. Despite the many termas he had revealed and the rituals he continually performed, Tertön Sogyal told his student Lama Trime that, "an unending wave of obstacles keeps coming, so now finding perfect conditions for spiritual practice will be difficult!" As part of his efforts to repel the invaders, he completed the consecration of the temple complex at Kalzang, as well as a strategically placed stupa at Deer Horn Junction. While white-lipped deer, blue sheep, and Himalayan pheasants roamed the forests of Kalzang Temple, feeding on the torma cakes the monks placed outside following daily rituals, the suffering and screams of war were just to the south.

People began asking Tertön Sogyal where they should go if they were forced to flee Tibet. He had been asked the same question when he was in Lhasa. With violence just south of Nyarong, the villagers packed their bags but did not know where to go. Tertön Sogyal began to receive messages in visions about hidden valleys—*beyuls*—sanctuaries where the Dharma would survive, even if Tibet were lost. Padmasambhava and the Dharma protectors told Tertön Sogyal specifically about the remote region of Pemakö on the southern slope of the Himalayas, a hidden land shaped like a lotus, renowned for its fierce creatures, dangerous terrain, and near-inaccessibility beyond glaciers and impassable waterfalls. Yet finding the portal to the hidden land would open the pilgrim to sublime, mist-wreathed valleys where herbs and animals held miraculous powers, and the efficacy of Dharma practice was greatly enhanced.

"There, in Pemakö, my followers, you should take refuge in the future," Padmasambhava told Tertön Sogyal.

Padmasambhava had concealed keys and maps to these hidden realms on earth, as termas, as well as specific meditation teachings and recipes for spiritual medicines. In dire times such as political upheaval, these sancta sanctorum were to be sought by yogis and pilgrims; the reason for finding the hidden lands was not so much to escape reality as it was to enter more deeply into the truth.

In the third month of the Wood Snake year (1905), Tertön Sogyal was performing a ritual when his normal perception ceased and he found himself in an unfamiliar place near a large rock in an open meadow while many people milled around him. A man approached and said, "The secret guidebook to Pemakö is hidden in that boulder." A month later, Tertön Sogyal had a similar vision where he was in the same meadow in a tent with his teacher Lama Sonam Thaye.

"Where is the hidden land?" he asked.

"I will give you the secret instructions in a fortnight," Lama Thaye responded in the vision.

Two weeks later, Tertön Sogyal encountered Jamgön Kongtrul in a dream. Kongtrul transformed into Padmasambhava and said, "All who desire to go to Pemakö should not postpone departure. As for those who do not wish to go, do not urge them. To find the passageway, you must perform the rituals perfectly in order to create the auspicious conditions."

Padmasambhava then enumerated a wide-ranging list of rituals for Tertön Sogyal and others to perform, and advised what behaviors the populace ought to adopt, such as reciting particular prayers, abandoning hunting, and not speaking ill of others. Tertön Sogyal was told to make medicinal pills from crushed gems and herbs, to empower the pills with mantras, and to distribute them to the public as spiritual protection. Additionally, the guru advised Tertön Sogyal to build a large stupa in central Tibet, underneath which to place piles of spears, arrows, and guns in order to ritually banish the current quarrels that plagued Tibet, and to construct temples dedicated to Padmasambhava, Tara, Milarepa, and Tsongkhapa. Padmasambhava advised additional prescriptive measures to purify past negative karma, protect Tibetans in the present situation, and remind them in the future of the correct course of action.

"As for you, Tertön, for the time being do not go to the hidden lands but be diligent in performing these rituals," Padmasambhava said. "Because these rituals are needed in order to protect the Dharma, even if they are only performed once, they will bring benefit, produce immeasurable virtue, and restore peace to Tibet."

"How can I really accomplish all of this?" Tertön Sogyal questioned.

Padmasambhava encouraged him to strive to enact the treasure prophecies he had already been given, and to propitiate specific Dharma protectors. Then Padmasambhava transformed into Khyentse Wangpo and said, "I will tell you how to get to Pemakö, and you must write it down."

Tertön Sogyal could not find paper to write on, so Khyentse handed him a scroll and said, "There has never been a reason for anyone to hesitate to accept the guru's instructions. But still, so many Tibetans in prominent positions and commoners have not done what Padmasambhava has told them. Why do they continue to disobey his commands?"

"So, what can we do now?" Tertön Sogyal asked.

"Nearly everyone is being deceived by the demons," Khyentse said in a severe tone as he took back the scroll that he had handed Tertön Sogyal.

He continued. "The Karmapa, Sakya Trizin, and Kongtrul have already done the prescribed prayers. Now you and Trime should perform the host of meritorious deeds; this will surely bring benefit. And whatever Jamgön Kongtrul has told you, go and personally inform His Holiness the Dalai Lama of what should be done. Because the populace did not practice the teachings nor enact Padmasambhava's prophecies in a timely manner," Khyentse said. "I myself am losing interest in termas, and Jamgön Kongtrul has also been saddened by those who are possessed by the samaya-breaking demon. So Kongtrul won't retrieve any more termas. As for you, be careful about mingling with negative people who abandon their samaya commitments; this will lessen your ability to accomplish fully your mission.

"Regarding the guidebook to Pemakö the extensive instructions are hidden at the holy site of Vajravarahi; you can obtain that if you perform offerings to the dakinis. And reciting the *Dispelling Flaws in Interdependence* liturgy is of particular importance."

Khyentse described the pure land of Pemakö, and how the pilgrim must abandon all attachment to any place and any wealth. "See them as mere illusion. Completely abandon, without any hesitation, all hopes and fears. And in an unelaborate manner, with fervent regard, fearlessly place your mind in the heart of the guru. Strive on with diligence!"

Khyentse then spoke about the ultimate meaning of the hidden lands. "Without any trace of hopes or fears, you should walk in the direction of Kongpo. Enemies and thieves will come upon you first, and then, after walking upon glaciers and through snow, you will meet angry animals and snakes in jungle gorges and on steep precipices. But, whatever appears, do not hold any attachment or aversion. Stamp out your attachments! Remain true to your commitment. Whatever experiences you might have that are seemingly good or bad, do not tell others; just let the experiences come and allow them to release themselves. Do not hold on to elation or painful experiences; with the practice of equal taste, the yogi should be fearless like a lion. Have no doubts about this! Do as I have stated, fortunate son. Samaya."

The last thing Khyentse did was to indicate how the ultimate hidden land is beyond geographical coordinates. "Be ever mindful! If the proliferations of desire and attachment cannot be cut off, then there will not be a moment when the deluded mind is at peace. If you want to search for the inner pilgrimage site, practice repeatedly the yoga of blazing and dripping. If you want to discover the secret pilgrimage site, gaze at the face of ultimate reality. If you want to find the innermost pilgrimage site, remain uncontrived in the union of space and luminous awareness. To say more is such a distraction. This is my heart advice, my heart-son. Samaya."

Khyentse Wangpo then vanished into the light.

# CHAPTER 17

# CHALLENGING *the* DEMONS

Nyarong and Dzogchen, Eastern Tibet

*Year of the Wood Snake to the Water Rat, 1905–1912*

Late in the Wood Snake year (1905), while Tertön Sogyal continued to reside in Nyarong, monks and farmers in Litang rose in armed rebellion against Butcher Zhao's armies. Though the Tibetans were initially successful in their fight, by the summer, additional Qing reinforcements from Chengdu arrived with German-made bolt-action Mauser rifles and transportable cannons, and crushed the Tibetan resistance, razing one of the largest monasteries in Batang and killing hundreds. Additional forces moved into Gyalthang farther to the south, and many defenseless monasteries were destroyed. Butcher Zhao was soon promoted to viceroy of Sichuan Province. The brutal accounts of destruction and beheadings continued to reach Tertön Sogyal from those fleeing the fighting. Tertön Sogyal remained at his hermitage conducting rituals.

Despite a bitterly fierce winter, Butcher Zhao's armies began cutting a bloody swath from Litang toward Chamdo, killing and burning along the way. It was feared they might move north into Nyarong. Atrin and Khandro Pumo came into Tertön Sogyal's retreat cabin; they had prepared the horses to leave. They told Tertön Sogyal they had to flee, and though Tertön Sogyal knew the hidden lands of Pemakö were to the southwest, they were forced to flee north. To disguise Tertön Sogyal as a pilgrim, Khandro Pumo presented a knitted hat to cover her husband's nest of hair and suggested that he don a tattered cloak. This would get them through Upper Nyarong. She did not want even the locals to know that their spiritual father was departing the region, for if Butcher Zhao caught wind that the Dalai Lama's teacher was within reach, certainly his army would pursue them. They zigzagged through northern-facing slopes where the forest was dense until they arrived on the Tromthar Plateau, where Tertön Sogyal had once run with the group of bandits. On mountain passes by the rock cairns and stacked yak skulls, they burned juniper branches and roasted barley flour as an offering to the local protectors, requesting safe passage through their domain. They stopped only briefly for tea and to let the horses rest, until they knew they were well beyond Butcher Zhao's army. Tertön Sogyal told his family and Atrin to continue north to Dzogchen Monastery while he went in search of the Vajravarahi dakini cave in Marong, toward the headwaters of the Drichu River, where he'd been told the guidebooks to Pemakö were hidden.

When he found the Vajravarahi cave, Tertön Sogyal entered into retreat to fulfill the practices that would allow him to find the concealed key and treasure maps. No sooner had he started the prescribed rituals than Padmasambhava appeared to him and told of the Dalai Lama's impending death seven years hence, in the Water Rat year (1912). Yet Tertön Sogyal was told he could remove the threat to the Dalai Lama's life by finding a prophesied companion who resided in the area and together discover a number of treasure statues and sacred plants. Tertön Sogyal immediately turned his attention away from the discovery of the Pemakö guidebook to saving the Tibetan leader's life. He quickly found the prophesied dakini and together they discovered the treasure and arranged for seven hand-size statues of Padmasambhava to be sent to Lhasa to protect the Dalai Lama. Tertön Sogyal placed another seven treasure statues in nearby temples as a defensive barrier. Before the prophesied companion departed, she gave Tertön Sogyal a protective ring with a coral stone and told him to blow mantras on it to increase its strength of magnetism.

Returning to the dakini cave and the search for the Pemakö guidebooks, Tertön Sogyal discovered a stone casket with esoteric maps to the hidden lands. As he started to decipher the cryptic maps, one evening, he had a series of eight visions. In each vision, he met a different dakini who empowered him and told of future treasure revelations that would protect his own life and prolong the longevity of the Buddha's teachings in Tibet. Each dakini dissolved into his heart after they offered their predictions. In the final vision, Tertön Sogyal understood that his two guides to the hidden lands would be Jamgön Kongtrul and Khyentse Wangpo. He was also told that during Kongtrul's and Khyentse's lifetimes, Tibet would not be conquered.

Tertön Sogyal was having many kinds of visions and meditative experiences at this time, with complex lists of rituals to practice, temples and stupas to erect, people to meet based upon astrological calculations and birthmarks, and long prophetic indications of how to transform the troubled times into peace. Some prophecies seemed to contradict others. Although Palden Lhamo had told Tertön Sogyal only to follow Padmasambhava's prophecies, he still listened intently and copied out every vision and prophecy, trying to understand its import. It was as Khyentse Wangpo had once said, "Prophecies are the tertön's downfall," because once a tertön hears of a prophecy, he or she is bound to the work of bringing its auspicious conditions together.

Although Tertön Sogyal now had the maps to the hidden lands of Pemakö, he was unable to move south because Butcher Zhao's troops occupied the region. And, as yet, Padmasambhava had not told him to do so. Tertön Sogyal traveled east from Marong through the spruce and fir forests, over the Trola Mountain pass, broke camp early each day before sunrise, and within a few days reunited with his family in Dzogchen. He met the throne holders of Dzogchen, from whom he requested one of the most elaborate series of tantric empowerments and transmissions, which he received along with Khandro Pumo, his son, and many monks. While the abbots were bestowing esoteric initiations in the great hall of Dzogchen Monastery with hundreds of monks sitting in rows, Tertön Sogyal's visionary experiences continued unabated. At one moment, Tertön Sogyal would see the tantric mandala scroll paintings hanging in the hall, and the next he would enter that very same mandala in a vision, finding himself escorted into massive celestial palaces, meeting Vajrakilaya in the flesh, and encountering playful dakinis who teased and fooled him. As he flowed in and out of these dream-like experiences and visions, the empowerments lasted for more than three months.

While Tertön Sogyal remained in and around Dzogchen Monastery, in the summer of the Earth Monkey year (1908), the Dalai Lama left Mongolia for Peking. He wanted to negotiate directly with the Qing emperor to have Butcher Zhao's armies desist from their attacks on monasteries in eastern Tibet and to halt their advance on Lhasa. Although the Tibetan leader was received with ceremony and respect by the emperor and empress of China, and performed Buddhist rituals on the Imperial Court's behalf, there were no significant political developments. While the Dalai Lama was staying at the Yellow Palace in Peking, both the emperor and empress died unexpectedly. The Dalai Lama was asked to perform the funerary rites for both. Knowing little could be accomplished now in Peking after their deaths, the Dalai Lama decided to return to Lhasa. Just as the Tibetan leader was returning home through northeastern Tibet, a force of 2,000 troops left Chengdu by the southern route to march on the Tibetan capital.

On the 29th day of the tenth month of the Earth Bird year (1909), Tertön Sogyal had a visionary conversation with the protectress Palden Lhamo. The tertön asked urgently what was in store for the Dalai Lama and how to protect the Tibetan ruler's life. The protectress gave an ominous forecast:

*When efforts were made in accord with the Guru's [Pad-
masambhava's] prophecies,*
*Some twisted individuals reversed the favorable opportu-
nities,*
*Thus laying the foundation for the destruction of Tibet.*
*Still today, their reliance on the deceptive allure of tempo-
rarily apparent wealth,*
*Like a dream, a shooting star, a flash of lightning, is mis-
taken.*
*The strength of demonic forces of the dark side is gaining
strength.*
*I see little chance for the well-being of the teachings and
living beings in Tibet.*
*The earlier predictions about your own longevity,*
*Through your connection with the "life-giving" dakini
revelation,*
*And the Dispelling Flaws in Interdependence treasure rev-
elation,*
*Was the grace of Oddiyana Padmasambhava—*
*Now, given the confluence of karma, present causes and
conditions, and these unfortunate times,*
*If the religious leaders are not convinced, what means re-
main?*
*Once the medicinal tree of physical health is sickened at
the root,*
*The foliage of beneficial activity will automatically dry
up.*
*Even if you meet apparent success through the religious
polity,*
*You must closely examine the signs.*
*If it is the final and unalterable result, remain in equa-
nimity;*
*If not absolutely final, the means of repair are those that
I have already prophesied.*
*There is nothing more than those. Obstacles will con-
tinue to hinder success.*

Then the protectress spoke in a foreboding tone. Predicting dire ends for the Tibetan people, who had nearly exhausted their storehouse of positive karma, she said:

*If you fail and descend between the jaws of two quarreling demons,*
*The light of the Buddha Dharma will be extinguished;*
*All the masters of the teachings will fade away like rainbows in the sky;*
*Nominal representatives may remain, but they will not serve the teachings.*
*When the teachings disappear, living beings will not know happiness,*
*The life span of masters who serve the teachings will dwindle in equal measure,*
*And some prominent individuals will attack the teachings.*
*The milk lake of the monastic assembly will be laced with black poison,*
*And some malign ones within your own ranks may go the way of the demons,*
*And as a result, even your worldly estate will be lost to demonic forces.*

A month after Tertön Sogyal's vision, the Dalai Lama arrived back in Lhasa. He had been in exile in Mongolia and China for five years. Butcher Zhao, after putting down resistance in Derge, continued west through pockets of the Tibetan army to Chamdo. The Nechung Oracle insisted that the Dalai Lama leave the capital again. With political allegiances altered, the Oracle advised the Dalai Lama to seek political refuge to the south in British India.

By early February, 2,000 troops approached Lhasa. Butcher Zhao remained with his battalion six days' ride from the capital. The night before the planned siege of Lhasa, the Dalai Lama and a small entourage left the Potala undetected and escaped. The Qing army realized only the next day that the Tibetan leader had fled and they were late in pursuit. While the Tibetan militiamen stalled the army, the Dalai Lama was able to cross the border into

Darjeeling where the British offered protection. Still, thousands of Chinese soldiers invaded Lhasa, and at least two Tibetan policemen and a Tibetan woman were killed. The Dalai Lama immediately petitioned the British and the Russians to support Tibet in the international political arena, though both governments refused in the face of possible backlash from Peking. Butcher Zhao turned back to eastern Tibet to resume his subjugation of the region, with the hopes of taking control of Nyarong, which had still eluded him.

Tertön Sogyal had received news of the Dalai Lama's safe arrival in Lhasa but did not know he had to immediately flee again in exile to India. The tertön asked Palden Lhamo, "In the Wood Dragon year [1904], outsiders invaded Tibet and His Holiness had to leave his seat. Will His Holiness have to depart Lhasa again?"

"The Iron Dog [1910] is a black year for His Holiness."

Tertön Sogyal knew the Dalai Lama was in danger again.

"How can these demonic people harm Tibet? Is it really possible that His Holiness the Dalai Lama will have to leave Tibet again? If there is something that can be done in advance to avert him from leaving Tibet, what should that be?"

"If a drop of poison falls in the lake, near and far and everywhere is threatened. The golden garuda has already reached the golden mountain."

Tertön Sogyal understood the Dalai Lama had arrived safely in India and so asked, "What can be done in order to bring His Holiness back to Lhasa? Please reply to me with clarity!"

Palden Lhamo advised prayers to Padmasambhava and to conduct the terma rituals Tertön Sogyal had already discovered, "Then His Holiness might soon come back in good form.

"Although Padmasambhava has been so compassionate as to offer prophetic advice for you Tibetans, as well as to conceal innumerable termas," the protectress said, "only a few Tibetans strive to carry them out. I myself have given you, as a mother would to her son, so much counsel and prophecies, but why has there been so little benefit? It is because of the beings' negative attitude. The community has used up all of their positive karma. Now it is important that you keep yourself safe—living long is important."

Padmasambhava had told Tertön Sogyal some years before that at the end of the Iron Dog year he should strive one-pointedly in the practice of *The Most Secret Wrathful Vajrakilaya* and of the Lion-Faced Dakini, and Khandro Pumo should constantly be nearby. In particular, he should practice Vajrakilaya's averting rituals by loading tormas with fierce mantras and throwing the missile in the direction of the obstacles to repel them—continuing until he received clear indications that it was successful. As Tertön Sogyal was conducting the rituals against Butcher Zhao, the Chinese army gained control of Lhasa, which marked the first time in Tibet's long history that a Chinese army directly controlled the Tibetan capital. But the Qing's stay in Lhasa was short-lived. Shortly after the Dalai Lama arrived in India, revolution broke out across China. By November 1911, with the Republican Revolution in full force, Sun Yat-sen rose to lead the Nationalist Party. The Qing dynasty dissolution was rapid, their troops in central and eastern Tibet mutinied, and Butcher Zhao retreated to Chengdu.

After weeks of Vajrakilaya practice, Tertön Sogyal received signs that the Chinese soldiers had been forced to leave Tibet and that Butcher Zhao ceased his campaign of terror. When the revolution reached Chengdu, Butcher Zhao put up a determined resistance but within three months surrendered and received the same treatment that he had inflicted upon so many across the Tibetan Plateau—execution by beheading in Chengdu. Though Zhao experienced a gruesome death, Tertön Sogyal told Lama Trime that he had liberated Butcher Zhao's consciousness into a pure realm where he could meet the Dharma.

With the Qing military command in disarray, central Tibet became free of Manchu troops, and the Dalai Lama left India in the Water Rat year (1912) and arrived in Lhasa early the next year. The Dalai Lama wrote during this period a declaration of independence, which in part read:

> During the time of Genghis Khan and Altan Khan of the Mongols, the Ming Dynasty of the Chinese, and the Qing dynasty of the Manchus, Tibet and China cooperated on the basis of patron and lama relationship. A few years

ago, the Chinese authorities in Sichuan and Yunnan endeavored to colonize our territory. They brought large numbers of troops into central Tibet on the pretext of policing the trade marts. I, therefore, left Lhasa with my ministers for the Indo-Tibetan border, hoping to clarify to the Manchu emperor by wire that the existing relationship between Tibet and China had been that of patron and lama, and had not been based on the subordination of one to the other. There was no other choice for me but to cross the border, because Chinese troops were following with the intention of taking me alive or dead.

Cutting off all diplomatic ties with China that had existed for centuries, the Dalai Lama declared Tibet's sovereignty, concluding: "Now, the Chinese intention of colonizing Tibet under the patron-lama relationship has faded like a rainbow in the sky." The Dalai Lama was free from an immediate external threat, but the internal demon remained.

# CHAPTER 18

# CAPTURING *the* LIFE-FORCE

Golok, Eastern Tibet

***Year of the Iron Dog, 1910***

The Dalai Lama had declared Tibet's independence from China. Upon his return to Lhasa after two and a half years in India, he quickly exerted unprecedented political authority not seen since the Fifth Dalai Lama. But, there were orthodox factions within his government that boycotted his attempts to modernize Tibet's education system and open the country to the outside world. These factions, which included the likes of Phabongka and his Dogyal cult, saw modernization as a threat to the Gelug hegemony. The pernicious sectarianism of Phabongka was strong. Never before had the worship of a cult spread so quickly in Tibet; it had infiltrated all levels of the Tibetan government and monasteries.

Before the Dalai Lama returned to Lhasa, Tertön Sogyal, with his wife and son and attendants, had crossed the Yellow River watershed and entered Golok. This gigantic landscape swallows travelers in dust storms and wind that can knock a sturdy Tibetan horse flat to the ground. Tertön Sogyal relied upon the treasure guardians to show the route. They steered the reins past the southern turnoff toward Kandze and ventured due east across the highland ranges with its rolling golden grasslands that extended as far as the eye could see. As they entered the sparsely populated region of southern Golok, the number of flat-roofed, stone-stacked houses in any village was no more than a dozen. Corn and barley sheaves hung among drying chilies from the three-story houses with the ubiquitous Tibetan mastiffs guarding the perimeter from sand foxes and wolves. Above the riverbanks where the barley terraces were planted, nomad children and women ran after Tertön Sogyal seeking his blessing, their devotion inspired by his tantric attire and nest of hair. In the high mountain meadows and pastures of rhododendron shrubs, and along the river basins, Tertön Sogyal's caravan passed herds of yaks numbering in the thousands, tended by nomads.

This was the first time Tertön Sogyal had come to Golok, a region that rivaled Nyarong in its reputation of rugged nomads and roaming bandits. When locals camped for the night in Golok, horses were picketed under strong guard and men slept with their boots laced and their weapons at hand. Outsiders, including the few British and Russian explorers or Christian missionaries who tried to move through Golok in the late 1800s, were told to turn around or quickly fell to the swords of the Golok warriors or roaming bandits. The warriors of Golok, clad in fox pelt and felt hats with thick yak-hide coats, were legendary in their warring prowess on horseback. Even the monasteries needed protection by the various ruling tribal chiefs. When frontier scouts, with their long rifles slung over their backs, approached Tertön Sogyal's party to question his entourage, the tertön quietly recited pacifying mantras.

Golok was never directly ruled by the Qing dynasty in Peking or the Tibetan government in Lhasa. The vast plains, upland pastures, and mountains were the domain of three prominent chieftains. Soon after Tertön Sogyal arrived in Golok, he met one of the powerful chieftains, Dorde of Upper Wangchen. There would have been little chance Tertön Sogyal could travel through, much less reside in Golok, without the protection of such a chieftain. It was known that Tertön Sogyal was Khyentse Wangpo's close disciple, which in Nyingma-strong Golok was as strong a credential for the tertön as being the Dalai Lama's teacher. Tribal chiefs like Dorde wanted the protection of powerful tantric yogis like Tertön Sogyal.

Tertön Sogyal was shown into Dorde's large tent. Armed guards stood on either side of the tent's entrance, long daggers hanging from their waist belts. Unlike the Nyarong warriors, who wind their hair in a single braid around their heads, these Golok warriors had two braids that extended down their backs and were tied together at the end with colorful red or blue silk string. Their faces were as weather worn as a saddlebag. They did not bow in respect when Tertön Sogyal walked past them. Their stoic silence was as fierce as the snarling mastiffs staked out around the tent's perimeter.

Dorde stood when Tertön Sogyal entered, and welcomed him to sit on the carpeted cushions that had been laid out in his honor. As tea was served, the chief's daughters offered bowls of thick curd with small wild yams. Dried goat and yak meat still on the bone was brought on a wooden tray with a large bowie knife laid to the side, followed by milky barley beer. Tertön Sogyal offered Dorde a white silken scarf with a blessed statue of Padmasambhava that he had discovered as a treasure en route to Golok, telling the chief to pray to Padmasambhava to avert the same troubles that befell Lhasa, Litang, and Batang. He said he had been guided to Golok by visions and prophecy regarding the need for him to reveal treasures in the region. And he said that the chief would certainly share in the positive merit should he grant refuge in Golok and support his treasure revealer's activity.

Dorde guaranteed Tertön Sogyal's security. The chief sent scouts to inform locals that if the tertön or anyone in his party passed through, they should be provided with tents and barley flour, and feed for their horses. Dorde in return requested Tertön Sogyal's spiritual guidance and protection.

Having secured patronage from the local chieftain, Tertön Sogyal's next stop was a visit to the scholar and highly realized practitioner, the Third Dodrupchen Rinpoche. Just as Khyentse Wangpo and Jamgön Kongtrul were the spiritual pillars in the

Derge region, Dodrupchen was a spiritual giant in Golok. Prophecy indicated that Dodrupchen and Tertön Sogyal would collaborate to enhance each other's Dharma activities. They had spent time together in their younger years when they studied under many of the same masters, including Khyentse Wangpo, Patrul Rinpoche, Khenpo Pema Vajra, and Ju Mipham Rinpoche. They made a strong connection at that time, but because Tertön Sogyal was traveling to and from central Tibet, their relationship did not develop. The time and conditions now presented themselves to bring the connection with Dodrupchen to full maturity, as well as with some of the hermit's seven brothers who lived in the region.

Dodrupchen, the son of the famed tantric adept Dudjom Lingpa, was an extremely learned master who lived his monk's vows purely and maintained a strict schedule of study, contemplation, and meditation in his hermitage. As one of the most highly realized masters on the Tibetan Plateau, he revitalized philosophical study and debate not only in Dodrupchen Monastery, but throughout eastern Tibet. His reputation as a scholar began as a boy when he was studying with the great Patrul Rinpoche. One day, Patrul Rinpoche asked the young Dodrupchen to give a teaching to a large public gathering on *The Way of the Bodhisattva*. After the teaching, Patrul Rinpoche was so inspired by the sermon, he wrote a letter to Khyentse Wangpo, saying, "Concerning the Dharma of learning, Dodrupchen has given teachings on *The Way of the Bodhisattva* at the age of eight. As for the Dharma of realization, Nyala Pema Dündul has just attained the rainbow body. So the doctrine of the Buddha has not yet been diminished."

Many years later, after Dodrupchen had established a monastery in Golok, he was teaching to the congregation in the late afternoon when dark clouds formed overhead; thunder crashed about them as the temple roof shook. Some say that the spirit of an evil sorcerer with perverse aspirations caused the storm. As lightning struck, Dodrupchen felt ill, and by the time the storm subsided, he was paralyzed on his small wooden throne. He could barely walk for the rest of his life. The monks moved their stricken teacher to the Hermitage of Fostering Virtue, above the monastery where the surrounding pine and juniper trees of

Dodrupchen Rinpoche, Jikme Tenpe Nyima, was one of the most outstanding
Tibetan masters of his time and collaborated with Tertön Sogyal.

the Forest of Many Birds provided shelter from the strong Golok
storms. There he began a life of seclusion among white-eared
pheasants and soaring eagles. Except for his attendants, the four
abbots of the monastery, and several incarnate lamas, few people
were allowed to visit Dodrupchen. He described his hermitage:

*It is raised as the crown of a high mountain,*
*Crowded with youthful men, the trees,*
*In whose laps women, the gentle birds,*
*Are singing their melodies.*
*In it there is a temple where virtuous fruitions are being*
     *fulfilled.*
*Its walls are smooth with the color of the moon.*
*Young plants of the forest are visiting to decorate it,*
*As if they are making curtsies of respect.*

When Tertön Sogyal arrived at Dodrupchen Monastery, he did not know of his Dharma brother's paralysis. He was taken immediately to his hermitage. It was a joyful reunion, as the two had not seen each other for more than 25 years. Tertön Sogyal and his family were offered a nearby house belonging to the Puchung family, which they would use as a base for the next decade.

After Tertön Sogyal and his family settled into their new accommodations at Puchung House, he and Atrin left for the holy mountains around Amnye Machen, the abode of one of the most important Dharma protectors, Magyal Pomra. Rising steeply at the edge of a prodigiously fertile golden prairie, like a saw blade facing toward the heavens, Magyal Pomra surveys all of northeastern Tibet from the glaciated peaks of her long mountain range. Crystalline lakes in the uplands are surrounded by sparse juniper forests—this was where Tertön Sogyal was told he needed to meditate in preparation for revealing a life-force stone that was meant for the Dalai Lama, and to find additional keys to the hidden lands.

Tertön Sogyal's life in Golok continued to be guided by visions and prophecy. He did not hesitate to enact what Padmasambhava told him, just as he had done in central Tibet during the last two decades. Signs indicated that his presence in Lhasa was no longer useful, for he had accomplished all that he could for the Dalai Lama's court and the Tibetan government. He had performed the rituals Padmasambhava prescribed and had revealed the prophesied treasure teachings. Tertön Sogyal was undoubtedly frustrated with the lack of proactive measures taken by the Tibetan government, and without a direct representative of Padmasambhava—a tertön, or even a strong voice from the Nyingma school—in the court of the Dalai Lama, the specific ritual protection for the nation, as Padmasambhava recommended, would be likely left unaccomplished. The elements within the Lhasa establishment and Gelug leadership who scorned Tertön Sogyal's advice had gained the upper hand. The tertön realized that for the rest of his days, his field of activity would be in the northeastern borderlands of Golok.

Even though the Qing had been expelled from Tibet, Padmasambhava still warned that an enemy from the east could rise again. Tibet was wounded and needed to restore its spiritual strength. But Tertön Sogyal saw how his countrymen were distracted from what is truly meaningful. Palden Lhamo said, "If the people of Tibet have no devotion and do not act in accordance with Padmasambhava's prophecies, the force of the demons will be difficult to subdue. The Buddha Dharma is like a flickering butter lamp. To prevent the return of the demonic forces from overcoming Tibet in the future, it is important to discover the life-force stone."

Tertön Sogyal had received clues about the existence of such life-force stones, but now he was being given specific directions. Life-force stones have the ability to protect and to extend one's life. Certain stones have a connection to a particular individual's life-force—that subtle energy within the body that is the support for a person's consciousness. The longevity of that life-force depends on vitality and strength, for when it wanes, sickness and death are imminent. Tantric practitioners like Tertön Sogyal became adept at specific longevity practices that fortified and enriched their own vitality and life-force, often referred to as capturing the life-force. They relied upon a host of tantric practices, such as mantra recitation, directed meditative concentration, and resting in the sublime view of the ultimate nature of reality, in order to capture the life-force. Coupled with these esoteric practices, it is believed that inanimate objects such as unique rocks or trees or animals associated with one's zodiac sign can impact the strength of one's life-force. Tertön Sogyal was told that he needed to find a handful of life-force stones, and that one in particular was meant to be in the possession of the Thirteenth Dalai Lama to protect his life.

Tertön Sogyal felt a great resolve to find the stones, the kind of urgency not held by most of his countrymen. With the Qing no longer a threat to Tibet, many Tibetans felt they could relax. Many of those who had been asking Tertön Sogyal about the location of the hidden lands now sensed there was no longer such a need. In Lhasa and other large towns, the population was lulled into thinking they had banished the demons. Tertön Sogyal knew otherwise. Tibet must recuperate its strength. Tertön Sogyal still carried the maps and directions to the hidden valleys because he knew they would one day be needed. For now, however, Tertön Sogyal was on a mission to find the life-force stones, and in particular, the one to extend the life of the Dalai Lama. As he traveled around Golok en route to the Amnye Machen Mountains, he urged the farmers and nomads to unite behind the Dalai Lama and to express this by continually reciting the mantra of Avalokiteshvara, compassion in the form of sound: *Om Mani Padme Hum.*

"Whether you conduct elaborate rituals of offerings and pray to Avalokiteshvara, or just simply recite the six-syllable mantra, *Om Mani Padme Hum,* this is what the great populace must do," said Tertön Sogyal.

In the Water Rat year (1912), Tertön Sogyal returned to meet with Dodrupchen. He had brought a recently discovered treasure casket with him, and Dodrupchen asked him to open it and reveal its contents. Within the casket was a guru yoga liturgy and spiritual medicine, as well as a prophecy about a companion who needed to travel with him in order to reveal the life-force stone. With Dodrupchen's encouragement, Tertön Sogyal departed immediately to meet the life-force-giving dakini named Kangwa

Ahga. Tertön Sogyal was particularly intent on finding the life-force stone, because he was given a prophecy that read:

> There will come a yogi who will be the lamp, the great dispeller of darkness, for outer and inner regions of Tibet, a great holder of the Dharma who will reveal precious, supreme, and profound termas, including the extraordinary *Wish-Fulfilling Jewel Guru Statue That Liberates Upon Seeing*, and many scrolls of dakini scripts. These teachings, found and practiced, will dispel obstacles. If the exceptional life-force stone is not found, however, then all of the treasure teachings already discovered will only serve to benefit a relative few. Strive with great effort to find the stone.

In the first month of the Water Ox year (1913), Tertön Sogyal had a vision of a sacred cave with a graceful monk standing at the entry. The monk had a dark reddish appearance, and his robes were iridescent with red and yellow orbs of light moving in and out of the fabric. Tertön Sogyal told his son about the vision: "In his right hand he held a rosary and he spoke in cryptic language about a secret cave. In the depths of that cave there is a White Lake, and that is the actual residence of the wrathful Hayagriva and the dakini Vajravarahi—the father and mother."

Tertön Sogyal knew the life-force stone treasure was hidden in that lake and that if he could find it, he could be empowered by the life-force of these two deities.

Tertön Sogyal was told by the graceful monk, "The yogi's friend will appear as a normal human being with the syllables *Ah* or *Pa* in her name. The right timing to search for the stone will come when you, the yogi, have a passing meditative experience."

Tertön Sogyal and his son Rigdzin Namgyal, Atrin, and the dakini Kangwa Ahga began a month of meditation and ritual offerings to the dakinis in order to purify any obstacles to the revelation of the life-force stone. They stayed in a shack at the base of a steep mountain, and one night Tertön Sogyal heard a voice say, "You need to make feast offerings to the dakinis in each of the four directions of the lake. When you see the life-force stone in the earth or in the lake, either you will be given it or let your friend retrieve it. You will know when the right time arises."

The group circumambulated the mountain to petition and make offerings to the terma guardians in the cardinal directions, until one evening Tertön Sogyal and his companion both felt an intense courage rise within them during a ceremony.

*You can't trust such ephemeral experiences in meditation,* Tertön Sogyal thought, but he also knew this was the meditation experience that the graceful monk had told him would occur. Now was the time to search for the life-force stone.

In the morning, they climbed the mountain and entered a cave. Their butter lamps could not illuminate the depths of the deep cavern that dropped below them. Rigdzin Namgyal hurried back to camp to find rope and returned to the cave. Tertön Sogyal was the first to descend into the cave, climbing down the yak-hair rope. At the bottom, he found the secret White Lake. The others descended the rope.

Tertön Sogyal heard a muffled voice say from underneath the ice, "I will give you the terma." He immediately struck the ice with a rock and told Kangwa Ahga to do the same with a hatchet. When the tool hit the surface, an enormous chunk of ice fell into the water. Tertön Sogyal's eyes bulged with clarity as he gazed into the dark water. He put his left hand into the lake. The others looked on in devotion. From under the water, Hayagriva and Vajravarahi placed in Tertön Sogyal's palm a life-force stone shaped like a half-moon.

"Bring me a piece of cloth."

As Kangwa Ahga gathered a scarf from her bag, Tertön Sogyal put his other hand into the lake, hoping for another treasure.

"Here, this is a secret casket," a terma guardian said, and handed him another treasure.

Tertön Sogyal set the life-force stone and the casket in his lap. As he inspected the stone and the casket, he noticed that the coral ring that he had worn since he was last in Marong was missing.

"I've taken your ring as a replacement," the treasure guardian said from under the water.

A tinge of sadness at the loss of the ring crossed Tertön Sogyal's mind, and then he heard the guardian tease him, saying, "Ha, ha! You think your ring is more precious than these treasures from Padmasambhava we just gave you?"

Tertön Sogyal wrapped the life-force stone and treasure casket in silk cloth and handed them to his companion.

"Nobody else besides me and Ahga should touch this stone before it arrives in the hands of His Holiness. Put this in a box and mark it with my seal."

Tertön Sogyal knew his efforts were protecting the Dalai Lama. The group rejoiced with songs that echoed throughout the grotto as Tertön Sogyal took some of the lustral water from the White Lake and sprinkled it on his and the others' heads, and he removed his phurba dagger from his belt and cleansed it. The group returned to camp and began weeks of thanksgiving feast offerings. From the treasure casket, Tertön Sogyal took out a manual that enumerated the rituals he needed to do to capture and activate the life-force stone, which in part read:

"This life-force stone is something that you can't do without. The origin of the life-force stone is an ordinary rock, four finger-widths high and three wide. On one side you can see two overlaid triangles, making a star, and within that the dakini mantra of the mother, Vajravarahi. On the other side you will make out the syllable *Hrih* and, if you look closely, see the image of the father, Hayagriva."

The significance of the life-force stone with Hayagriva and Vajravarahi, including their mantras, related directly to the Thirteenth Dalai Lama. Hayagriva was not only the principal deity that the Thirteenth Dalai Lama meditated upon, it is a wrathful form of Avalokiteshvara, of whom the Dalai Lama is a manifestation. The dakini Vajravarahi is considered to be a form of Tara, another deity that the Thirteenth Dalai Lama relied upon. With the blessings of Guru Padmasambhava, the principal deity Hayagriva, and the dakini Vajravarahi, this particular stone would enhance the vitality and dispel obstacles to the Dalai Lama's life—if it could arrive in his hands.

Tertön Sogyal began the intensive practice of capturing the life-force of the deities Hayagriva and Vajravarahi so as to empower himself and enact the power in the stone. The stone itself was already consecrated and displayed spontaneously appearing images of the deities indicating its natural magnetism that attracted the blessing of the mother and father. With stable meditative concentration that did not waver for even a moment, and by summoning the deities by chanting their heart essence mantras, Tertön Sogyal soon met Vajravarahi and Hayagriva face-to-face, and they bestowed spiritual attainments upon him. Tertön Sogyal prayed that he would himself be able to fiercely liberate from their violent ways those beings who cannot be hoisted out of ignorance by the rope of compassion.

# CHAPTER 19

# *The* SOURCE *of* BLESSING

JENTSA AND XINING, NORTHEASTERN TIBET

*Year of the Water Ox to the Wood Tiger, 1913–1914*

After revealing the life-force stone, Tertön Sogyal traveled from Golok to Xining, the largest city in the region, on the frontier with China. He was following a prophecy delivered by a raven-faced Dharma protector who indicated that if he could make an auspicious connection with a Muslim warlord's daughter, he would reveal a wrathful practice needed to ward off future invasions by the Chinese. Following the fall of the Qing dynasty in 1911, and with the Nationalist government in its infancy, Muslim warlords ran China's borderlands. International political allegiances were repositioning, with Outer Mongolia and Tibet recognizing each other's independence. China's northwestern frontier with Tibet—where Tibet, Mongolia, central Asia, and China meet—was the realm of the Ma warlord clan, who had been in power for generations and had now reasserted themselves, forging bonds with Mongolians and Tibetans. In 1912, the Northern Warlords Alliance appointed Ma Qi as the military commander of Xining.

Tertön Sogyal wrote a message to Ma Qi and sent it by attaching the letter to a raven's neck for delivery. The letter indicated Tertön Sogyal's intention to meet and practice treasure rituals with his daughter. After a few days, the raven returned with a curt message from the warlord, saying, "You, a vagabond, ask me to trust you with my daughter! I highly doubt I would trust you with my dog. Still, I am an honest man and have read your request. Should you prove yourself worthy, I will allow my daughter to meet you. But you must prove yourself before my eyes."

Tertön Sogyal snarled at the warlord's message but took it as a challenge. "It is clear that the general does not know who he is dealing with." Tertön Sogyal began the long journey with Atrin to Xining in the Water Ox year (1913). They would travel east through the fertile grasslands of Dzoge, follow the Machu River northeast to the sun-blasted badlands near Rebkong, and then head north toward Xining. Halfway into the journey, intense fighting broke out between warring Tibetan tribes near Rebkong. Tertön Sogyal was advised not to proceed to Xining by the yogis he had met in Lhasa on his first trip to the capital in 1888, when they were conducting ritual protection for the Tibetan government. The yogis introduced Tertön Sogyal and Atrin to Alak Gurong, who invited them to stay in the Jentsa area and provided all provisions and lodging.

Alak Gurong was a charismatic polymath who used to boast that he had electricity while the powerful Muslim warlords in Xining were still using candles. After traveling throughout China and touring factories, Gurong was proficient in handling photography and electrical equipment, and set up printing houses and invented a type of Morse code for the Tibetan language for his personal use. He was also a deeply devout man who had spent seven years in his youth studying with the great master Ju Mipham Rinpoche, built a stupa in memory of his teacher at Wutai Shan, and was appointed titular head of the Nyingma school by the president of China in 1916, during which time he performed Vajrakilaya rituals in Peking.

Alak Gurong and the yogis in the area requested Tertön Sogyal to teach the *Secret Essence Tantra* and bestow empowerments, including his Vajrakilaya termas. The lay tantric community took Tertön Sogyal in as one of their gurus; prayers were written to invoke his blessing, and his image was painted in *thangka* scrolls in the traditional Rebkong style, with elaborate use of gold and consistent use of rainbow spheres for nimbuses and aureoles. While there were prayer halls and small temples in the area, most of the tantric practitioners in the region were married, lived at home with their families, and gathered in the temples only on specific ceremonial days for rituals. The yogis spent the time before dawn in meditation, then worked the fields or moved their sheep and yaks before noon. Before sundown, a deep drum and chant could be heard from within each adobe-walled household as the inhabitants made offerings to the lineage gurus and the Dharma protectors. Tertön Sogyal stayed most of the time in retreat in hermitages or in the southeast-facing caves that overlooked the wide Machu River which flowed east. Devotees and yogis sought his meditation instructions and visited him daily.

One chilly morning, Tertön Sogyal told his host he needed to go to Nyenbo Dzari Lake to conduct a ritual. Alak Gurong and a few of his attendants and monks saddled the horses and they left straightaway. Arriving at the high mountain lake known for its medicinal qualities, the group made camp while Tertön Sogyal began a ceremonial offering of beer and juniper smoke to the tellurian spirits and treasure guardians. He instructed everyone to leave him alone and told them to walk to the center of the frozen lake and to break open a large hole. When they returned, he told them to stay at the campsite; he then walked to the center of the lake. No sooner had Tertön Sogyal arrived at the hole than he dove headfirst into the frigid water. The group ran to save Tertön Sogyal from certain hypothermia. But they could see nothing when they looked into the cold water. They did not know what to do. Worried and anxious, some began to cry. Minutes seemed like hours.

"What have we done?"

"Our refuge has died."

As if a lion were roaring, Tertön Sogyal emerged from the lake with a rush of wind. He held in his right hand a Buddha statue and in his left hand a bejeweled treasure casket and a smaller stone casket. The group stood in stunned silence that transformed into devotion. As they prostrated upon the ice to Tertön Sogyal, whom they saw as Padmasambhava, the tertön walked away, saying nothing. At the campsite, Tertön Sogyal celebrated the occasion with offerings and prayers of thanksgiving, and he had Alak Gurong return to the hole in the ice and drop golden coins bound in a silk scarf to the bottom of the lake for the terma guardian.

Back at Gurong's residence of Mandigar at Drakga a few hours east of Achung Namdzong, the group was overjoyed and wanted to mark the occasion of seeing Tertön Sogyal reveal a treasure. Alak Gurong suggested taking a photograph of the tertön to celebrate. He attempted to explain to Tertön Sogyal what a photograph was and proudly showed off his tripod and gear. Tertön Sogyal wondered what he was hiding under the black cloak but kept quiet. As Gurong adjusted the tripod and readied the camera, Atrin laid out Tertön Sogyal's ritual instruments on a ceremonial table, including a hand drum, a five-pronged dorje scepter, a bell, and a *kapala* cup containing spiritual medicine. To the right side, Tertön Sogyal placed the recently discovered jeweled treasure casket. Alak Gurong requested that Tertön Sogyal sit in meditation posture and hold his prayer beads. As if to show how little time Tertön Sogyal ever spent in one place, there was no brocade, scroll painting, or other wall hangings behind him. A thick dark maroon cloak was wrapped around the tertön's upper body with long sleeves falling over his hands and knees, his posture at ease. The shadows that fell on Tertön Sogyal's high cheekbones under his yogic crown of hair accentuated his eyes and high forehead. Tertön Sogyal looked directly into the camera, his gaze at once piercing and vast. This was the face of determination, of resoluteness, of fearlessness. With a flash, the photo was taken; Gurong immediately went to his darkroom to develop the negative and returned to show Tertön Sogyal the photograph. Tertön Sogyal looked on without a change in his expression.

Tertön Sogyal photo taken circa 1913.

Tertön Sogyal and Atrin returned to their retreat cabin for a few months, and when the fighting to the north abated, they decided to continue to travel to Xining. Tertön Sogyal told Alak Gurong of his intent to meet the daughter of the Hui Muslim warlord

205

Ma Qi. Alak Gurong was a close friend of Ma Qi's closest advisor, Li Dan, a scholar and Buddhist aristocrat from Hunan who spoke and translated Tibetan. Alak Gurong wrote a letter of introduction to Li Dan and asked him to assist Tertön Sogyal in meeting the warlord's daughter. Tertön Sogyal was sent off with fresh horses and an escort.

Tertön Sogyal and Atrin followed the caravan route north, passing traders carrying wool, hides, deer horns, musk, medicinal herbs, and precious stones to the great market and temple city of Xining. It was unlike any city they had ever visited. Turbaned traders and light-skinned foreigners fresh off the Tsaidam Basin of the Silk Road tended to their Bactrian camels, caravan horses, and pack mules on the outskirts of the city. Tibetan, Monguor, and Mongolian Buddhist monks; Han Taoist sages; and Salar and Hui imams walked with their acolytes through the shops to acquire provisions for their religious communities far and near. Bearded Uighur, Turkish, and Kazakh traders bartered their wares; spice and vegetable sellers hollered from the street side; and paupers mixed with ragged refugees from Xian, who sat along the road begging for food escaping China's civil war. Tertön Sogyal and Atrin were led to the walled compound of Ma Qi in the center of Xining. The three-story-high sprawling complex with its curved, Ming-style pagoda roof and glazed tiles looked like a jeweled fortress.

The Ma family was famous in the region, and in Peking, as skilled military strategists. For generations they had commanded the tough Muslim horsemen whom even the Golok tribes were cautious to battle. When Tertön Sogyal arrived in Xining, it was Ma Qi who was the patriarch of the family, renowned warlord, and soon-to-be appointed Governor General of Gansu. On the advice of his most trusted confidant, Li Dan, the warlord maintained close relations with the Tibetans and Mongolians. Ma Qi had even taken an interest in reading Li Dan's translation of Tsongkhapa's *Praise of Dependent Origination* and Mipham Rinpoche's *Treatise on Advice to Rulers: Specifically the King of Derge*. Like many of the Hui Muslims in the area, Ma Qi was not beyond consulting Tibetan divinations or making offerings to local spirits. Of all the Ma family warlords, Ma Qi was the most open and curious about others' religions and cultures, albeit often for use in governing or ruling others.

Ma Qi remembered Tertön Sogyal's message delivered by the raven and read Alak Gurong's letter of introduction. The six-foot-tall burly warlord, with his Fu Manchu moustache, high-collared silken gown, and black skullcap, welcomed Tertön Sogyal. He was impressed by the tertön's willingness to travel the great distance to meet his daughter and was surprised when Tertön Sogyal told him that he knew her name was Shinya and that she was an Earth Rat. Tertön Sogyal reiterated his purpose for coming to see Ma Qi—that his daughter was prophesied to assist him in revealing treasures. Ma Qi invited him to stay, and Li Dan took a great interest in the tertön.

Tertön Sogyal was introduced to the 25-year-old Shinya, who had a natural disposition for spiritual practice. Two nights after meeting her, Tertön Sogyal had a vision of the One-Eyed Protectress, who said, "Oh, the seed of goodness and virtue has been planted since you have been able to find this companion with little effort. Such a connection is rare." When Tertön Sogyal awoke from the vision, his wisdom mind blazed with the recognition of ultimate reality, and when he arose from that state, a wave of memory flooded his mind. He recalled profound teachings that he had received in past lives as well as the location of many termas in the area.

Tertön Sogyal stayed for two months as a guest of the large Ma family, meeting the warlord's children, including Ma Qi's second son, the ten-year-old Ma Bufang. Tertön Sogyal performed rituals to bring peace to the region and revealed a number of treasures with the assistance of Shinya. They traveled together to pilgrimage sites and consecrated a number of temples, leaving behind treasure statues and stones that Tertön Sogyal blessed with the life-force stone which he carried constantly on his person. Tertön Sogyal was greatly inspired by Shinya's enthusiasm for practicing the Dharma and continually bestowed teachings and empowerments upon her.

One evening, Atrin gifted Ma Qi and Shinya with a copy of the photograph of Tertön Sogyal that Alak Gurong had taken. Ma

Qi greatly appreciated the offering. Not to be outdone by Gurong in showing off technological wonders, the warlord asked Tertön Sogyal if he would perform a *chö* ceremony, because he wanted to make an audio recording of it. Tertön Sogyal did not understand what was meant by recording his voice, but he agreed to the teaching and ceremony all the same. The next morning, in front of a small gathering, Tertön Sogyal sat in his room, wrapped in his thick felt cloak, with his large hand drum and other ritual items before him. He asked Shinya to sit next to him. Ma Qi had a shellac gramophone-recording cylinder wheeled into the room and placed in front of the tertön.

Tertön Sogyal spoke to the small group about chö, a contemplative practice that progressively destroys self-cherishing, which is the source of obstructions to enlightenment. Tertön Sogyal taught the group how to visualize and meditate upon a method that destroys clinging to one's body as something everlasting, destroys habitual addiction to harmful emotions, destroys the fear of change, and destroys craving for pleasure. By severing these obstructive forces and the self-cherishing that is at their core, Tertön Sogyal taught that the practitioner can quickly progress along the spiritual path.

Then Tertön Sogyal cleared his throat. When he started to chant, he chimed a bell rhythmically in his left hand and, in unison, slowly beat the double-sided leather drum with his right hand. As the tertön's chant continued, a technician made sure that the cylinder continued to turn and etch the vibrations of Tertön Sogyal's voice and the sounds of the ceremony onto the shellac. At the conclusion of the ceremony, Ma Qi and the technician adjusted the phonograph's funnel to play back the recording. First the scratching and static sound of the 78 rpm came, and then Tertön Sogyal could hear himself coughing.

"He thinks that my clearing my throat is part of the ceremony?" Tertön Sogyal questioned Li Dan, who just smiled. Then his voice came clear:

*"Phat! By abandoning all attachment to this body held so dear, the demonic forces of seduction through desire are destroyed."*

Tertön Sogyal listened closely to the meaning of the words, as if receiving the instruction himself. The recorded teaching continued. With the final words of the liturgy, Tertön Sogyal actualized the instructions and dissolved the visualization into the vast expanse of his Dzogchen meditation with a long exhalation, *"Ahh."* There he remained in an effortless equipoise of the ultimate nature of his mind, spacious and luminous like the clear sky.

Tertön Sogyal broke his meditative silence and spoke to Ma Qi, "Indeed that voice machine sounds like my voice. And yes, that photograph is a likeness of me. But whether you receive the blessings is not dependent upon external factors. It depends on you yourself destroying your self-cherishing, opening your heart, and recognizing that ultimately your mind is nothing other than the wisdom mind of the guru. Everything else is a fabrication."

Tertön Sogyal knew it was time to depart Xining. The profound connection that he made with Shinya would continue, he told her, but for now, he needed to return to Golok. He and Atrin were offered mounts by Ma Qi. They rode west into the lands mostly inhabited by Mongols, toward the uninterrupted plains as vast as the ocean. They stayed in the area for some weeks, circumambulated the largest lake in all of Tibet and China, the holy Tso Ngonbo—Kokonor in Mongolia—and made smoke and feast offerings, before they turned south toward the Amnye Machen Mountains.

# CHAPTER 20

# LIBERATING *a* SINGLE THOUGHT

Soon after Tertön Sogyal returned to Puchung House, his first grandchild was born. Tertön Sogyal asked Dodrupchen to bless and name the child. The boy would be known as Pema Chöpel Gyatso. Unlike his father and grandfather, Chöpel Gyatso would become a fully ordained monk.

Tertön Sogyal spent increasing amounts of time upon his return to Golok with Dodrupchen, because the One-Eyed Protectress told him it would benefit both of them if they discussed Dzogchen practice. The collaboration of the two lamas resulted in one of the definitive commentaries on the *Secret Essence Tantra*, the foundational Vajrayana scripture of the Nyingma school. For days the scholar-hermit spoke about the origin of the tantric teachings in this world, and laid bare the most sublime meaning of mantra, *mudra*, mandala, empowerment, samaya, and other elements crucial to a yogi's practice. Tertön Sogyal sat by his side working as the scribe with a bamboo quill and rice paper. The commentary was entitled *The Key to the Precious Treasury,* and Dodrupchen would say after they finished composing the treatise that it exposed his heart.

In another of Dodrupchen's unique expositions, *Wonder Ocean,* a book on the treasure tradition of Tibet and authenticating tertöns and termas, he relied upon Tertön Sogyal to elucidate difficult points. During their work together, Tertön Sogyal presented four dakini scripts that he had discovered but had not decoded. While Dodrupchen was not known publicly as a tertön, he and Tertön Sogyal decoded them together, with Dodrupchen serving as the scribe. In the second month of the Wood Hare year (1915), Tertön Sogyal offered Dodrupchen the empowerments and oral transmissions for all of his treasure revelations, at that time more than a dozen volumes. Their time was spent alone without any attendants. Dodrupchen infrequently allowed visitors, and only a handful of monks who stayed at the hermitage ever saw him.

One exception was a young and talented scholar-monk named Tsultrim Zangpo from nearby Shukjung Monastery. Tsultrim Zangpo, or Tsullo, was learned in the Gelug tradition, known for upholding his monk's vows, and also an excellent scribe. He copied many texts for Dodrupchen's personal library and used the work as an opportunity to obtain access to the teacher and to receive clarifications on esoteric practices. In Tsullo's own scholarship, he demonstrated a unique way of explaining the ultimate truth using the different vocabularies of the Gelug and Nyingma schools. Tsullo refined his experiential-oriented understanding of the Dharma under Dodrupchen and Tertön Sogyal, whom he considered his root gurus.

Soon after he met Tertön Sogyal, Tsullo invited him to his monastery to give teachings and a series of empowerments. At the conclusion of the empowerments, Tsullo said, "I bow down to you as my guru, for having heaped compassion and the precious jewel of wisdom upon us. This is very rare. Until now, my negative karma has befallen me and I could not differentiate between what to abandon and what to adopt. Now I am beginning to cross over

Tsultrim Zangpo, also known as Tsullo, was Tertön Sogyal's student and biographer.

the ocean of samsara with your quintessential teachings. I am riding a supreme steed toward the beautiful house of enlightenment so as to release others and myself from suffering. Until then, please be my protector."

Khandro Pumo told Tertön Sogyal that she also very much wanted to receive teachings from Dodrupchen. She rarely asked for anything, but she felt a connection to the great master. It was widely known that Dodrupchen preserved his hermitage as a monastic residence where no women were allowed. One of the reasons why Dodrupchen was strict in this regard was a vow made during his previous life when he was a married yogi; in his next life, he wanted to be a pure monk. Tertön Sogyal made the request to Dodrupchen.

"My spiritual wife strongly wishes to make a Dharma connection with you. Is this possible?"

"I guess it is all right if I don't go beyond my retreat cabin, for no woman has ever crossed my doorstep."

The next day, Tertön Sogyal and Tsullo assisted him to the entryway and he gave teachings to Khandro Pumo, likely the only female disciple that Dodrupchen accepted while he lived at his retreat.

While staying at Puchung House, Tertön Sogyal received additional prophecies associated with the life-force stone and a prophecy that he should build a retreat facility especially dedicated to the yogic practice of Kalachakra. He was told financing was not an issue because a benefactor would step forward. When Tertön Sogyal met Dorde, the chieftain who had originally guaranteed his safety in the region, he told him about his intention to establish the yogic retreat. They traveled together to an uninhabited valley near the Khemar Plains. Tertön Sogyal decided to build a small temple, and Dorde sponsored the construction. Wangrol nomads in the area were pleased to donate their time and energy in building the timber and earthen walls. The temple was small, with intricately carved motifs and a few simple rooms for the yogis, around which was a fenced enclosure where meditators remained undisturbed for months on end. Tertön Sogyal appointed the Dzogchen yogi Pushul Lama to be in charge as a retreat manager.

While staying at the temple, Tertön Sogyal had a pure vision of Khyentse Wangpo, who prescribed building a number of other temples and statues, reminding Tertön Sogyal, "It is important that all the upholders of our tradition who are still living strive to strengthen the Dharma now so that its practice does not diminish. You in particular have to be ready to face any and all difficulty. With strong resolve, strive to strengthen the Buddha Dharma. Do not lose hope. Be diligent!"

Tertön Sogyal stayed near the temple in a retreat cabin to carry out rituals and to write out liturgies from his recently discovered treasures. He also gave teachings and blessed four yogis to enter long-term retreats in the newly constructed temple.

From his small cabin, Tertön Sogyal could hear the yogis' morning rituals, their drums rumbling like distant thunder. Smoke from smoldering pinesap and mustard seeds filled the one-room chapel where they chanted. A golden chalice of thick rice wine stood on the altar between chunks of barley cakes dripping blood red dye. The wide-eyed tantric yogis intoned chants to invoke Vajrakilaya to take his honorary seat for the ritual feast. Lances, chain mail, clubs, swords, and a victory banner hung from the chapel's single pillar, reminding the deities and practitioners alike of the weapons of choice for Vajrakilaya. For the four yogis, Vajrakilaya was as present and vivid as the Amnye Machen Mountains towering on the horizon. The deity was partaking of the offerings on the shrine, and fulfilling the yogis' requests—a tantric process of cause and effect whereby the wrathful Vajrakilaya assists yogis in liberating the negativity within their hearts.

Tertön Sogyal closed his prayer book. The words of his last prayer permeated the space like rising incense smoke:

> *For as long as space exists*
> *And sentient beings endure,*
> *May I too remain,*
> *To dispel the suffering in the world.*

He could hear the adepts chanting in the nearby chapel. Tertön Sogyal knew that the power of the Vajrakilaya practice would transform their perception of reality and alter the way they engaged with the world. His disciples were sealed for three months of continuous tantric practices, secured by their oath not to walk beyond the confines of the small temple room. Tertön Sogyal silently commanded the local mountain spirits to assist the yogis in their practice.

Atrin entered the master's meditation chambers with a full pot of salted butter tea. Tertön Sogyal sat on a wolf-skin pelt on the floor with a simple prayer table in front of him. After pouring the steaming brew into Tertön Sogyal's wooden cup, Atrin placed the blackened pot on a mound of hot coals.

"I will see the two mendicants now," Tertön Sogyal said, before Atrin could inform him that two pilgrims had arrived requesting an audience. The attendant was used to Tertön Sogyal reading his mind.

Atrin motioned for the two young monks to enter the room. They touched their foreheads to the feet of Tertön Sogyal and nervously presented him with a tattered silk offering scarf along with their only money—two silver coins—and a small bouquet of purple flowers they had picked along a nearby streamside.

Both monks had long heard of Tertön Sogyal. This was the meditation teacher of the Dalai Lama. This was one of the most powerful tantric masters of his day. This was a representative of none other than Padmasambhava himself. The two monks had heard that Tertön Sogyal could halt hailstorms with mantra, summon rain for crops, and exorcise demons from possessed villagers. By now, many in Golok spoke of the tertön's ability to predict the future. Trust in his clairvoyance was such that devotees would travel months to seek the opportunity to ask Tertön Sogyal for a single divination.

The monks Lobsang and Gelek were not seeking such clairvoyant answers. They came with the heartfelt wish to receive a blessing from one they considered a buddha in the flesh, and to ask for advice for their pilgrimage.

Scroll painting of Tertön Sogyal circa 1915
that has the tertön's thumbprints on the back.

"We will begin tomorrow prostrating to Lhasa," Gelek said to Tertön Sogyal of their impending seven-month, 1,000-mile pilgrimage, body-length by body-length, from Golok to sacred shrines in central Tibet.

"I have prayed for years for the opportunity to meet you, precious master," Lobsang said. "Please give us advice for our spiritual practice."

"Whether you are sitting quietly in a meadow, conducting elaborate tantric rituals, or bowing continuously all the way to Lhasa, your mind must never part from that state we call meditation." Tertön Sogyal never wasted a moment to strike the crucial point.

He continued, "In meditation, you take care of your mind like a mother looks after her baby."

Atrin called Khandro Pumo and Rigdzin Namgyal from the kitchen. They sat on their heels in the door frame with keen attention to Tertön Sogyal's advice to the pilgrims.

"But if at the time of meditation, the nature of your mind, your *rigpa*, is not radiantly aware, then you will not be able to liberate even one single thought."

Tertön Sogyal sat upright, eyes unblinkingly still, his shoulders spread downward like an eagle getting ready to take flight. He demonstrated with his body and mind how to rest in the innermost nature of mind, where, when the clouds of turbulent thoughts and emotions dissolve, the sky-like nature of the mind is revealed.

Atrin and Khandro Pumo never knew when Tertön Sogyal would expound on Dzogchen or introduce disciples to the nature of mind. It seemed Tertön Sogyal recognized when an auspicious moment arose, and then whoever was present, be it one student or hundreds of disciples, would receive the precious instructions. To Lobsang and Gelek, two students he had never before met, Tertön Sogyal was offering the view of Dzogchen meditation.

"What is it your mind must liberate?" Tertön Sogyal asked the two monks, who had lifted their gazes to his face.

Holding his thumb and forefinger in the air, he said, "Attachment to good and aversion to bad circumstances. These two." The firm hand gesture reassured the two monks.

"Seemingly good circumstances can creep in stealthily, like thieves, and if you are not on guard, to notice them and liberate them, they will become a demonic force, enticing and seducing you, leading you into mindless distraction.

"Bad circumstances will come more obviously, aroused by lustful attachments to forms, or aversion toward an enemy. If your mind is not able to liberate your attachment or aversion at that precise moment, then, when you meet the actual circumstances themselves, your true failing as a spiritual practitioner will be exposed."

Tertön Sogyal emphasized to his disciples the importance of diligently applying themselves in practicing the Dharma in formal meditation sessions so that when they were off their meditation carpets, awareness would be integrated into all actions of thoughts, words, and deeds. The point was not that disciples mechanically repeat mantras and prayers, or mindlessly perform rituals, or simply sit peacefully in meditation posture. Rather, the vital point was maintaining undistracted awareness every moment, regardless of the activity.

"Now, what is it that liberates?" Tertön Sogyal asked, his eyes widening like those of the wrathful deities painted in the temples. "The wisdom of rigpa—the nature of mind."

Tertön Sogyal sat unmoving like a mountain. Simply hearing the word *rigpa* from the famous teacher's mouth suspended the moment for the two monks, their minds expanding like space. In the silence, any rising thoughts in the minds of the two monks evaporated like mist in the sun. Devotion rose within Lobsang's and Gelek's hearts.

In the adjacent chapel, the yogis continued beating a drum as part of their daily rituals. Lobsang's mind wandered from Tertön Sogyal's meditation instructions and followed the percussion. He pondered if he might know the yogis and what liturgy they were reciting, and he began thinking of his schedule for the coming weeks. Like a leaping monkey, his mind jumped toward the future and back to the past. Lobsang's awareness was everywhere but in the present moment.

Tertön Sogyal slammed his hand on the table, causing his cup of tea to spill on the floor.

"What is it you liberate?" he yelled.

Lobsang did not say a word, but the clarity of his own awareness struck like lightning illuminating itself. Tertön Sogyal was not teaching about meditation, he was giving them the experience of meditation. He caused Lobsang's razor-like awareness of the nature of mind to slice through thinking, leaving his mind unaltered in a state of equipoise. Tertön Sogyal was bestowing the most profound instruction of liberating thoughts upon arising—for it is thinking about thoughts, as in the links of an iron chain, one after another, that prevents a meditator from abiding in wakeful awareness.

"What is it you liberate?" Tertön Sogyal asked again. "All these rising thoughts in your mind, whether good or bad. That is what is liberated—thoughts themselves."

He continued with the severing of the monk's habitual tendency to chase after each rising thought. Tertön Sogyal asked, "How do you liberate them? Upon its arising, allow each thought to move like a wave dissolving back into the vast ocean from which it came."

Tertön Sogyal paused again, hands resting on his knees. He offered the two monks a lasting impression of his face for their pilgrimage, to remind them of their glimpse of pure awareness—the true, unchanging nature of mind. Indeed, it was this stoic impression of Tertön Sogyal resting in the most profound state of meditation that the monks carried in their hearts and minds for the rest of their lives.

Tertön Sogyal told the monks they would surely encounter hardship day after day while on their journey to Lhasa, but this meditative tool—liberating thoughts upon their arising—would be their refuge.

"The real, true sign of whether you can liberate thoughts or not is when you actually meet negative circumstances face-to-face. When thoughts arise like a blazing fire or bubble up like boiling water, if, at that very moment, you are able to liberate them, then that is truly the same as a miracle.

"If you are able to liberate one attachment, one aversion, one negative thought, then many lifetimes of negative karma are purified."

Tertön Sogyal's ability to transmit experientially, viscerally, the power of his meditative mind was born of his own profound realization of the Buddha's teachings, the devotion of his disciples, and the authentic blessings he carried. Whether he was teaching two wandering monks in eastern Tibet or the Dalai Lama in Lhasa, students cherished Tertön Sogyal's pith instructions on meditation as dearly as their own hearts. And this single instruction—liberating thoughts upon their arising—was one such meditation tool that Tertön Sogyal felt was more powerful than any mantra, any prayer, or any ritual.

"Such a person who can liberate thoughts upon their arising," Tertön Sogyal declared, "I call the greatest of meditators; such a person I call clairvoyant—even omniscient."

CHAPTER 21

# CREATING PEACE
### *between* TIBET
### *and* CHINA

DODRUPCHEN AND DZOGCHEN, EASTERN TIBET

*Year of the Wood Hare to the Water Dog, 1915–1922*

At the beginning of the Wood Hare year (1915), a request came
from the tribal chiefs and lamas from the neighboring province
of Sertar to Tertön Sogyal to give teachings and consecrate a recently built stupa. The request confirmed what Tertön Sogyal had
seen in a vision a few months earlier. In the vision, he had met
three girls adorned with many jewels circumambulating a massive
stupa. The girls asked Tertön Sogyal, "Will you be able to remove
the difficulties for our guru? They are formidable!"

"Who is your guru?" Tertön Sogyal asked.

"Our guru is the omniscient Thubten. He is under the spell of
obstacles." And they told Tertön Sogyal to recite various practices
at a newly constructed stupa for the benefit of Thubten Gyatso,

the Thirteenth Dalai Lama, and for all of Tibet. Such practices accomplished in front of the stupa had the power to subdue evil intention. The stupa was one of the largest to have ever been built in eastern Tibet. Dodrupchen told Tertön Sogyal that he too would perform the consecration at the same time, but from his hermitage.

In the sixth month of the year, Tertön Sogyal went with Atrin, Khandro Pumo, and others to the stupa on the southern edge of the one-road town of Sertar. The enormous four-story, white-washed, conical-shaped brick reliquary, with a golden spire on top, could be seen rising out of the golden plains from 50 miles away. Surrounded with prayer wheels that devotees turned as they cir-cumambulated, the structure's base was a temple that could hold more than 100 monks, and there was a second floor that could be reached by ladder. The inner sanctum housed representations of enlightened body, speech, and mind—hundreds of statues, thou-sands of volumes of scripture and mantra, and relics of the histori-cal Buddha and saints.

Tertön Sogyal was met miles before reaching the town by an escort party who hoisted flags, waved white scarves, and hollered greetings from their horses. They were taken to their hosts in a large nomad tent that served as their residence. With the grass plentiful in the summer pastures, the yogurt and cheese offered were sweet and abundant. Thousands of nomads and farmers ar-rived for the ceremony, setting up their own tents on the edge of the town's meandering river, racing horses during the day and bartering rope, reins, and saddles. The consecration of the stupa brought together the entire community; women and men wore their finest dress and coral and turquoise jewelry, danced and sang in the evening, and caught up on gossip from the nearby valleys.

The ceremony lasted for a week, which included rituals in the morning and Tertön Sogyal teaching to the thousands gath-ered in the afternoon. He sat on a throne under a tent outside of Auspicious Temple in front of the stupa. Hundreds of monks sur-rounded him. During the consecration, Tertön Sogyal held a large mirror and slowly moved it through the space in front of him to catch the reflection of the sacred stupa and the whole of the environment—the sky, hills, stupa, village, people. Tertön Sogyal then took a ritual vase with consecrated water and, while chanting purifying mantras, poured water over the mirror to cleanse and empower all that had been reflected. Tertön Sogyal and the monks prayed and invoked blessings from the buddhas and bodhisattvas in all directions to rain down. At various points during the ceremony, Tertön Sogyal took a handful of rice and barley grains and tossed them toward the stupa, visualizing a descent of blessings from the lineage masters. At one point, Tertön Sogyal and others saw grains of barley fall from high in the western sky and land on the stupa. He knew that these were the blessed substances that Dodrupchen had cast in the direction of the stupa from his hermitage three days' ride away.

On the final day of the ceremony, Tertön Sogyal saw 21 dakinis in the sky make offerings—perfumed water, flowers, incense, butter lamps, and sumptuous food and drinks—to the stupa. He took this as a sign that the consecration was successful. The following day, Tertön Sogyal was asked to perform a blessing in an adjacent village. During the ceremony, Tertön Sogyal again saw many dakinis in the sky— thousands of them—their bodies made of rainbow light. They were singing and dancing in silk dresses with flowing hair, holding many kinds of nourishment and adornments and ritual implements. The dakinis began to merge into one another, as when mist becomes raindrops, eventually leaving 16. Tertön Sogyal recognized some of the 16 dakinis he had met in Amnye Machen, Lhasa, and elsewhere, and some he had met only in dreams. Tertön Sogyal recognized two of the dakinis in the vision from 20 years before, when they had persuaded him against his will to dance in order to deepen his Dzogchen realizations.

Then Shinya, his companion from Xining, stepped forward with two Chinese friends on either side. "I was quite difficult for the tertön to meet," she told the other dakinis. "But I have extraordinary qualities."

"If you are all manifesting like this together," Tertön Sogyal asked, "tell me, what can help the difficult relationship that Tibet has with China? Please tell me!"

Shinya and her two friends discussed it between themselves. Tertön Sogyal could not understand Mandarin, so Shinya translated.

"What they are saying is that all the monks in the monasteries should have the resolute intention only to follow the Dharma, and to keep it all on track they should recite the mantras of Shakyamuni Buddha and the *Essence of Dependent Origination*, and make offerings to those guardians who really protect the Dharma." Then they started singing the mantras, *Om Mune Mune Mahamunaye Svaha* and *Om Ye Dharma Hetu Prabhava Hetun Tesam Tathagato Hayavadat Tesam Ca Yo Nirodha Evam Vadi Mahasramanah Svaha.*

Some of the other dakinis discussed the importance of promoting peace between Tibet and China, and how disparaging thoughts between the monks and lamas of the various traditions are what actually blocks them on their own spiritual path. Tertön Sogyal heard them say it was important to strengthen the root of the Dharma and to spend less time on the minor rituals. Then the dakinis spoke in poetic verse about the happiness of beings and the stability of the Dharma, some of them gesturing to Tertön Sogyal for his attention.

Tertön Sogyal was engrossed in the vision when a dakini named Tsukye stepped forward and said, "Of all the holy places, the location where one's spiritual master is staying is the most holy!" Then she whispered in Tertön Sogyal's ear a riddle in dakini verse that only he could understand. Another moved to the foreground and said, "All of us have the power to enhance friendship between China and Tibet because we are blessed by our previous prayers and karma. But we all know that there are obstacles to this friendship. So listen now to what we have to say!"

The dakini named Tsephel said, "If China and Tibet fight in the future, everyone will lose, but in the end Tibet will succumb! But I will be sure to protect you and your son when you go into retreat in the mountains!" Before she returned to dancing, she told Tertön Sogyal that she had continually appeared to Atrin over the years and guided him.

The dakini Gomchik, who said that she was charged to protect the borderlands of Tibet, sang in a verse, "Wisdom dakinis are born due to the sacred tantra, so do not hesitate to accept what we say. If Tibet and China go to war, your side will be defeated. Have no doubt about that. Thubten Gyatso [the Dalai Lama] should command the monks from the Gelug, Sakya, Kagyu, and Nyingma monasteries, big and small, to be unified in their aspirations. This is the solution! If the great beings and lamas are not harmonious among each other, and if the public and monasteries do not listen to the Dalai Lama, at least the Nyingma should be of one mind. At least you and Jikdrel [Alak Gurong] are doing patch-up work now for the Nyingma; this is good, and it is enhancing each other's longevity."

As the dakinis swirled and danced among clouds of offerings and orbs of lights, the dakini Nemkye told Tertön Sogyal, "Dealing with China or Tibet is one matter. But it is important that you fearlessly stay true to your mission. Practice the phurba dagger and the Lion-Faced Dakini; there is nothing more superior at this time. Do these practices in the region of the Amnye Machen Mountains, not moving here and there." She indicated that he should not go to the hidden valleys of Pemakö at this time.

Then all the other dakinis came forth, one after another, to offer more prophecies, advice, prescriptions for practice, and inspiration for Tertön Sogyal; finally, they began to dissolve into one another, like light merging into light. Shinya dissolved into the last remaining dakini, named Samdrun, who offered Tertön Sogyal counsel for his personal practice:

"Go and establish a sacred place to live and meditate, and conduct rituals for peace and harmony—the sooner the better. But, before that, strive to reveal yet another life-force stone, a wrathful life-force stone. If you work to create peace between China and Tibet before you find that second life-force stone, it could be dangerous for your own life. Do not tell anyone else about the life-force stones except Thubten Gyatso [the Dalai Lama]. Keep this advice close to your heart."

As Samdrun radiated light into Tertön Sogyal, she advised him to send people in all directions to monasteries and towns with the instructions that the dakinis had told him. They were to look for the right people, those who were unafraid and could skillfully assist him. In particular, she reminded Tertön Sogyal,

"The religious and political policies of the supreme one, Thubten Gyatso, must firmly take root. Encourage all to be nonsectarian, to have resolute intention, and to emulate the lives of the great saints of the past."

Glowing with tremendous light, she merged into Tertön Sogyal's heart. An intense wave of happiness and bliss pervaded his being. He arose from the vision and immediately wrote down what each of the dakinis had told him. He knew that he needed to make plans to return to Lhasa to see the Dalai Lama. But first he would have to find the second, wrathful life-force stone.

Tertön Sogyal returned to Dodrupchen to inform him about the visions, and they discussed the meaning of some of the riddles and difficult points. Tertön Sogyal told Dodrupchen that in the near future, he might have to leave his hermitage for a visit to Lhasa to meet the Dalai Lama.

"Why is that? I am unable to walk."

"If I can teach the *Secret Essence Tantra* to His Holiness, to you, and to Atrin and Tsullo, together as a group in the Potala Palace, then this will provide additional protection to central Tibet from being attacked in the future." Tertön Sogyal said he would tell them when the time was auspicious to travel to central Tibet. Dodrupchen agreed, although he would have to travel for months in a palanquin and on horseback.

Undoubtedly the number of prophecies that Tertön Sogyal was being told to carry out from many different sources was close to overwhelming. He received encouragement and inspiration and even teasing from the dakinis and protectors; still, Tertön Sogyal was a stern man who wanted to leave nothing incomplete. At one point, he questioned Padmasambhava in a visionary conversation: "There are so many terma prophecies and special experiences and advice I have had that I have not been able to enact or fulfill them all. The ones that come later make me forget the earlier ones. It is difficult enough to differentiate them all—the time, place, and liturgies—let alone actually have the time to practice them all. I certainly have confidence in them all, but each newer one seems better than the one before. I sometimes don't know what is most critical to practice."

"With devotion, there is no difference between me and the prophecies, remember this," Padmasambhava replied. "Continually maintaining the view of Dzogchen automatically creates the auspicious circumstances. Just to follow the words of prophecies sometimes can miss the point!"

"Even to maintain my home, with family tasks and yaks, much time can be squandered in worldly affairs," Tertön Sogyal admitted. "Is it true that I should go to the Amnye Machen Mountains to practice? If so, tell me directly what I should practice."

The answer came: "If you focus merging your mind with the wisdom mind of the guru, all will be accomplished."

For the next three years, Tertön Sogyal moved constantly around the region, completing many projects and responding to the requests of his disciples. When Dodrupchen's health waned, Tertön Sogyal returned to Puchung House to perform longevity rituals for his Dharma brother. Other times, Tertön Sogyal traveled with Tsullo to Sertar to oversee the carving and printing of his collected terma revelations, which would eventually fill 20 volumes, the most of any tertön of his day. He was also discovering new termas and completing the deciphering of others, some of which he had in dakini script for over two decades.

At the end of the Iron Monkey year (1920), when Tertön Sogyal was 65 years old, he received indications of the location of the second life-force stone; he needed to return to the caves in Marong. Tertön Sogyal and his son traveled on horseback through northern Trehor for two weeks to find the dakini cave, a place where many previous treasures had been revealed. En route, Tertön Sogyal was given a prophecy that told him of his immediate duties upon his arrival.

A dakini who spoke the prophecy said, "The removal of obstacles for everyone is the practice of *Dispelling Flaws in Interdependence*. Now is the time to complete the revelation of its elaborate, medium-length, and short liturgies. Cherish it thereafter."

A few nights after the prophecy, Tertön Sogyal dreamed of the Dalai Lama's chief household officer, who told him to conduct a number of meditation retreats in central Tibet and said, "You and Lama Trime should eliminate the obstacles to Dodrupchen's life by performing the *Wisdom Flame* rituals. Write down the additional *Dispelling Flaws in Interdependence* practices near Dzogchen Monastery and practice them in Marong, in Derge, and en route to Lhasa. Take the road through Chamdo to Lhasa."

Tertön Sogyal sent a message to Lama Trime that he would be arriving soon at his hermitage. Meanwhile, Tertön Sogyal and his son stayed in Marong and revealed additional termas, including *Names of the Thousand and Two Buddhas of This Fortunate Age.* After a few weeks, the protectors led Tertön Sogyal to Black Lake. Tertön Sogyal sat by the shore, and the terma guardian delivered the wrathful life-force stone into his hands. Tertön Sogyal's preparatory rituals and prayers had removed obstacles to the treasure's retrieval, and he sensed that he was strengthening a protective sphere around the Dalai Lama. Tertön Sogyal placed the wrathful life-force stone in the box with the other mother-father stone so that nobody else would lay eyes on it. He gathered some of the water from the Black Lake to use for ablution rites, washed his phurba dagger in the lake, and then departed to Lama Trime's hermitage, known as the Turquoise Fortress of the Mighty Lion, to perform the requisite rituals to ignite the energy in the newly discovered stone.

As soon as he arrived at the hermitage, Tertön Sogyal told Lama Trime to write a message to Dodrupchen, Tsullo, and Atrin. They should prepare to leave for Lhasa so as to fulfill Tertön Sogyal's own prediction that he teach the group the *Secret Essence Tantra* in the Potala. And he would be able to personally deliver the life-force stones to the Dalai Lama. They sent the message by horse-man to Golok. When Tsullo received the message, he departed for Lhasa straightaway to make preparations for the others. The Dalai Lama had already received a message from Tertön Sogyal and re-sponded that the group should come to Lhasa as soon as possible.

After Tertön Sogyal completed the rituals at the Mighty Lion Hermitage, he traveled to Dzogchen to await Dodrupchen's arrival. Khandro Pumo and Atrin soon arrived at Dzogchen. While staying at the monastic college, Tertön Sogyal had a vision of a child wearing white garments, who said, "Hold this secret sealed guidance for the government. It is their main path." Just before disappearing, the child gave him a scroll with three syllables written on it. Tertön Sogyal knew the scroll was meant for the Dalai Lama, with advice on how to skillfully merge politics and Dharma. Then Tertön Sogyal heard a voice: "From the top of the Potala, he who is the all-powerful, may the gods be victorious! *Lha Gyalo!*" Tertön Sogyal immediately redacted the meaning from the three syllables in the form of a guru yoga practice to Padmasambhava—yet another means to strengthen the Tibetan government that Tertön Sogyal knew he would be passing to the Dalai Lama within weeks.

While Tertön Sogyal was staying in the area, one of the reincarnations of Khyentse Wangpo arrived—his name was Jamyang Khyentse Chökyi Lodrö. Even before Chökyi Lodrö met Tertön Sogyal, merely hearing the tertön's name caused the incarnate lama to feel deep and uncontrived devotion. Marking yet another chapter in the continuity of their student-teacher relationship, which had begun many lifetimes before, Tertön Sogyal bestowed empowerments and transmissions upon Chökyi Lodrö, including *The Razor of the Innermost Essence.* After he received the transmission for *Dispelling Flaws in Interdependence,* Chökyi Lodrö felt such an intense devotion for Tertön Sogyal that he requested Tertön Sogyal to decipher the very brief liturgy of the practice, which begins:

> *Greatest among teachers, Buddha and lord of sages, Shakyamuni,*
> *With the one thousand and two buddhas to attain complete enlightenment in this "Fortunate Age,"*
> *You who dwell in pure realms pervading the whole of space and time,*
> *To all the victorious buddhas, I offer the ultimate homage!*
> *To Manjushri, Avalokiteshvara, and Vajrapani, and*
> *To all the bodhisattvas, I offer homage!*

*To the exalted ones among the shravakas and pratyeka-*
*buddhas,*
*And to all you who in this world of ours are worthy of*
*reverence, in devotion I offer homage!*
*Let your power cleanse and purify all inauspicious,*
*harmful circumstances—every single one!*

Like many treasure teaching cycles that include a variety of liturgies and ritual practices, *Dispelling Flaws in Interdependence* was set into writing over the course of decades. Tertön Sogyal had already fully revealed the elaborate and medium-length *Dispelling Flaws* liturgies. With Chökyi Lodrö's encouragement, Tertön Sogyal wrote the last, very concise liturgy, concluding the *Dispelling Flaws* revelation cycle. Before they departed, he granted permission to Chökyi Lodrö to transmit the entire collection of his treasure revelations.

Meanwhile, Dodrupchen had left his hermitage in Golok for Lhasa. The monks from Dodrupchen Monastery and many of the villagers were extremely concerned about their teacher departing the area. Many people followed the caravan as it made its way westward. At one point, the group came to a difficult river crossing. The horses and yaks were losing their footing and falling into the current. Leather saddlebags were swept away. Dodrupchen watched from the banks as the handlers whipped the horses and beat the yaks to rush through the raging waters.

"My travel is not so uncomfortable, but so many people and animals are coming along. We have only traveled a short distance and have already caused so much suffering to the others and especially to the animals," Dodrupchen lamented. "Imagine how much suffering will happen if I travel as far as Lhasa. Turn around!"

By the time Tertön Sogyal received the news that Dodrupchen had returned to his hermitage in Golok, Atrin had fallen gravely ill. The auspicious circumstances for the transmission in the Potala Palace had fallen apart.

Such disappointments did not remain in Tertön Sogyal's mind, for he focused on the task in front of him—his loyal attendant's imminent death. Atrin had served Tertön Sogyal for more than 25 years. Now Tertön Sogyal was sitting by his disciple's side, guiding him through the most important moment in his life. Tertön Sogyal calmly reminded Atrin that his conceptual mind and its delusions were dying and that, upon the dissolution, he should merge his unbound awareness with the sky-like nature of mind that he would encounter. This unconditioned natural state, which Tertön Sogyal had introduced to Atrin repeatedly throughout his lifetime, was the backdrop to the whole of life and death. Atrin had trained for decades in his meditation practice for this very moment, to recognize timeless awareness that is deathless. He expelled his last breath in a state of meditation.

# CHAPTER 22

# RESTING INSEPARABLY
## *in the* GURU'S
## WISDOM MIND

G OLOK, E ASTERN T IBET

*Year of the Water Dog to the Wood Rat, 1922–1924*

Tertön Sogyal knew that Padmasambhava's matrix of prescriptive measures—averting practices, geomantic stupa and temple building, reconsecrating power places, making spiritual medicine, informing yogis how to perform wrathful ceremonies, and empowering and spreading life-force stones—was needed in its entirety to accomplish fully the future protection of Tibet. The repetitive frequency with which Tertön Sogyal was being told how he and others needed to work for the benefit of all Tibetans was testament to the fact that the pool of positive karma for Tibet was depleted. The menacing Dogyal worship continued in Lhasa, and some of Tertön Sogyal's own disciples and treasure revelations were targeted by Dogyal worshipers. Stories swirled in Lhasa that the father of a prominent council minister to the Thirteenth Dalai Lama had been killed at the age of 37 by Dogyal because he practiced Tertön Sogyal's treasure teachings alongside his Gelug meditations. Had Tertön Sogyal traveled to Lhasa, he would have confronted Phabongka face-to-face to back up the Dalai Lama's directives to desist from promoting sectarian beliefs. While many Tibetans were relaxing in the apparent freedom from conflict with Tibet's neighbors, Tertön Sogyal and the other treasure revealers were growing increasingly frustrated. It was as the powerful confession prayer read:

> *How utterly mistaken are the minds of ignorant beings!*
> *They reject the truth and put their energy into harmful deeds,*
> *Spurning the Buddha's words, they fall prey to life's addictions,*
> *And apply their intelligence toward meaningless distraction.*

It was against a backdrop of recent disappointments that Tertön Sogyal began to streamline his activity, concentrating only on the specific goals of extending the life of the Dalai Lama and ritual protection for Tibet. He abandoned divinations and astrological calculations for the many people who came asking for worldly advice. He stopped using his own prescience for others, or relying on predictions from reading his dreams, unless they concerned the Dalai Lama, Dodrupchen, or his immediate family. When Tertön Sogyal heard that Ma Qi had sent his troops to fight Golok tribes after the warlord occupied Labrang Monastery, Tertön Sogyal merely sent a message to Shinya to encourage peace, instead of going there in person. Tertön Sogyal refrained from normal conversation or idly speaking, and he no longer visited homes of patrons. Tertön Sogyal practiced his own termas and taught from his memory and experience. And whenever he was unclear about a particular direction to travel or there was some question about his work, Tertön Sogyal invoked Noble Tara and other dakinis for guidance and protection.

Tertön Sogyal continued using the two life-force stones, for he believed that this method in particular was critical to the Dalai Lama. The tertön traveled to various pilgrimage locations associated with the two stones to continually activate their power. At caves and high peaks, he would engage in three days of silence in which he practiced yogic breathing throughout the day and night, harmonizing the movement of his breath with the mental recitation of the syllables *Om, Ah, Hum,* a method to recognize nonconceptually the innate nature of the mind. He would then perform tantric rituals and recite the appropriate mantras to capture the life-force of the deity, empowering himself and the stones. After he finished a few days of such practice, he sometimes offered an empowerment of Avalokiteshvara to the public, or blessed them by reciting the terma *Names of the Thousand and Two Buddhas of This Fortunate Age.*

As he continued his effort to purify Tibetans of their transgression against their lama's instructions and laziness toward fulfilling the prophecies of Padmasambhava, Tertön Sogyal made feast offerings before the two life-force stones. He repeatedly recited short prayers such as "All the ocean-like buddhas and bodhisattvas, please accept this offering," or "*Hum.* Guru, devas, dakinis, and treasure guardians, all of you, accept this offering." While there was food and drink placed on the shrine, it was the tertön's mind that multiplied the offerings to fill the whole of space with inexhaustible delights to enlightened beings from the past, present, and future.

Tertön Sogyal also empowered other rocks as emissaries of the two principal life-force stones. He painted or carved the names and images of the mother and father deities, Vajravarahi and Hayagriva, one on each side, and then directed the blessings and life-force of the deities toward the new stones. Spontaneously arising syllables would sometimes appear on the new rocks. At other times, with newly consecrated stones, fresh with blessing, the mother and father deities appeared in visions to Tertön Sogyal, saying, "The fortunate owner of me is you!" Tertön Sogyal took this as a significant indication that the consecration of the life-force stones was successful. There were some stones that did not take the blessings, and he simply returned those rocks to their original location lest he annoy a local spirit for disturbing the environment. As for other stones that he imbued with the life-force of the mother and father deities, Tertön Sogyal sent them by messengers across Tibet, to Lhasa and Nyarong, and Litang and Chamdo, and elsewhere. He instructed that the stones be strategically placed in temples and monasteries and given to specific lamas. Sometimes he buried the stones as offerings to the treasure guardians. Tertön Sogyal was trying to single-handedly resupply the whole of Tibet with the spiritual fortitude that it had lost.

One early spring evening in the Water Pig year (1923), Tertön Sogyal met Guru Padmasambhava in a vision. Sometimes his visions were mixed with dream-like states, so that he had to be diligent in assessing the validity of the visions. On this occasion, he believed that Padmasambhava actually appeared to him in reality. There were a host of dakinis surrounding the Great Guru, and one of them spoke for Padmasambhava, saying, "Within the expanse of rigpa's self-manifesting clarity, the darkness of grasping ignorantly at duality is completely abolished. The means for accomplishing this is both the Peaceful Guru and the one known as the Wildly Wrathful Guru with nine heads and eighteen arms." Tertön Sogyal then saw five teachers—Jamyang Khyentse, Jamgön Kongtrul, Nyala Pema Dündul, Tertön Rangrik, and Dudjom Lingpa—emanate into the space before him.

The dakini continued. "If you can unite all of the lamas of the past, present, and future, together, as Padmasambhava, then the blessing will be swift. In these degenerate times, this is the method to remove all obstacles; there is no other method superior to this. While you still have an ordinary physical body, you should conduct wrathful practice to accomplish your aim. You will see that this is true. The time is ripe now!"

After her quintessential instruction, the dakini dissolved into the heart of Padmasambhava. Tertön Sogyal received in his mind-stream different liturgies associated with the five lamas. As he began to write the liturgies down, Tertön Sogyal heard the sounds of the liturgies themselves resounding from the heavens:

> *Dudjom Lingpa can be accomplished as the Wildly Wrathful Guru;*
> *Khanyam Lingpa [Nyala Pema Dündul] is accomplished as Dharmakaya Samantabhadra.*
> *Dongak Lingpa [Khyentse Wangpo], as Sambhogakaya Vajradhara;*
> *Pema Garwang [Jamgön Kongtrul] is for the accomplishment of Nirmanakaya Vajrasattva;*
> *and Kusum Lingpa [Tertön Rangrik] is to accomplish Padmasambhava Pema Tötreng Tsal.*

The five lamas appeared in the sky as fully accomplished buddhas, as Tertön Sogyal heard each of their names. Each master repeated the same phrase as he appeared: "I am the great holder of all the *Complete Gathering of Teachings*. If you accomplish me, then you accomplish all the buddhas." Then the lamas each dissolved into Padmasambhava and the retinue of dakinis dissolved into a single enriching dakini who wore green silk garments. With only the guru and the enriching dakinis left, she spoke, "The sixteen joys fuel the flame of clear realization of what to adopt and what to abandon. If you do not dispel obstacles with diligence, black magic and other harmful spirits will hurt you. If you can dispel them, at that moment good fortune will abound. As for the black magic directed toward you, the Lion-Faced Dakini is the antidote, and performing prayers to Tara. Continue doing Vajrakilaya to combat the demons and obstacles, and to purify any harm that has already befallen you from others' contaminated views, practice the three long-life dakinis."

Then, in an instant, the entire vision dissolved into Tertön Sogyal's heart, and an overpowering bliss surged through his body and mind.

> *All you masters of the lineage of the ultimate heart essence,*
> *To you I pray! Shower down your blessings!*
> *May all my dualistic perceptions vanish like clouds in the sky!*

*May I realize directly, here and now,*
*The face of the ultimate guru, my very own rigpa.*

That evening, he wrote the liturgies by the light of a butter lamp. Just as he was passing into the sleep state, he felt as though he were in a cave, when a lama stepped forth and gave the final instructions associated with the vision: "For your own well-being, visit the Crystal Cave and do this guru yoga practice, especially this year. The next year and into the Wood Ox year [1925], concentrate on your own Vajrakilaya treasure revelation. Then, until the Fire Rat year [1927], cherish the dakini practice to purify any and all negativity."

In his 68th year, Tertön Sogyal embarked upon what would become his last tour of Golok and the Derge regions. He was receiving invitations from monasteries and lamas in Trehor, Marong, and Dzogchen to teach and to give empowerments. There were indications that Tertön Sogyal could encounter sickness the following year, so he wanted to fulfill his disciples' requests to teach before any health problems arose. Lama Trime and Tertön Sogyal's son accompanied their teacher to assist him on this sojourn, as they had stepped into the role of Tertön Sogyal's attendants after Atrin's death. They were also doing practices to elongate Tertön Sogyal's life and to repel any spells or black magic directed toward him. Tertön Sogyal taught extensively wherever he went, and after he bestowed empowerments, the monasteries performed long-life ceremonies for him. The teaching tour lasted six months, and upon his return to the Puchung House, exhausted from the travel, Tertön Sogyal fell ill. The most skilled doctors visited and purification ceremonies were performed, but improvements did not manifest quickly. There was a prophecy regarding this episode of sickness that said, "In order to eliminate the obstacles for everyone, Tertön Sogyal will take upon himself sickness and harm."

In his sickened state, Tertön Sogyal practiced the instructions known as *tonglen*, or "giving and receiving." Tonglen is training in generating great compassion for all. Using the medium of the in-breath and out-breath, the practitioner repeatedly offers his own well-being to others and takes their suffering upon himself. The practitioner trains continually to reverse the habitual tendency of cherishing only his or her own happiness. Instead, the practitioner cultivates authentic concern for others. In the case of Tertön Sogyal, a yogi who had reached the pinnacle of Dzogchen realization, he understood that from the perspective of the fundamental ground of being, there was no separation between himself and other beings. Even if there appear to be myriad types of sufferings, if the basic nature of all beings is the same, then there is only one thing called suffering. Meditating deeply on the nondual state of his own and other beings' suffering, the realization of the highest truths dawned in Tertön Sogyal's mind. And at that moment, he reduced the suffering of all beings. Such a practice was the ultimate antidote to sickness.

When Tertön Sogyal recovered and returned to Golok, he went to see Dodrupchen in the summer of the Wood Rat year (1924). The termas that he had revealed in the previous two years, including *Names of the Thousand and Two Buddhas of This Fortunate Age*, he offered to Dodrupchen. While he was reciting the liturgies of the terma revelations, a dakini appeared. She gave him a prophecy, but it was a riddle in numbers. Dodrupchen assisted Tertön Sogyal in deciphering the meaning, which concerned where the tertön should go to practice and who should accompany him. And there were other signs that they both understood but did not discuss. At the conclusion of their meeting, both Tertön Sogyal and Dodrupchen uncharacteristically took out long white offering scarves. Normally, such a scarf would be offered upon meeting, not at the time of departure, to mark the occasion as auspicious. But they both knew they would not see each other again in this life.

"We will meet each other again in the pure realms," Tertön Sogyal said.

"The great Khyentse prophesied that I would live only to be fifty years old," Dodrupchen said. "But I have crossed well beyond my sixtieth year. Tertön, this is thanks to you."

"You should not think of going to the pure realms anytime soon," Tertön Sogyal encouraged his spiritual brother. "I too will also try to live long."

The two masters touched their foreheads together in a mutual sign of respect and love. Tertön Sogyal rose quickly and departed.

# CHAPTER 23

# *The* NYARONG LAMA'S LAST ENCAMPMENT

Nyagar, Golok, Eastern Tibet

*Year of the Wood Rat to the Fire Tiger, 1924–1926*

Tertön Sogyal and Khandro Pumo with their family and Lama Trime departed Puchung House to travel to Shukjung Monastery. Tsullo had returned from his trip to Lhasa and escorted the group to his monastery. There he requested that Tertön Sogyal consecrate a newly installed statue of Padmasambhava. After the consecration, Tertön Sogyal announced to the monks and villagers that he was authorizing Tsullo to give empowerments and the oral transmission for all of his treasure revelations and teachings. Tertön Sogyal spoke about Tsullo's becoming a lineage holder.

"The time and circumstance did not align for the two prophesied holders—Jamyang Khyentse Wangpo and Thubten Gyatso, His Holiness the Dalai Lama—to receive my collected treasure revelations in their entirety. But this devoted student, Tulku Tsultrim Zangpo, who has the correct view, has also been prophesied to become a lineage holder."

Tsullo accepted his role and said, "As I have seen your golden face in reality, Tertön Sogyal Rinpoche, I accept this fortune you have bestowed."

While staying in Shukjung Monastery, Tertön Sogyal met with Dodrupchen's nephew, Kunzang Nyima. They already had a close relationship, and Tertön Sogyal had earlier recognized him as a reincarnation of his teacher, Lama Sonam Thaye. Kunzang Nyima brought to Shukjung the chieftain of the Washul Kaduk tribe to meet Tertön Sogyal. The chieftain told Tertön Sogyal that he was offering him a permanent residence and that he had already built a small temple and housing for the tertön and his family in a valley called Nyaknyikil Peldeu near Sertar. Tertön Sogyal saw that the chieftain benefactor's offer accorded with the prophecies that told him to find a place to settle down. Tertön Sogyal accepted and said they would depart in a fortnight.

When they were packing their few belongings and loading the yaks for the move, a monk named Namgyal from Khamgon Monastery arrived. He respectfully offered a quill pen and paper and requested the tertön to write a prayer for causing the Buddha's teachings to flourish.

Tertön Sogyal was just beginning to write when a vision of a red dakini appeared and said, "Wait! When the time comes, I'll speak the prayer to you!" Tertön Sogyal placed the pen on the table and told Namgyal that he would have to wait for the prayer, and then invited him to come and live with his family.

Tent poles on the backs of yaks formed a V silhouette against the skyline as the caravan moved out from Shukjung to the new encampment. Black yak-hair tents and other cargo were strapped to the sides of the animals. Mastiffs used to protect the camp from wolves and bandits barked and ran alongside the caravan. A dozen yogis and yoginis in the party walked. Proceeding slowly on a white horse, after a quarter century of travel and pilgrimage, Tertön Sogyal knew he was riding to his last encampment.

When they arrived a few miles from the encampment, Tertön Sogyal dismounted to rest and have tea. Facing south and west on the hillside, the Ja Valley was deep and thick with pine and juniper forests. To the northwest, a single yak trail disappeared into the windswept pass that leads to Larung Valley. From the east, glacial water flowed from the peaks of the eight holy lakes of Dzongdün. The sky was vast, the air thin.

Tertön Sogyal sent Khandro Pumo and their son ahead to prepare the house by burning purificatory juniper smoke in all of the rooms, and to instruct the monks to begin praying in the temple. After cleaning the rooms, Khandro Pumo unrolled in the small shrine room the wolf pelt that Tertön Sogyal had used for decades as his meditation rug. Their few belongings were unpacked. Tertön Sogyal remained on the hillside in meditation for some hours. It was as Tertön Sogyal had told one of his students:

> At this, the time for discovering Buddha directly, you must remain alone, without companions, in an isolated mountain retreat. With a staff to the right, a container of grain to the left, a copper pot in front, and a cave behind. From now until the attainment of enlightenment, you must look upwards, entrusting yourself to the teacher and Three Jewels, and downwards, into the naked unity of awareness and emptiness. At all times and in all situations, you must guard the fortress of the view, just as you would cherish a diamond. And you must continue meditating until, your eyes turned lifeless and blue, you breathe your very last breath.

Tertön Sogyal rode toward the hillside that would become known as Nyagar—the Nyarong Lama's encampment. Near the perimeter, where the mastiffs guarded, Tertön Sogyal dismounted and circumambulated the site 21 times, with everyone following him in a slow movement of prayer, Kunzang Nyima holding Tertön Sogyal's hand to keep him steady. Tertön Sogyal approached his two-room stone house from the east, and Khandro Pumo, Rigdzin Namgyal and Sonam Dolma and their son, Chöpel Gyatso, Tsullo, Lama Trime, Kunzang Nyima and the chieftain, and a dozen disciples with pure samaya and devotion gathered around their teacher. With folded hands, Tertön Sogyal led them in a prayer to Tara before entering the house:

*We pray to you who are like the moonlight, the one who
 pacifies all fear:
Of doubt, desire, envy, and avarice,
Of wrong views, hatred, delusions, and pride.
Jetsun Tara, mother of all the buddhas, we pay homage
 to you!*

After bowls of yogurt and roasted barley were served, the
Washul chieftain appointed two scouts to remain at the camp
as guards while the newcomers became acquainted with the valley. The chieftain asked if he could take his leave. Tertön Sogyal
thanked him for offering him a home, saying, "This house made
of earth and stone with a beautiful appearance and its colorful
painting is like my own illusory body; they both will collapse and
dissolve without a trace."

"May you live one hundred and eight years," the chieftain
said, bowing his head.

Tertön Sogyal reminded his patron that a person cannot escape the impending results of his actions, so one should never
cease in striving to benefit others. "Endeavor with all your might
to make great use of your precious human birth!"

Later that day, Tertön Sogyal called Kunzang Nyima into the
house and said, "Take my black yak-hair tent with you. It is yours
now." Kunzang Nyima was overjoyed and immediately set up
the tent next to Tertön Sogyal's house. He would later say, "Why
would I sleep in a house when I can sleep every night in the home
of the Dalai Lama's guru!"

Tertön Sogyal settled into a routine of meditation and ritual
practice. Sometimes he would teach in the morning if his students
had questions, especially regarding yogic exercises to gain mastery over the subtle body, rendering the body a perfect vessel for
the mind to recognize its own clarity. For his own practice, he
concentrated on long-life deities and making offerings to the dakinis. In the evening, he would have a barley torma set out and
call his wife and family into his room to chant and offer a ritual
feast. There were other wrathful practices and mantras that he
recited, to which nobody was privy. When yogis and monks from

the region would arrive, Tertön Sogyal taught them whatever they requested if they promised to apply the teachings he gave.

At the end of the Wood Ox year (1925), monks from Nubzor Monastery arrived and requested that Tertön Sogyal come to give empowerments and transmissions; despite the arduous horseback journey, Tertön Sogyal agreed. An escort party returned two weeks later to take Tertön Sogyal on a white horse decorated with colorful silk tassels to the monastery; there he dismounted onto a *svastika* design—the ancient Indian symbol of deathlessness—drawn with white rice powder on the ground. Though Tertön Sogyal tired quickly, he finished all the empowerments, including *The Most Secret Wrathful Vajrakilaya* and *Dispelling Flaws in Interdependence*, concluding with the long-life empowerment of Amitayus, the Buddha of Infinite Life. Tertön Sogyal and his family returned to Nyagar after the few days of empowerments at Nubzor.

Soon after they returned home, Tertön Sogyal called his daughter-in-law to help him walk above the dozen stone huts at Nyagar. Sonam Drolma held the hand of the 71-year-old tertön as they circumambulated mantra-carved stones on the north end of the encampment and then continued up the grassy knoll to take in the expansive view. Tertön Sogyal's breath was labored, but his eyes were clear and soft. Among the black-lipped pika, musk deer, and soaring lammergeier of Nyagar, Tertön Sogyal sat quietly looking into the distance with Sonam Drolma by his side. After some time, he told her that he was going to die within a week, but that she should not despair.

"All that is born must die. I have done all that I could for the people of the Land of Snows." He told Sonam Drolma not to cry.

"As for the twelve treasure teachings of mine that remain unfinished, I will summon the treasure guardians and they will return the treasure objects among the lakes and grottoes of all the places I have traveled throughout Tibet. My future incarnations will rediscover them."

That evening, Tertön Sogyal prepared the two life-force stones that still needed to arrive in the hands of the Dalai Lama. He wrapped them in five-colored silk cloth and placed them inside a box and sealed it shut with his wax seal. Tertön Sogyal told his son to accompany them to Lhasa and make sure that the Dalai Lama personally received the stones.

For the next week, Tertön Sogyal sat unmoving in meditation throughout the day and into the night. He called Khandro Pumo into his room one morning and handed her a piece of paper with a prayer written on it, and said, "I dreamed I was in the Crystal Cave of Padmasambhava last night when a dakini appeared and spoke this to me. Please be sure that young monk Namgyal receives a copy." She looked down at the prayer Tertön Sogyal had written, touching it to her crown.

> *Buddha, Dharma, and Sangha, and the Lord of the*
> *Shakyas, Shakyamuni Buddha,*
> *Avalokiteshvara, Manjushri, Vajrapani, and Maitreya,*
> *The sixteen Great Elder Teachers,*
> *And Padmasambhava—*
> *Through your power and through your truth,*
> *May the lives of the masters be secure!*
> *May the spiritual community increase and dwell in har-*
> *mony!*
> *May all circumstances hostile to the Dharma be pacified!*
> *May the activities of study and practice grow and spread!*

"These words are the mother's last advice," Tertön Sogyal said, referring to the One-Eyed Protectress of Mantras, who had guided and assisted him throughout his life. "There is still much more to this, and it will be explained, when the time is right."

On the tenth day of the first month of the Fire Tiger year (1926), Tertön Sogyal was helped by Khandro Pumo and Sonam Drolma to sit upright in his bed and cross his legs in meditation posture on his wolf pelt. Rigdzin Namgyal and Tsullo and Kunzang Nyima sat on the floor. Khandro adjusted a wool blanket over Tertön Sogyal's shoulders. A profound peace settled as the tertön rested his hands on his knees and entered a deep stillness. His body was like a mountain, his gaze as vast as the sky.

Khandro Pumo and her family and the close disciples sat in silent prayer with Tertön Sogyal. They all knew their teacher's mind would soon be released from his body. Emotions arose and washed over them. Precious moments in their life with Tertön Sogyal flashed through their minds—his wordless teachings, his fierce love, and his undying compassion. Tears of devotion and longing fell from their eyes.

> *In the heavenly palace of All-Encompassing Space*
> *Dwells the embodiment of all buddhas, past, present, and*
> *future,*
> *To you who have shown me the ultimate nature of my*
> *mind.*
> *To you, my root guru, I pray!*

> *The texts of the Kama, Terma, and pure visions,*
> *Their empowerments, instructions, transmissions, au-*
> *thorizations, and blessings,*
> *You who have given them out of your compassion,*
> *To you I pray, grant me spiritual attainments, ordinary*
> *and supreme!*

> *Glorious root guru, precious one,*
> *Dwell on the lotus seat on the crown of my head,*
> *Look upon me with the grace of your great compassion,*
> *Grant me spiritual attainments of body, speech, and*
> *mind!*

The great tertön was motionless, abiding in the expanse of the luminous clarity of his mind. His piercing eyes were at once gazing outwardly to the world with compassion, while inwardly abiding in natural great peace, resting in his own pure nature. As the valley's mist blew into the encampment and dissolved in the morning sunlight, Tertön Sogyal exhaled his last breath.

> *The innermost, profound meaning is crystallized here, so*
> *take it to heart:*
> *Utterly beyond all thoughts and thinking,*
> *All-penetrating rigpa awareness arises naturally by itself.*

*Unmoving, unchanging, once this intrinsic self-cognizance
Is recognized with no mistake, within its uncontrived ex-
    panse of naturalness,
Clarity, stability, and deep confidence are secured. And in
    this state
All risings keep liberating, by themselves, just as they
    arise.*

*Everything is perfected within the primordial ground, lib-
    erated beyond duality.
When the roots of all flaws and failings are severed like
    this,
You will have seized the fortress of the utter purity of all
    appearance and existence!*

# CHAPTER 24

# CONTINUATION
## *of* BLESSING

Khandro Pumo was the last to leave the deep peace that pervaded the tertön's room. For the next three days, few words were spoken. Others in the encampment knew that Tertön Sogyal's consciousness had left his body, though nobody spoke of it. Prayers and rituals were being conducted in the temple. Khandro Pumo and Rigdzin Namgyal prayed near the body, and Tsullo, Lama Trime, and Kunzang Nyima sat in meditation as well. A messenger was dispatched to Nubzor Monastery summoning Trashe Lama to come with his monks.

Rigdzin Namgyal and Tsullo bathed their teacher's body after a week with consecrated saffron water, and then they attached various written mantras, drawn mandalas, and tantric texts to the energetic centers, such as the heart and crown. The body was wrapped in a white shroud and scented with herbal water before being dressed in tantric attire and positioned in the meditation posture, with the legs crossed in the lotus position, and a bell and dorje placed in the hands. Tertön Sogyal's consciousness had arrived in the Luminous Sphere of Padmasambhava's Pure Land, which is no other place than the ultimate fruition of meditative realization, buddhahood itself. Although the tertön's mind had departed the body, the final rites were an opportunity for the disciples to accumulate positive merit, purify their minds, and confess any misdeeds. The adorned body was placed on a simple throne in the temple, and for weeks the yogis, yoginis, monks, and nuns chanted rituals and made offerings to the lineage. When the senior lamas and monks of Nubzor Monastery arrived, a cremation stupa was built next to Tertön Sogyal's house. On the day of the cremation, the body was placed on a wood pyre in the conical-shaped dome, rainbows arched over the Ja Valley, and melodious singing was heard from the sky. A sweet aroma descended like mist.

Lamas and monks sat in the four cardinal directions of the stupa, arranged like a mandala with the guru in the center. As prayers and verses of purification were chanted, Rigdzin Namgyal set the pyre alight. Offerings of grains, butter, flowers, and other substances were made into the raging fire that consumed the tertön's body. Villagers circumambulated the ceremony and prayed to Tertön Sogyal. The cremation ritual lasted for half the day, after which time the stupa was sealed for three days. When the cremation stupa had cooled and was opened, many spherical relics—both small white *ringsel* and the pearl-size, five-color *dung*—were found within the ashes, an indication of Tertön Sogyal's attainment of the five wisdoms of buddhahood. Tertön Sogyal had transformed his ordinary existence and the death of his body into evidence of enlightenment for the devoted. The relics were distributed to close disciples, and some were placed inside a newly constructed stupa at Nyagar. In the 1960s, the Chinese Communist army destroyed the stupa and small temple at Nyagar after they invaded Golok. Tertön Sogyal's devotees rebuilt the stupa in 2008.

Within a month of the cremation, Khandro Pumo and Rigdzin Namgyal and his family, along with other students, collected Tertön Sogyal's belongings and left Nyagar, traveling southwest to Trango, through Kandze, and finally home to the Kalzang Temple in Nyarong. Woodblocks of Tertön Sogyal's 20 volumes of collected treasure revelations were housed at Kalzang Temple.

Sogyal Rinpoche is one of the most prominent Tibetan Buddhist teachers in the world, one of the two simultaneous reincarnations of Tertön Sogyal, and author of *The Tibetan Book of Living and Dying.*

The lineage holders of Tertön Sogyal's treasure teachings, some of whom were also his own teachers, included the Thirteenth Dalai Lama (Thubten Gyatso), Jamyang Khyentse Wangpo, Jamgön

253

Kongtrul Rinpoche, the Fifth Dzogchen Rinpoche (Thubten Chökyi Dorje, Dzogchen Khenpo Pema Vajra, Ju Mipham Rinpoche, Nyoshul Lungtok, Dza Choktrul Rinpoche, Lama (Tertön) Trime, Katok Situ, Minyak Khenpo Kunzang Sönam, the Third Dodrupchen Rinpoche (Jikme Tenpe Nyima), Demo Rinpoche, Dorje Drak Rigdzin Nyamnyi Dorje, Minling Trichen Rinpoche, Sakya Trichen, the Fifteenth Karmapa (Khakhyab Dorje), Tertön Kunzang Nyima, and Jamyang Khyentse Chökyi Lodrö.

Dodrupchen Rinpoche passed away at the age of 62, a few months after Tertön Sogyal left his body. After 49 days, Dodrupchen's body was cremated amid wondrous signs. His remains were preserved in a two-story-high golden stupa near his monastery.

The Thirteenth Dalai Lama continued to rule Tibet from Lhasa. In the year preceding the Thirteenth Dalai Lama's passing, he urged his countrymen to prepare for hostile forces that would attack Tibet. His concerns were consistent with Padmasambhava's prediction and exactly as Tertön Sogyal had repeatedly warned. The Tibetan leader was well aware of the Communist Revolution in Mongolia, as refugees arriving in Lhasa from Ulan Bator spoke of Stalin's atrocities. And the civil war that had destabilized China eventually gave rise to Mao Zedong's rule. At a teaching at Reting Monastery in the year of the Water Monkey (1932), the Dalai Lama told the congregation that he was speaking as a father would advise his son:

> I am now in the fifty-eighth year of my life. Everyone must know that I may not be around for more than a few years to discharge my temporal and religious responsibilities. You must develop a good diplomatic relationship with our two powerful neighbors: India and China. Efficient and well-equipped troops must be stationed even on the minor frontiers bordering hostile forces. Such an army must be well trained in warfare as a sure deterrent against any adversaries.
>
> Furthermore, this present era is rampant with the Five Degenerations, in particular the Red ideology. In Outer Mongolia, the search for the reincarnation of Jetsün

Dampa was banned; the monastic properties and endowments were confiscated; the lamas and monks forced into the army; and the Buddhist religion destroyed, leaving no trace of identity. Such a system, according to the reports still being received, has been established in Ulan Baatar.

In future, this system will certainly be forced either from within or from outside the land that cherished the joint spiritual and temporal system. If, in such an event, we fail to defend our land, the holy lamas including the triumphant father and son [the Dalai Lama and the Panchen Lama] will be eliminated without a trace of their names remaining; the properties of the reincarnate lamas and of the monasteries along with their endowments for religious services will be seized. Moreover, our political system originated by the three ancient kings will be reduced to an empty name; my officials, deprived of their patrimony and property, will be subjugated as slaves for the enemies; and my people, subjected to fear and misery, will be unable to endure either day or night. Such an era will certainly come.

The Dalai Lama died in the year of the Water Bird (1933), a year after giving this speech, six years after Tertön Sogyal's passing. Mao Zedong's Communist armies invaded Tibet less than 20 years later.

The Hayagriva-Vajravarahi life-force stone was delivered to the Thirteenth Dalai Lama in Lhasa within a year of Tertön Sogyal's passing, in 1926 or 1927. Tsullo says it was Rigdzin Namgyal who delivered it, while Keutsang Rinpoche's biography claims that he was sent by the Dalai Lama to retrieve it in 1926. Dilgo Khyentse Rinpoche said that as the stone approached Lhasa, the Dalai Lama determined with astrological calculations the exact time to receive it and summoned abbots and monks from the Sera, Drepung, and Ganden monasteries, senior government officials, and other spiritual masters to ceremonially escort the stone into the city. The Dalai Lama came down from Keutsang Monastery to the Norbulingka Palace and received the stone. The stone, which was said to have the warm breath of the dakinis still upon it, was kept in the inner sanctum of the Kelsang Dekhyil chamber of the Chenling Palace, protecting the Thirteenth Dalai Lama until his death. When the 19-year-old Fourteenth Dalai Lama fled Tibet in 1959, he took the Hayagriva-Vajravarahi life-force stone as his protection from the bullets of the Chinese army. His Holiness recalls, "There were quite a number of sacred things that remained in Potala, but I left from Norbulingka. So when I left, those things that were available in Norbulingka, I took them. I carried with me that life-force stone, [which] the Thirteenth Dalai Lama kept in the Norbulingka, and one vajra and one phurba."

Tertön Sogyal's spiritual wife, Khandro Pumo, spent her later years in a simple hermitage high in the mountains of Nyarong. She was a great practitioner of Vajrakilaya and recited *Om Vajra Kila Kilaya Sarwa Bighanen Bam Hum Phat* 300 million times during her life. Khandro Pumo became renowned for her clairvoyance and her ability to avert frost or bring rain. She often recommended healing prayers or rituals to the sick who came to her. Sometimes she would tie a protection cord around their necks; it was noticed that if she gave such a protection cord, it meant the person would live, but if she gave them spiritual medicinal pills, it meant that their illness was fatal. Khandro Pumo died in 1949; there is a stupa with her remains at Kalzang Temple.

Rigdzin Namgyal and his wife, Sonam Drolma, lived near Khandro Pumo. Their child, Pema Chöpel Gyatso, became famous in Nyarong and Kandze as a scholar-monk and used to stay for long durations at Lumorap Monastery. The Chinese Communists jailed him in Dartsedo in 1957, along with many other incarnate lamas. Ama Adhe, the heroic Khampa resistance fighter, was in prison with Chöpel Gyatso. She said that seven incarnate lamas, including Chöpel Gyatso, died one evening in prison, but that it was not at the direct hand of the prison guards—rather, the lamas decided to eject their consciousness and die so as not to allow the Chinese Communists to incur negative karma by beating them. There is a stupa dedicated to Chöpel Gyatso near Kalzang Temple.

Tsullo lived at his monastery of Shukjung in the Do valley for the rest of his life, traveling to teach in the region on occasion, and became a great scholar, authoring eight volumes, including the secret biography of Tertön Sogyal. The secret biography was based on the tertön's journals of his mystical visions and prophecies and his wide-ranging travels, and includes many of his own words. Upon the completion of the biography in 1942, Tsullo concluded with an homage to Tertön Sogyal that in part reads, "The secret life story of the liberation of Tertön Sogyal, which is like a miracle, is now complete. You, my guru, will take other miraculous rebirths according to your wishes. In all direction and in all times there will be billions of places where you will manifest to benefit beings; may I simultaneously attain the power to see you on all those occasions and in all those realms. Now, to you who are in the Luminous Sphere of Padmasambhava's Pure Land, in the presence of the Great Guru from which all the buddhas emanate, purified from all defilements, where there is great bliss, I emanate a great host of boundless offerings, and through this I pray that I will remain inseparable from you."

Three people in particular urged Tsullo to write the biography of Tertön Sogyal—Chöpel Gyatso, Tertön Sogyal's grandson, made his request with a "cloth of the gods," Yamantaka and Vajrakilaya texts, and a new set of monk's robes; Khenpo Lekshe Jorden, an important teacher from Katok Monastery, accompanied his request to Tsullo with an offering of a bell and dorje; and the nun Jamyang Chodren, the aunt of Garje Khamtrul Rinpoche, made her request with a white offering scarf, representations of enlightened body, speech, and mind, along with precious turquoise and sapphire, and, importantly, with paper, pens, and ink. Jamyang Chodren's request especially inspired Tsullo to write about the immense kindness of Tertön Sogyal as demonstrated by his life.

The last lines of the colophon of Tertön Sogyal's 725-page secret biography states, "People like us have a hard time fathoming the profound minds of realized beings like Tertön Sogyal, whose life cannot be framed conceptually. His accomplishment and qualities are like a vast heap of precious gems equal to space that emanate light rays of enlightened activity. In this world where there are an infinite number of scholars and yogis, the life story of someone like Tertön Sogyal, whose clarity and perfection are

Khenpo Jikme Phuntsok, holding a phurba that belonged to
Tertön Sogyal, was the most prominent teacher who emerged from
the Cultural Revolution to teach and revive Buddhism in Tibet. He was
one of the two simultaneous reincarnations of Tertön Sogyal.

without compare, justifies being told. His entire life was lived
to benefit all beings through accomplishing the intent of the
undeceiving treasure prophecies. This secret biography is based on
the terma prophecies themselves; it is not just random stories or

what people have said here and there. I, Tsultrim Zangpo, known as Shilabhadra, who has received the particles of dust from the feet of the great Tertön Sogyal Rinpoche upon my head, who is the lowest of all of his disciples, completed his secret biography nearby the great monastery of Dzogchen Samten Orgyen Choling, at the retreat mountain of Osel Lhundrup, in the spring of the year of the Water Horse [1942] on a very auspicious day. May it be auspicious. *Sarvada Kalyanam Bhavantu.*"

Tsullo died in the year of the Fire Bird (1957). He had two reincarnation: Chökyi Nyima Rinpoche of Nango Gonpa in Trango and Tulku Nyoshul Lungtok of Tawo; both are students of the late Khenpo Jikme Phuntsok from Larung Gar.

Regarding the reincarnations of Tertön Sogyal, there were a number of prophecies. Tertön Sogyal indicated he would emanate beneficial activity through hundreds of future practitioners. He also predicted that there would be two principal reincarnations. Tertön Kunzang Nyima revealed a prophecy about these two incarnations that reads:

> *Nanam Dorje Dudjom [previous incarnation of Tertön Sogyal] will certainly ripen into two fruits:*
> *One, a turquoise dragon holding up a jewel for all to see,*
> *The other, his voice resounding everywhere like a lion's roar.*

It is believed that Khenpo Jikme Phuntsok was the "turquoise dragon" and Sogyal Rinpoche has the "voice resounding everywhere like a lion's roar."

Khenpo Jikme Phuntsok was born in the Water Bird year (1933) in a valley between Dodrupchen and Shukjung monasteries near Padma Township in Golok, and received his training from the Dzogchen scholar-hermit Thubten Chöpel before taking up residence at Nubzor Monastery, where he was the chant leader. He later founded the famous Larung Gar Buddhist Academy, which grew to house more than 10,000 monks, nuns, and lay practitioners at its height in early 2001. In June 2001, the Chinese government demolished a large portion of the academy and expelled more than 3,000 students. Despite the Chinese government's restrictions, Larung Gar remains the largest center of Buddhist studies in the world. Khenpo Jikme Phuntsok was the single most influential lama in Tibet since the liberalization of religious policy by Chinese authorities in the late 1980s. He died in January 2004 at the age of 71.

Sogyal Rinpoche, born in the Lakar Tsang family in Trehor, was recognized as the reincarnation of Tertön Sogyal by Jamyang Khyentse Chökyi Lodrö. Sogyal Rinpoche and his family fled Tibet with Khyentse Chökyi Lodrö in the 1950s and eventually settled in Sikkim in northern India. Sogyal Rinpoche was raised like a son by Khyentse Chökyi Lodrö, and after the great master's passing, he studied with Dilgo Khyentse Rinpoche, Dudjom Rinpoche, and Nyoshul Khenpo Rinpoche, eventually establishing one of the largest networks of Dharma centers in the West— Rigpa Fellowship. His book *The Tibetan Book of Living and Dying* has been translated into 34 languages.

In August 1993, the two principal reincarnations of Tertön Sogyal—Khenpo Jikme Phuntsok and Sogyal Rinpoche—met for the first time at Sogyal Rinpoche's retreat center of Lerab Ling in southern France. Khenpo Jikme Phuntsok said at the time, "So, it was said, Dorje Dudjom was to have two incarnations. One of them was to be a monk [turquoise dragon], who would benefit beings through the Vinaya monastic discipline [the jewel], and the other was to be one who would spread the secret mantra Vajrayana [lion's roar] far and wide. When I saw this, I thought that Sogyal Rinpoche must be the one to spread the secret mantra Vajrayana, and I might be the monk."

Khenpo Jikme Phuntsok went on to say, "In the predictions of Tertön Sogyal's *The Tathagata Practice of the Gathering of Drolö* it says that during his own lifetime, his teachings would not spread very far, only to a small extent in central Tibet around the Thirteenth Dalai Lama. During his second incarnation, however, his teachings would flourish and become known all over the world. Now, when I see the work of Sogyal Rinpoche, I am convinced that he is the reincarnation of Tertön Sogyal, and I am filled with faith and confidence in him. Tertön Sogyal predicted that if his two main reincarnations were harmonious and helped each other, then their benefit for the Dharma and for sentient beings would be as vast as space, but if there were any disagreement or conflict between them, this would be a disaster for the Dharma and for beings. Yet suppose we were to consider that Sogyal Rinpoche and I were the reincarnations of Tertön Sogyal, then I declare that our minds are inseparable, and that all our spiritual and material things are one. Consider that we are one."

Khenpo Jikme Phuntsok and Sogyal Rinpoche at Lerab Ling in southern France upon their first and only meeting in August 1993.

# *In* GRATITUDE

With deep gratitude for teaching the profound doctrine of the Great Perfection, and for having given me a glimpse of the teachings and mind of Tertön Sogyal, I bow to His Holiness the Dalai Lama, Sogyal Rinpoche, Khenpo Jikme Phuntsok Rinpoche, Khenpo Namdrol Rinpoche, Garje Khamtrul Rinpoche, and Lodi Gyari Rinpoche. May the masters' aspirations for the Dharma, for Tibet's unique wisdom culture, and for the world manifest spontaneously!

I am grateful for the blessing and guidance that I have received from lamas who are no longer with us, including Trulzhik Rinpoche, Khenpo Akhyuk Rinpoche, Chagdud Rinpoche, Adeu Rinpoche, Sherab Özer Rinpoche, Lama Wangde of Kalzang, and Amchi Chime of Lumorap. I am immensely appreciative to the teachers who have given me instructions, protection, and advice while researching *Fearless in Tibet,* including Dodrupchen Rinpoche, Tenzin Gyatso Rinpoche, Khenpo Tsodargye, Tromge Konchok Wangpo, Ajam Rinpoche, Osel Dorje Rinpoche, Tertön Wangchen, Neten Chokling Rinpoche, Tsikey Chokling Rinpoche, Orgyen Tobgyal Rinpoche, Tulku Thondup Rinpoche, Jamphel Sherab Rinpoche, Chökyi Nyima Rinpoche, Rabjam Rinpoche, Tsoknyi Rinpoche, Arjia Rinpoche, Lama Zopa Rinpoche, Gelek Rinpoche, the Medium of the Nechung Oracle Thubten Ngödrup, Venerable Matthieu Ricard, Khenpo Gyurme Tsultrim, Lama Chonam, Sangye Khandro, and Mayum Tsering Wangmo of Lakar. And I am grateful to Patrick Gaffney in particular for his guidance and wisdom, and for being an example to us all of a true Dharma practitioner. May all obstacles to the flowering of the Dharma be vanquished!

I am indebted to the learned translator-practitioners who have given their energy to this project, and grateful for their friendship. Thanks especially to Venerable Tenzin Choephel of Nechung Monastery and Lotsawa Adam Pearcey; both translators opened for me the meaning of Tsullo's biography of Tertön Sogyal. Deep appreciation also goes to Venerable Jampa Tenzin (Sean Price), Gyurme Avertin, and Venerable Lozang Zopa, who translated teachings and interviews for me in Nepal, India, France, and the United States, and provided critical feedback. I also relied upon Antonio Terrone's linguistic skills in Nyarong, Lhasa, Larung Gar, and elsewhere; thank you. May the Dharma continue to be communicated in skillful and diverse ways!

A number of scholars have generously given their time to discuss with me Tibet's religious history, and the life and times of Tertön Sogyal, including Gen Pema Wangyal, Tashi Tsering, Gray Tuttle, Matthew Akester, the late E. Gene Smith, Heather Stoddard, Erik Pema Kunsang, Venerable Gyaltsen of Nechung Monastery, Phelgye Kelden, my professors at the School of Oriental and African Studies, including the late Alexander Piatigorsky and Tadeusz Skorupski, and S. K. Pondicherry. Thanks to those who maintain the Rigpa Archive, and those who provide the excellent material at Lotsawa House (www.lotsawahouse.org), Rigpa Shedra Wiki (www.rigpawiki.org), Rangjung Yeshe Wiki (rywiki.tsadra.org), and the Treasury of Lives (www.treasuryoflives.org).

I want to thank the kind people at Hay House, especially my editor Patty Gift, who believes in the transformative power of the written word. Thanks also to Kendra Crossen Burroughs and Laura Gray for excellent copyediting. Many drafts were read both by my mother, Francey Pistono, whose support is always there for me, and by the poet James C. Hopkins, whose feedback I value highly. My family in Wyoming and Colorado has been understanding of my being away for years on end in Tibet and the Himalayas, for which I am grateful. I could not ask for better literary agents than Gail Ross and Howard Yoon. And thanks to Jocelyn Slack and John Wasson, who rendered the map of Tibet; Jamyang Dorjee Chakrishar, who digitally retouched the seal of Tertön Sogyal; and Robert Beer for his kind permission to use his art from his *The Encyclopedia of Tibetan Symbols and Motifs* for the section breaks.

I always felt the support and appreciated greatly my Dharma brothers and sisters at Rigpa and elsewhere for their directed prayers. And a special thanks to Josh and Ali Elmore and Mark Rovner for their generosity. The International Campaign for Tibet supported my travels to Tibet, Nepal, and India on various occasions; I thank Richard Gere and all of the ICT board of directors and staff for their trust and support.

The research and writing of *Fearless in Tibet* has taken more than 15 years. It is the culmination of many people's blessings, guidance, and efforts. To those I have mentioned here, and many others in Tibet and around the world, I am forever grateful. Thank you. But of all the people I owe my deepest gratitude, it is to my wife, Monica, whose support and love and encouragement have been unceasing. I could not have written this book without her. With love and devotion, I pray that all of her aspirations manifest spontaneously.

Finally, to Sogyal Rinpoche, our precious teacher, who tirelessly guides countless beings in skillful and manifold ways to abide in the natural state of primordial awareness; any benefit and merit accrued from writing this book about the life of your previous incarnation, I dedicate to the realization and spontaneous fruition of your aspirations and prayers.

Matteo Pistono
The full moon of the tenth month of the Wood Horse year
March 16, 2014

# DRAMATIS PERSONAE

**Alak Gurong, Orgyen Jikdrel Chöying Dorje** (1875–1932) Tibetan polymath; sponsor of Tertön Sogyal around Jentsa and Rebkong; photographer of the tertön in 1913.

**Amgon, Gonpo Namgyal** (d. 1865) Chieftain from Tertön Sogyal's home region of Nyarong. He perpetuated a culture of violence in Nyarong and forcibly took over much of eastern Tibet.

**Atrin** (d. 1922) Loyal attendant to Tertön Sogyal, who traveled and served him for more than 25 years.

**Avalokiteshvara** (Sanskrit; Tibetan *Chenrezik*) The Buddha of Compassion, who embodies the compassion of all the buddhas. The Dalai Lamas are believed to be manifestations of Avalokiteshvara, who is regarded as the progenitor of the Tibetan people and the patron deity of their country.

**Chenrezik** *See* Avalokiteshvara.

**Chöpel Gyatso, Pema** (1914–1959) Tertön Sogyal's grandson, who was a fully ordained monk and renowned teacher in Nyarong and Kandze region.

**Dalai Lama, Thirteenth: Thubten Gyatso** (1876–1933) Spiritual and political ruler of Tibet (beginning in 1895) and a disciple of Tertön Sogyal.

**Dalai Lama, Fourteenth: Tenzin Gyatso** (b. 1935) Reincarnation of the Thirteenth Dalai Lama, who ruled Tibet until 1959, and currently resides in exile in northern India.

**Dargye** Father of Tertön Sogyal.

**Demo, Ngawang Lobsang Trinley Rabgye** (1855–1899) Regent of Tibet before the Thirteenth Dalai Lama's accession to power in 1895; head of Tengyeling Monastery; implicated by association in an assassination plot against the Thirteenth Dalai Lama.

**Dodrupchen, the Third: Jikme Tenpe Nyima** (1865–1926) One of the most outstanding Tibetan masters of his time; collaborated with Tertön Sogyal to compose philosophical treatises. He was the teacher of many great lamas, including Jamyang Khyentse Chökyi Lodrö.

**Dorje Dudjom, Nanam** (8th century) Previous incarnation of Tertön Sogyal; minister of religion in Tibet; close disciple of Padmasambhava; accomplished Vajrakilaya practitioner.

**Drolma, Orgyen** Mother of Tertön Sogyal.

**Dza Choktrul Kunzang Namgyal** Learned master associated with Katok Monastery; teacher of Tertön Sogyal; student of Jamyang Khyentse Wangpo and Jamgön Kongtrul.

**Jamgön Kongtrul Lodrö Thaye** (1813–1899) Eminent master and tertön who inspired the Rime (ecumenical) movement; teacher to Tertön Sogyal. Also known as Jamgön Kongtrul the Great, and as Pema Garwang.

**Jamyang Khyentse Chökyi Lodrö** (1893–1959) Reincarnation of Jamyang Khyentse Wangpo; student of Tertön Sogyal; recognized Sogyal Rinpoche as the reincarnation of Tertön Sogyal.

**Jamyang Khyentse Wangpo** (1820–1892) Eminent master and tertön who inspired the Rime (ecumenical) movement; teacher of Tertön Sogyal. Also known as Dongak Lingpa.

**Khandro Pumo** (1865–1949) Spiritual wife of Tertön Sogyal and accomplished meditation master.

**Khenpo Jikme Phuntsok** (1933–2004) One of the two simultaneous reincarnations of Tertön Sogyal, who remained in Tibet throughout the Cultural Revolution, and later in the 1980s, established Larung Buddhist Academy; teacher of current Fourteenth Dalai Lama.

**Kunzang Nyima, Tertön** (1904–1958) Student and attendant of Tertön Sogyal in Golok; grandson of Dudjom Lingpa; nephew of Dodrupchen; teacher of Khenpo Jikme Phuntsok.

**Lama Trime** Student of Tertön Sogyal; was also a tertön whose revealed termas fill six volumes.

**Lerab Lingpa** Another name for Tertön Sogyal.

**Ma Qi** (1869–1931) Prominent Hui Muslim warlord in northeastern Tibet. Tertön Sogyal had a spiritual connection with his daughter, Shinya; he also had a son, Ma Bufang.

**Nechung Oracle** State Oracle of Tibet; the Oracle communicates through possessing a medium, who is always a monk from Nechung Monastery; responsible for protecting the Dalai Lama and strengthening the Tibetan nation.

**Norbu Tsering** (d. 1899) Mastermind behind the failed 1899 black magic assassination plot of the Thirteenth Dalai Lama; nephew of Regent Demo of Tengyeling.

**Nyagtrül** (d. 1899) A Nyarong yogi who, taken over by dark forces, attempted to assassinate the Thirteenth Dalai Lama with sorcery in 1899. Also known as Nyarong Tulku or Shiwa Tulku.

**Nyala Pema Dündul** (1816–1872) Visionary and meditation master; first teacher of Tertön Sogyal; founded Kalzang Temple in 1860; attained rainbow body. Also known as Khanyam Lingpa.

**Nyoshul Lungtok Tenpe Nyima** (1829–1902) Meditation master and supreme among Patrul Rinpoche's students; the teacher with whom Tertön Sogyal refined his Dzogchen practice.

**Padmasambhava** (8th century) Indian tantric master who established Buddhism in Tibet and concealed treasure teachings throughout the land, to be revealed when most needed. Also known as Guru Rinpoche.

**Rigdzin Namgyal** (1891–1950s) Son of Tertön Sogyal and Khandro Pumo.

**Shinya** (b. 1888) Daughter of the Muslim warlord Ma Qi; assisted Tertön Sogyal in the revelation of termas in northeastern Tibet.

**Sogyal Rinpoche** One of the two simultaneous reincarnations of Tertön Sogyal, based in Lerab Ling in France; student of Jamyang

Khyentse Chökyi Lodrö, Dilgo Khyentse Rinpoche, and Dudjom Rinpoche; author of *The Tibetan Book of Living and Dying*; founder and spiritual director to Rigpa International.

**Sonam Thaye, Lama** One of the two heart-sons of Nyala Pema Dündul; an accomplished yogi who oversaw Tertön Sogyal's early meditation training.

**Tertön Rangrik Dorje** (1847–1903) One of the two heart-sons of Nyala Pema Dündul; founder of Lumorap Monastery in Nyarong; senior spiritual brother to Tertön Sogyal. Also known as Kusum Lingpa.

**Tertön Sogyal** (1856–1926) One of Tibet's great mystics and a teacher to the Thirteenth Dalai Lama. His birth name, Sonam Gyalpo, means "King of Merit." The name was contracted to produce "Sogyal." Also known as Lerab Lingpa.

**Trisong Detsen, King** (742–797) The 38th king of Tibet; invited Padmasambhava to Tibet.

**Tsultrim Zangpo** (1884–ca. 1957) Lineage holder and biographer of Tertön Sogyal; student of Dodrupchen Jikme Tenpe Nyima; abbot of Shukjung Monastery. Also known as Tsullo.

**Vajrakilaya** (Sanskrit) A wrathful enlightened deity who embodies the activity of all the buddhas and whose practice is utilized to remove obstacles, destroying forces hostile to compassion, and purifying the spiritual pollution; commonly depicted with six arms and three faces, standing in a raging inferno and wielding a phurba (Sanskrit *kila*) that is used to vanquish the self-cherishing ego.

**Yeshe Tsogyal, Lady** (8th century) The spiritual consort of Padmasambhava, a realized practitioner who assisted him in the concealment of treasure teachings.

**Zhao Erfeng** (1845–1911) General of the late Qing era, nicknamed Butcher Zhao, who led military campaigns throughout eastern Tibet. His troops eventually reached Lhasa in 1910, forcing the Thirteenth Dalai Lama into exile.

# NOTES

Page xvi–xvii Map drawn by Jocelyn Slack.

Page 1 *"Shall we take him to the master Nyala Pema Dündul . . ."*: Nyala Pema Dündul (1816–1872) is also known as Trulzhik Changchub Lingpa, Orgyen Khanyam Lingpa, and Drupchen Nyida Kunze. For a biography in English, see Yeshe Dorje 2013.

Page 2 *"Dargye had no intention of allowing his son . . ."*: The characterization of Dargye is based upon Sherab Ozer Rinpoche interview 1998; Ajam Rinpoche interviews 2001, 2007. For Sogyal's childhood, see Tsultrim Zangpo 1942, pages 17–22.

Page 2 *"Amgon was a brutal fighter . . ."*: The stories about Amgon (Gonpo Namgyal Tashi) are from Sherab Ozer Rinpoche interview 1998; Ajam Rinpoche interviews 2001, 2007. See also Yudru Tsomu 2006 and Tashi Tsering 1986.

Page 2 *"Among those he waged battles against . . ."*: The Tibetan government in Lhasa maintained influence in certain areas of Kham through monasteries that represented their interests, mostly by collecting taxes for Lhasa. The Qing's influence in eastern Tibet was in the form of granting ceremonial titles, known as *tusi*, to the various Tibetan kings and chiefs, though the Qing were never able to truly exert authority. Any authority in Kham by the Lhasa government, like that of the Qing, was nominal and indirect. In the centuries before Amgon, various decentralized kingdoms and tribal chieftains of Kham in eastern Tibet maintained a balance of power, despite regular armed battles with one another. None of the Khampa kings from Derge, Nangchen, Ling, or Chala were ever able to exert significant control beyond their own tribal area. The vast area of Kham provided a nearly impassable buffer zone between the Tibetan government in Lhasa and the Qing in Peking.

Page 3 *"In a surprise attack, Tibetan government cavalry . . ."*: See Petech 1973, page 56; Tashi Tsering 1986, page 211. Also, Amgon's death was taken as an ominous forecast for the future of Tibet, as Do Khyentse predicted (Do Khyentse 1997):

> *When there is a war between devils,*
> *The weasel-headed Chinese slaughterers and the red-faced*
> *    Nyarong fiend [Amgon],*
> *They will gain victory or lose according to their own actions.*
> *. . . there is no reason to assist or to harm them.*

> *In the future when there is this war,*
> *Should the Chinese devil gain victory,*
> *The Buddha's teachings will certainly be harmed.*
> *If the devil from Nyarong is triumphant,*
> *Innocent sentient beings will face calamity.*
> *Therefore, be neutral towards both.*

Page 3 *"When Sonam Gyalpo began speaking . . ."*: Ajam Rinpoche interviews 2001, 2007.

Page 3 *"Commit not a single unwholesome action. . ."*: Praise to Shakyamuni Buddha *(rgyud chags gsum pa)* translation courtesy Rigpa.

Page 4 *"Drolma was surprised . . ."*: Khamtrul Rinpoche teachings 1992 (a), 1992 (b). Khamtrul Rinpoche (b. 1927) is a tertön and Dzogchen master, close associate of the Fourteenth Dalai Lama in Dharamsala, lineage holder of Tertön Sogyal and Nyala Pema Dündul's treasure teachings, and former ritual master at Namgyal Monastery.

Page 4 *"Pema Dündul saw not only a child . . ."*: Tsultrim Zangpo 1942, pages 3–8. In Tertön Sogyal's previous incarnations, he appeared as numerous great bodhisattvas and vidyadhara, including the bodhisattva Vajragarbha, who compiled the Dzogchen teachings given by the Buddha Samantabhadra in the heavenly realm of Akanishtha. Later he appeared as Buddha Shakyamuni's aunt and stepmother, Prajapati Gotami, the founder of the order of nuns, and in Tibet he appeared as Nanam Dorje Dudjom in the 8th century, Trophu Lotsawa in the 12th century, and the great Rigdzin Gödemchen (1337–1408), founder of the Northern Treasures (*byang gter*) tradition. Tertön Sogyal was also considered the body emanation of Nanam Dorje Dudjom, the speech emanation of Vajravarahi, and the mind emanation of Guru Padmasambhava.

Page 5 *"Although you will not let your son . . ."*: Khamtrul Rinpoche 1992 (a) teaching. According to Yeshe Dorje 2013, chapter 9, Nyala Pema Dündul said that Sonam Gyalpo had "an excellent system of energy channels, and without doubt he is an emanation. He should therefore follow me, which will certainly help both the Doctrine [Dharma] and all beings."

Page 7 *"An emanation of the tantric adept Dorje Dudjom . . ."*: *Mirror of Astonishing Manifestations (ngo mtsar 'phrul gyi me long)*; Tsultrim Zangpo 1942, page 12; Khenpo Namdrol Rinpoche teaching 2007.

Page 8 *"The king beseeched the venerable . . ."*: Yudra Nyingpo 2004, pages 85–86.

Page 8 *"Padmasambhava's life was one of miracles . . ."*: There are many accounts of the life of Padmasambhava written by great scholars or revealed by the tertöns. Some of the most famous of his biographies are the *Tsullo Zanglingma (The Zanglingma Life Story)*, named after the Copper Temple at Samye, where it was discovered as a terma by Nyangrel Nyima Özer; the *Padme Kathang* or *Tsullo Sheldrakma (The Life Story from the Crystal Cave)*, revealed by Orgyen Lingpa; the *Kathang Serthreng (Golden Garland Chronicles)*, discovered by Sangye Lingpa; and the *Tsullo Yikyi Munsel (The Life Story That Dispels Mind's Darkness)*, by Sokdokpa Lodrö Gyaltsen; and Patrick Gaffney's *The Life of Guru Padmasambhava* in Rigpa 2004. Guru Rinpoche's life is also recorded in the histories of the different teaching cycles; there exists a famous Indian version compiled by Jetsün Taranatha, and biographies are also found in the Bön tradition of Tibet. Professors Cantwell and Mayer provide insightful academic historical analysis of Padmasambhava in their "Representations of Padmasambhava in early Post-Imperial Tibet" (Cantwell and Mayer 2013).

Page 10 *"My father is the pure awareness of rigpa. . ."*: Rigpa 2004, page 26.

Page 10 *"In the* Tantra of the Perfect Embodiment . . .*"*: Yeshe Tsogyal 1993, page v. *Tantra of Perfect Embodiment of Unexcelled Nature (bla med don rdogs 'dus pa'i rgyud)*. Also, the coming of Padmasambhava to the world was predicted in the exoteric sutras, including in the *Immaculate Goddess Sutra,* which states (Yeshe Tsogyal 1993, page 8):

> *The activity of all the victorious ones of the ten directions*
> *Will gather into a single form,*
> *A buddha's son, who will attain marvelous accomplishment,*
> *A master who will embody buddha activity,*
> *Will appear to the northwest of Oddiyana.*

Page 10 *"The Buddha's gradual approach . . ."*: According to this common approach of Buddhism, the story of the historical Buddha Shakyamuni begins upon his awakening more than 2,500 years ago in the Indian village known today as Bodhgaya. It was there where Prince Siddhartha had vowed not to move from his seat until he penetrated the ultimate truth of reality and understood the source of suffering. That night, deep in meditation, he saw how all suffering has a cause and how the very root of suffering is ignorance, like the dimming of the light of awareness. When awareness is dimmed, we are ignorant of the fact that all of existence is in a constant state of flux and that emotions ultimately result in suffering. Continually being in the dark about the truth of impermanence results in an endless cycle of suffering. But, Siddhartha logically understood, if the cause of suffering is removed, then the result will not arise, thus severing the cycle of suffering. While he sat in meditation, Siddhartha conquered the self-cherishing ego that veiled his indwelling light of wisdom. Realizing that the whole of existence is played out in an interdependent web of cause and effect, Siddhartha saw reality as it is and became the Awakened One, a buddha. The historical Buddha did not receive anything when he awakened; instead, he got rid of what was obscuring his innate enlightenment.

Page 11 *"In the Great Guru's supernatural duels . . ."*: Ju Mipham Rinpoche describes this in his *Kagye Namshe (dpal sgrub pa chen po bka' brgyad kyi spyi don rnam par bshad pa dngos grub snying po)*

(Ju Mipham Gyatso 2000). Thanks to Zach Beer for sharing his unpublished translations of the *Kagye Namshe.*

Page 11 *"The multitude of spirits . ."*: Later, with royal support and Padmasambhava's blessing, teams of scholars began translating the vast corpus of Buddhist scriptures and commentaries from the famed universities in India such as Nalanda and Vikramasila; philosophical colleges were founded for monks to study the inner science of consciousness; and communities of lay tantric practitioners took root in every valley of the plateau. As Padmasambhava journeyed across Tibet, he bestowed tantric empowerments and offered teachings and instructions to enable his students to fully manifest their true potential.

Page 12 *"Termas serve as portals . . ."*: Tsultrim Zangpo 1942, page 635.

Page 12 *"The Great Guru bound various spirits . . ."*: Ibid., page 637.

Page 12 *"Tibetans are indebted to Padmasambhava . . ."*: The Dalai Lama said of Padmasambhava (March 21, 2004, in Dharamsala), "It was because of his [Padmasambhava's] overarching power and strength that the Buddha Dharma was really established in Tibet, and then developed so that all the teachings of the Buddha, including the Mantrayana, were preserved as a living tradition, and have continued down to the present day." (Note: Mantrayana is often equated with Vajrayana Buddhism.) See Rigpa 2004, page 14.

Pages 12–13 *"Padmasambhava declined, invoking what Shakyamuni Buddha had told . . ."*: Translation courtesy Rigpa.

Page 13 *"Do not forget that life flickers by . . ."*: Yeshe Tsogyal 1993, page 185.

Page 13 *"Have you understood this . . ."*: Ibid., page 207.

Page 15 *"When Sonam Gyalpo was strong enough . . ."*: About Sogyal's hunting and marksmanship, see Tsultrim Zangpo 1942, pages 17–18; Nyoshul Khenpo Rinpoche teaching 1985; Nyoshul Khenpo 2005, pages 513–514; Khamtrul Rinpoche teachings 1992 (a), 1992 (b).

Page 16 *"Sonam Gyalpo recognized the letters . . ."*: Tsultrim Zangpo 1942, page 17.

Pages 17–18 *"We are what we think . . .":* Byrom 1993, verses 1–2, "Choices," pages 1–2.

Page 19 *"As a caravan wove its way in single file . . .":* Nyoshul Khenpo Rinpoche teaching 1985; Khamtrul Rinpoche teachings 1992 (a), 1992 (b).

Page 20 *"O sublime and precious bodhichitta . . .":* Translation of prayer courtesy Rigpa.

Page 20 *"The monk's prayer of* bodhicitta . . .": The stories of the monk-pilgrim, and the pregnant mare, are from Nyoshul Khenpo Rinpoche teaching 1985; Khamtrul Rinpoche teachings 1992 (a), 1992 (b), interview 2008.

Page 21 *"It was as Nyala Pema Dündul had once written . . .":* "Signs that the Common Preliminary Practices Have Penetrated the Mind." Translator: Adam Pearcey. www.lotsawahouse.org/tibetan-masters/nyala-pema-dundul/signs-practice-penetrating-mind.

Page 21 *"Dargye scolded his son . . .":* Tsultrim Zangpo 1942, page 21.

Page 22 *"Carve* Om Mani Padme Hum . . .": Ajam Rinpoche interviews 2001, 2007.

Page 23 *"Standing on tiptoes . . .":* Tsultrim Zangpo 1942, pages 20–21.

Page 24 *"I have promised to constantly survey . . .":* Yeshe Dorje 2013, page 103.

Page 24 *"The One-Eyed Protectress captured . . .":* Tsultrim Zangpo 1942, pages 20–21.

Page 25 *"As his condition improved . . .":* Ibid., page 22. Sogyal wrote down the liturgy for a practice of the Lion-Faced Dakini (*seng ge gdong ma*). Because he had no ink or paper, he dusted an oiled wood slat to write upon and thereafter memorized it.

Pages 27–28 *"Pema Dündul frequented many hermitages . . .":* The peak is referred to as the "conch-colored crystal rock piercing the sky," and villagers tell pilgrims that merely hearing, seeing, recalling, or touching the mountain has the power to bring one to realize his innermost nature. It is also known as Lhang Lhang or Shangdrak. See also http://www.lotsawahouse.org/tibetan-masters/nyala-pema-dundul/heaven-of-solitude for a translation by Adam Pearcey of Pema Dündul's poem entitled "The Heaven of Solitude."

Page 28 *"The last years of retreat in his cave . . ."*: Ajam Rinpoche interview 2001; Sherab Ozer interview 1998. This is the cave where Pema Dündul discovered the treasure text known as *Self-Liberation that Encompasses Space* (*mkha' khyab rang grol*). Lama Sonam Thaye was the scribe.

Page 28 *"Pema Dündul wasted no time in securing sponsorship . . ."*: See Yeshe Dorje 2013, page 173, regarding frescoes in Kalzang Temple.

Page 31 *"Pema Dündul decided that Sogyal should first . . ."*: Lama Sonam Thaye, Chomden Dorje, was one of the two heart-sons, or chief disciples, of Nyala Pema Dündul, the other being the senior Tertön Rangrik Dorje. Sonam Thaye was renowned as an emanation of Gyalwa Chokyang, one of the 25 disciples of Padmasambhava. Born into the family of Akalbu, he became a yogi who dressed in white and wore his hair in a topknot. He assisted in the construction of Kalzang Temple and took responsibility for many of Pema Dündul's disciples after their master attained the rainbow body.

Page 32 *"He and his students were a hard-nosed . . ."*: The lineage of Nyala Pema Dündul's teachings passed to his two main disciples, Tertön Rangrik Dorje of Lumorap and Lama Sonam Thaye, and these were known respectively as the "sun" and "moon" lineages. The "sun" lineage passed down through Tertön Rangrik Dorje and eventually to Minling Trichen Rinpoche, while Lama Sonam Thaye transmitted the "moon" lineage to Tertön Sogyal, and to Sempa Dorje, the reincarnation of one of Nyala Pema Dündul's first masters. Sempa Dorje transmitted the teachings to Anye Tulku Pema Tashi. Sempa Dorje's reincarnation was Sherab Özer Rinpoche (1922/3–2006), abbot of Kalzang Temple. On August 12, 1998, Sherab Özer Rinpoche performed a ceremony in Lerab Ling in southern France, during which he offered the throne of Kalzang Temple to Sogyal Rinpoche as the heir to Tertön Sogyal.

Pages 32–33 *"Whether the darkness of delusion has been eliminated
. . ."*: Excerpted from "Advice Revealing How Our Faults Become
Clear." Translator: Adam Pearcey. http://www.lotsawahouse.org/
tibetan-masters/nyala-pema-dundul/advice-on-faults.

Page 34 *"Drikok is west, over that mountain pass . . ."*: Tsultrim Zangpo 1942, pages 22–24. Drikok is near Dzongshö Deshek Dupe, a
sanctuary set among limestone cliffs in a steep northern tributary
of the Dzi Chu, east of Ragchab and south of Terlung. Jamgön
Kongtrul opened the site and revealed treasures in association
with Chogyur Lingpa and encouraged the establishment of a hermitage. See Jamgön Kongtrul 2012, pages 191–192.

Page 34 *"Sonam Thaye accepted and directed . . ."*: Lama Sonam
Thaye taught Sogyal the main terma revelation of Tertön Longsal
Nyingpo (1625–1692), whose name is also the title of the terma:
*klong gsal snying po* (The Vajra Heart Essence of the Luminous Ex-
panse). Thanks to Venerable Ngawang Senge for sharing his un-
published translation of *The Vajra Heart Essence of the Luminous
Expanse*, and his insightful comments on Tertön Sogyal. See also
Ronis 2009.

Pages 35–36 *"You will place no importance on home . . ."*: Tsultrim
Zangpo 1942, pages 27–29.

Page 36 *"As Pema Dündul had said to Sogyal . . ."*: Ibid., page 27.

Page 36 *"By contemplating how his ultimate contentment . . ."*: Ibid.,
pages 24–26.

Page 37 *"Give it all away—offer it to your guru . . ."*: Ibid., pages
28–29.

Page 37 *"Pema Dündul bestowed tantric empowerments . . ."*: Ibid.,
pages 35–37. All together, Sogyal received about a volume's worth
of transmissions from Nyala Pema Dündul in visions. This included principally Nyala Pema Dündul's main treasure, *Self Liberation
that Encompasses Space* (*mkha' khyab rang grol*), a mind treasure of
the One Hundred Peaceful and Wrathful Deities (*zhi khro rigs brg-
ya*), Guru Drakpo (*gu ru drag po*), among others. Sogyal said, "They
all arrived like a mind treasure."

Pages 37–38 *"Emaho! The View is like the sky . . ."*: Rigpa International 2000.

Page 40 *"Pema Dündul's realizations surpassed . . ."*: For "rainbow body," see Tulku Thondup 2011, pages 78–93; Sogyal Rinpoche 1992, pages 167–169.

Page 41 *"Though the tertön may know of the location . . ."*: For a general discourse on treasures and their revelation, see Tsultrim Zangpo 1942, pages 638–655; Tulku Thondup 1986.

Page 41 *"In the first month of the Wood Dog year . . ."*: Tsultrim Zangpo 1942, page 37.

Page 43 *"Hum. Padmasambhava and your hosts of dakinis . . ."*: This prayer is found within the Le'u Dünma—A Prayer in Seven Chapters to Padmakara. See also *www.lotsawahouse.org/topics/leu-dunma* and Ngawang Zangpo 2002.

Page 43 *"This is the special method of tertöns . . ."*: Tsultrim Zangpo 1942, page 635.

Pages 44–45 *"Spontaneously perfect, illusory manifestation . . ."*: *Vajrakilaya Lineage Prayer* composed by Tertön Sogyal. The colophon reads, "Sogyal, who holds the name of a tertön and who has the great fortune to have been cared for by this supreme of all yidam deities throughout the course of several lifetimes, wrote this during a break in retreat. Jayantu!" Translation courtesy Rigpa.

Page 45 *"Sogyal one-pointedly practiced* The Most Secret *. . ."*: Tsultrim Zangpo 1942, pages 40–41.

Page 45 *"Indeed, Padmasambhava had warned tertöns . . ."*: Yeshe Tsogyal 1993, page 145.

Page 46 *"The purpose of Vajrakilaya's wrath . . ."*: Khenpo Namdrol 1999, page 25. There came to be three traditions that stemmed from Padmasambhava's original transmission of the Vajrakilaya instructions. They are referred to as "The Tradition of the King" (through Trisong Detsen), "The Tradition of Jomo" (through his Tibetan consort, Yeshe Tsogyal), and "The Tradition of Nanam" (through Nanam Dorje Dudjom, Tertön Sogyal's previous incarnation). The Vajrakilaya terma revelations by Tertön Sogyal belong to "The Tradition of Nanam" as well as those revealed by Khenpo Jikme Phuntsok.

Page 47 *"The most important role of the treasure holder . . ."*: Treasure holders, guardians, or custodians, teach the text themselves and/or arrange for the textual transmission from a qualified master. They also have the responsibility of publishing the treasure teaching, an expensive endeavor involving woodblock carving, and purchasing paper and ink.

Page 47 *"In the treasures' prophetic guide . . ."*: Tsultrim Zangpo 1942, page 42.

Page 48 *"Khyentse, along with his close friend . . ."*: See Ringu Tulku 2007; Smith 1970. Also, in his *Overview of the Philosophical Foundations of the Different Buddhist Traditions*, Dungkar Lobsang Thinley explains the different implications of what it means to be Rime or nonsectarian: "The phrase 'non-sectarian unbiased approach to Dharma' can be understood in two ways. According to the first, rather than point to a single tradition as your own, you practice all traditions, Sakya, Nyingma, Gelug, Kadam, et cetera, and hence you are said to have 'a catholic approach to Dharma,' as exemplified by the Great Fifth Dalai Lama. As he practiced the philosophies of all traditions, there are different opinions as to what his actual view was. Gelugpas say the Great Fifth's was a Gelug view while Nyingmapas say the Great Fifth's was a Nyingma view. Why the discrepancy? His collected writings contain many Nyingma, Gelug, Kagyu works, and more besides, all of which are consistent with the distinctive views held by the relevant traditions. Thus, when you read his Nyingma writings, you get the impression he really subscribed to the Nyingma view and when you read his Sakya writings, you get the impression he really subscribed to the Sakya view. As for the second way to understand the phrase 'non-sectarian approach to Dharma,' if you are a Gelugpa, for example, then while regarding other traditions like the Nyingma as authentic, you remain impartial to them and never disparage, refute, criticize, or look down upon them, you are said to have 'an unbiased approach to Dharma.'" Translation courtesy Venerable Lozang Zopa. The four lamas most often associated with the Rime are Jamyang Khyentse Wangpo, Jamgön Kongtrul, Chogyur Lingpa, and Ju Mipham Gyatso. There were other great lamas as well, including the great Dzogchen Bön master Shardza Trashi Gyaltsen (1859–1934).

Page 48 *"While respecting other approaches . . ."*: Though Khyentse held a position in the hierarchy of the Sakya school, and Kongtrul was raised in the Bön tradition, the indigenous religion of Tibet, and was a lineage holder in the Kagyu school, both lamas were above all Dzogchen adepts.

Page 49 *"But nothing came of the ruffians' challenges . . ."*: Lama Wangde interview 2001.

Page 50 *"It was believed that some such charlatans . . ."*: Tulku Thondup 1986, page 154.

Page 50 *"I have compared the script on the golden parchment . . ."*: Tsultrim Zangpo 1942, pages 43–44. The other terma scrolls were from Nangrel Nyima Ozer, Guru Chowang, and Chogyur Dechen Lingpa.

Page 50 *"Tertön Sogyal and Khyentse spoke . . ."*: Tsultrim Zangpo 1942, page 44. Also, Tertön Sogyal said that "the moment the sublime great being [Jamyang Khyentse Wangpo] received this terma teaching, all the obstacles to my future general and specific treasure revelations were eliminated, allowing my activity to flourish in the ten directions" (Tsultrim Zangpo 1942, page 42). Orgyen Topgyal Rinpoche (teaching 1996) said, "There were five disciples of Jamyang Khyentse Wangpo who were great tertöns: Chogyur Dechen Lingpa, Lerab Lingpa [Tertön Sogyal], Bönter Tsewang Drakpa, Khamtrul Rinpoche Tenpe Nyima, and the old king of Ling, Lingtsang Gyalpo."

Page 51 *"Rather, stay true to your mission . . ."*: Tsultrim Zangpo 1942, page 43. Khyentse also told Sogyal, "From now on, you shall be a great tertön due to your vast aspirations from earlier times, and you will encounter great connections with karmically aspired friends, and you will find favorable circumstances for the Dharma—this you will accomplish."

Page 51 *"Should she become your spiritual consort . . ."*: Ajam Rinpoche interview 2001; Lama Wangde interviews 2001, 2004.

Page 52 *"Such consorts ensure that no obstacles . . ."*: Tsultrim Zangpo 1942, pages 100–130, 635.

Page 52 *"Tertön Sogyal practiced yoga to gain control . . ."*: See Tsultrim Zangpo 1942, pages 105–115. Because carnal desire is the predominant characteristic driving mundane sexual engagements, the end result is normally loss of vitality. Yogic practices in this context are meant to reverse this norm. Transcending carnal desires, tantric yogis engage in union whereby both male and female practitioners melt vital essence of the subtle body and drip it into the central meridian; then, instead of the usual outward energy-depleting current, the flow of essences is reversed. Pulling the vital essence up the central meridian, the life-force is spread throughout the intersecting chakras, increasing the intensity of nonconceptual bliss, which fans the flames of wisdom realization of the nature of reality.

Pages 52–53 *"Inner signs were evident . . ."*: Ibid., page 367. Conceptual thoughts move upon the body's karmic winds, just like a rider upon a horse. Tertön Sogyal was able to gather and contain his karmic winds in his central meridian, thereby arresting the flow of thoughts, allowing his timeless awareness to pervade.

Page 54 *"Don't prolong the past . . ."*: This story of Patrul Rinpoche in Katok is from "The Enlightened Vagabond" (Ricard, n.d.). *Words of My Perfect Teacher (kun bzang bla ma'i zhal lung).*

Page 57 *"At that moment, Nyoshul Lungtok's conceptual mind . . ."*: This story can be found in Sogyal Rinpoche 1992, pages 155–157; Nyoshul Khenpo 2005, page 241; Tulku Thondup 1996, pages 223–224; Ricard, n.d. ("The Enlightened Vagabond").

Page 58 *"At the end of Nyoshul Lungtok's nearly three . . ."*: Nyoshul Khenpo 2005, page 238. When Tertön Sogyal eventually met Patrul Rinpoche, according to Tsultrim Zangpo 1942, page 65, the elder master said, "Last night I had a dream and in the sky a dragon released a thunder that resonated all through the earth and sky, and it was an indication that you would be coming. Earlier when another tertön, Chogyur Lingpa, came to see me, I also dreamt that from the top of a high mountain there was a flag that was swept far away. It seems that I have different type of dreams for the different tertöns." From Patrul Rinpoche, Tertön Sogyal received the crucial points of the *Secret Essence Tantra (rgyud gsang ba'i nying po)* and clarified difficult points. Tertön Sogyal said, "I received many common and extraordinarily profound teachings from Patrul Rinpoche, whom I hold in great esteem. I am very grateful for the kindness that he showed."

Page 58 *"From now until I realize unsurpassed enlightenment . . ."*: Tertön Sogyal wrote this verse. See Tsultrim Zangpo 1942, page 130.

Page 58 *"Upon arrival at Nyoshul Lungtok's encampment . . ."*: For Tertön Sogyal's time with Nyoshul Lungtok, see Tsultrim Zangpo 1942, pages 47–48; Khamtrul Rinpoche teachings 1992 (a), 1992 (b); Nyoshul Khenpo Rinpoche teaching 1985; Nyoshul Khenpo 2005, page 513; Ajam Rinpoche interviews 2001, 2007.

Page 58 *"That Tertön Sogyal was wearing white . . ."*: Nyoshul Khenpo Rinpoche teaching 1985; Khamtrul Rinpoche interview 2008. Khamtrul Rinpoche said that the verse that Nyoshul Lungtok was reciting was from the *Manjushri-nama-samgiti* (*Chanting the Names of Manjushri*). Nyoshul Lungtok taught Tertön Sogyal from the *klong chen snying thig* (Heart Essence of the Vast Expanse).

Page 59 *"First, contemplate the preciousness of being free . . ."*: Translation courtesy of Nalanda Translation Committee.

Page 63 *"Listen here, Tibetan yogis endowed . . ."*: Yeshe Tsogyal 1993, pages 170–171.

Page 64 *"One morning, Tertön Sogyal saw in his mind . . ."*: Tsultrim Zangpo 1942, page 35.

Page 65 *"Studying alongside Tertön Sogyal . . ."*: Tertön Sogyal and Ngakchen met when they studied with Lama Thaye and would sometimes attend teachings and empowerments of other high lamas, such as when the Great Getse of Katok gave the *Secret Essence Tantra*. Ngakchen would come to be known as Orgyen Tutop Lingpa; see Nyoshul Khenpo 2005, pages 511–512.

Page 66 *"After flirting briefly with the girls . . ."*: Khamtrul Rinpoche, n.d. ("A Brief Biography . . ."); Khamtrul Rinpoche interview 2008.

Page 66 *"One day Nyoshul Lungtok decided to send . . ."*: Khamtrul Rinpoche's biography suggests that it was Kongtrul who sent Tertön Sogyal, though Ajam Rinpoche (interview 2001) said it was Nyoshul Lungtok.

Page 69 *"Now, all forms that appear are the wisdom deities . . ."*: Prayer known as *The Unending Flow of the Yoga* found within *The Razor of the Innermost Essence* terma. Translation courtesy Rigpa.

Page 69 *"The master called his disciple into his tent . . ."*: Nyoshul Khenpo Rinpoche teaching 1985; Ajam Rinpoche interview 2001.

The phurba dagger is often placed on a personal shrine and used as an aid in tantric visualization. In some extraordinary cases, when the yogi's meditative power imbues the dagger with profound blessing, the dagger actually becomes the deity and performs empowerments and other activities such as subduing negative forces.

Page 69 *"Padmasambhava advised tertöns like me . . ."*: Tsultrim Zangpo 1942, page 49.

Page 70 *"And because he diligently applied his teacher's pith . . ."*: Ibid., page 25. Tsultrim Zangpo also writes that Tertön Sogyal "swiftly realized the mind of the Buddhas" and "embodied the greatness of the teachings." Also, see Tsong-kha-pa 2000, pages 46–54.

Page 70 *"One of the principal goals of a Dharma practitioner . . ."*: Tsultrim Zangpo 1942, page 55.

Page 72 *"Padmasambhava told Tertön Sogyal in one vision . . ."*: Tsultrim Zangpo 1942, pages 74–77.

Page 72 *"Jamgön Kongtrul once told Tertön Sogyal . . ."*: Ibid., page 75.

Page 73 *"One evening, by candlelight, Tertön Sogyal wrote . . ."*: Ibid., page 84.

Page 73 *"When Khyentse heard this . . ."*: Nyoshul Khenpo Rinpoche teaching 1985.

Page 74 *"One morning Khyentse called for Tertön Sogyal . . ."*: Tsultrim Zangpo 1942, pages 85–87.

Page 76 *"Some months later, after Khyentse had bestowed . . ."*: Ibid., pages 90–91; see also 632–655. Regarding other termas, Jamgön Kongtrul (2012, page 144) writes about Khyentse and Tertön Sogyal, stating, "It seems that the most important of the profound treasures which this master [Khyentse] was to reveal in this incarnation was the *Tsasum kadü chenmo* at the Tsi-ki Lhakhang temple in Tsang Yéru, but as he did not achieve this, [there are only] the auxiliary teachings, the scrolls of the *Particular accomplishment of the unconditioned bliss [Tro-tral déchen göndrup]* which Tértön Lérab Lingpa revealed at Ka-tok, the Sadhana cycle of the 'eight close sons' from Tsangrong Tashi Lhatse which I got hold of, and the *Individual Sadhana-s of the eight Vidyadhara-s [Rikdzin gyéki gödrup]* from the 'Palace of assembled Sugata-s' at Dzongshö, none of which were transcribed." Kongtrul (2003, page 461) notes further about these revelations, writing, "On the basis of an omen in my dreams, I sought the help of Lerab Lingpa [Tertön Sogyal]. Lord Khyentse Rinpoche issued an injunction to the guardian of the termas and instructed Lerab Lingpa. Accordingly, Lerab Lingpa and I were together able, in Pal De'u [Cave at Dzongshö], to reveal individual sadhanas for the eight Indian vidyadharas and samaya substances that were associated with these practices. If my precious lord guru were to have revealed *The United Commands of the Three Roots,* these sadhanas would have constituted an auxiliary part of this cycle."

Page 76 *"Nearing the end of the Fire Dog year . . .":* Tsultrim Zangpo 1942, pages 90–93. Kongtrul had requested Khyentse to bestow the *Collection of Nyingma Tantras* (*rnying ma rgyud 'bum*) and other transmissions. Regarding the *Chetsun Nyingtik* (*lce btsun snying thig*) commentary, see Matthieu Ricard interview 2004. Khyentse gave the title of the work as *The Great Chetsun's Vimala's Profound Heart Teaching Commentary.*

Page 78 *"At the conclusion of the empowerments and transmission . . .":* Tsultrim Zangpo 1942, pages 93–95.

Page 81 *"The ill will that some people directed . . .":* Tsultrim Zangpo 1942, page 130. Garje is the home monastery of Khamtrul Rinpoche. The Garje region is bordered to the north by Palyul, to the east by the Tromthar plateau, to the south by Sangenrong, and to the west by the Dri River. See Khamtrul Rinpoche 2009.

Page 82 *"He contemplated repeatedly the verse . . .":* Seventh verse of "Eight Verses on Mind Training." See Thubten Jinpa 2005, pages 275–289.

Page 82 *"As Jamgön Kongtrul stated . . .":* Jamgön Kongtrul 2012, page 106.

Page 82 *"Villagers were relieved of their worries . . .":* Tsultrim Zangpo 1942, page 130. The implication is that the constellation Rahula captures the moon during a lunar eclipse. The moon is symbolic of wisdom, and in this case, Tertön Sogyal is equated with the moon, while Rahula is equated with obstacles and sickness.

Page 82 *"Tertön Sogyal told him . . ."*: Ibid., pages 97–98. Nyoshul Khenpo Rinpoche teaching 1985, which also says, "Jamyang Khyentse predicted that if she became his secret consort, it would be of very great benefit in the future, for she was the manifestation of Vajravarahi."

Page 83 *"Your clairvoyance is correct . . ."*: Ibid., pages 100–101.

Page 84 *"As the yogis passed through mountain hamlets . . ."*: Khamtrul Rinpoche interview 2008.

Page 84 *"We can see this letter comes from Master Khyentse . . ."*: Nyoshul Khenpo Rinpoche teaching 1985.

Page 85 *"On the morning following a prophetic dream . . ."*: Ajam Rinpoche interview 2001.

Page 85 *"Hum. In the northwest of the land of Oddiyana . . ."*: Translation courtesy Rigpa.

Page 86 *"Before sunrise the next day . . ."*: Tsultrim Zangpo (1942, page 101) writes that a similar ceremony marking Tertön Sogyal's spiritual union with Khandro Pumo took place after they returned to Tromthar.

Page 87 *"At the beginning of the Earth Rat year . . ."*: Tsultrim Zangpo 1942, pages 130–133. Tertön Sogyal had just revealed several termas, including a five-pronged vajra, a cycle of Avalokiteshvara teachings in association with a small statue of Khasarpani. He offered the statue to Nyoshul Lungtok.

Page 90 *"Tibet used this lama-patron bond . . ."*: The roots of this lama-patron relationship in Tibet reach back to the 13th century, when the Mongol descendants of Genghis Khan, namely his grandson Prince Goden and later Kublai Khan, ruled over the largest land-based empire in the history of the world, extending from southern China to Korea, throughout Central Asia, into modern-day Russia, Iran, and eastern Europe. Kublai Khan in 1240 invited a leading Tibetan religious hierarch to his Yuan court and subsequently adopted Tibetan Buddhism as the empire's state religion, and thus began the lama-patron relationship. Contacts between Tibet and Ming China rulers were limited throughout the 14th through the 16th centuries, but the lama-patron relationship did endure. In 1644, the foreign Manchus established the Qing dynasty and overthrew the Chinese Ming emperors. The Qing dynasty ruled China until 1911. In the last years of the Qing, the Thirteenth Dalai Lama's life and the existence of Tibet as an independent nation were threatened. Yet, both the Thirteenth Dalai Lama and Tibet outlived the Qing. Whether it was with the Mongol Yuan, Chinese Ming, Manchu Qing, or even into the early Republican period in the 20th century, Tibetan Buddhist leaders bestowed teachings, tantric empowerments, and blessings upon these foreign benefactors who in turn gave economic and martial support as well as conferring imperial titles upon the religious hierarchy. This was a mutually beneficial relationship. See also Tuttle 2005; Ruegg 1991; Jagou 2009.

Page 91 *"The incarnation lineage of the Dalai Lama . . ."*: The title of "Dalai Lama" became associated with the line in 1578 when the Mongolian ruler Altan Khan bestowed it upon the Third Dalai Lama, Sonam Gyatso. The title was retroactively given to Sonam Gyatso's two predecessors.

Page 91 *"It is no coincidence that the Great Fifth . . ."*: The Great Fifth Dalai Lama studied with two other Dzogchen masters. The first was Khonton Paljor Lhundrub, who is regarded as the incarnation of the great translator Kawa Paltsek. His proper name is Sonam Namgyal and he is also known as Phabongka Paljor Lhundrub because he was abbot of the Phabongka Retreat above Sera Monastery. He was outwardly Gelug but a great Dzogchen practitioner. The other important Dzogchen master was Menlungpa (or Draktsampa) Lochok Dorje, an incarnation of the great Pandita Vimalamitra. He practiced in the Northern Treasure tradition of Rigdzin Gödemchen and Legden Dudjom Dorje.

Page 91 *"The First, Second, and Sixth . . ."*: The Third Dalai Lama did not meet with a karmically connected tertön, but his activity was nonetheless significant.

Page 93 *"The holder of the lotus . . ."*: Tsultrim Zangpo 1942, page 136.

Page 94 *"Meditate by means of the recognition . . ."*: From Tertön Sogyal's personal notations after having received the *Chetsun Nyingtik* teaching from Jamyang Khyentse Wangpo; translation courtesy David Christensen. Tertön Sogyal concluded the treatise with the humble colophon: "I, the most lowly among the ranks of the many learned and powerful disciples of my Master [Khyentse Wangpo], who holds the terma name of Lerab Lingpa, wrote this as notes from the key points of all the profound teachings, based on what I understood. May it be totally virtuous."

Page 96 *"The Dalai Lama was overjoyed . . ."*: For the prophecies and meeting, see Tsultrim Zangpo 1942, pages 134–136.

Page 97 *"Additionally, yogis like Tertön Sogyal and a group from Reb-kong . . ."*: See also Thupten Jampa Tsultrim Tendzin 1998, pages 194–198, 582–583; Stoddard 2006.

Page 97 *"While staying a few weeks in the Potala Palace . . ."*: Tsultrim Zangpo 1942, pages 134–135. Tertön Sogyal stayed in the Fifth Da-lai Lama's sleeping room in the Potala Palace and copied treasure scrolls of Avalokiteshvara and Tara, and decoded a treasure text that he had discovered en route to Lhasa after a local spirit had told him to dive into the Secret Dakini Lake. Tertön Sogyal also stayed at the Sixteen Arhats Chapel on the roof of the Jokhang Temple and decoded some of the liturgies from the Avalokitesh-vara treasure he had taken in Gonjo.

Page 98 *"Another prophecy told Tertön Sogyal . . ."*: Ibid., pages 242–243. In addition to sectarianism, any influence on the Dalai Lama beyond the officials' tightly controlled circles was a threat to the economic control they held through vast monastic estates, corvée labor, and the taxes they collected.

Page 99 *"The Dalai Lama agreed that such a rare event . . ."*: Nyoshul Khenpo Rinpoche teaching 1985; Khamtrul Rinpoche teaching 1992 (a), interview 2008.

Page 103 *"Soon the Dalai Lama began to have pure visions . . ."*: The Thirteenth Dalai Lama's terma revelations included the liturgy *gling bzhi 'khor ba* as well as the treasure items of Je Tsongkhapa's hat and robe.

Page 104 *"Before Padmasambhava left Tibet, he hid a number of stat-ues . . ."*: Tsultrim Zangpo 1942, page 157. Before Padmasambhava hid the *Wish-Fulfilling Jewel Guru Statue That Liberates Upon See-ing (sku tshab mthong grol yid bzhin nor bu)*, he placed three bone relics of the Buddha inside the statue, as well as substances such as hair and bodhichitta pills from other great Dzogchen masters including Prahevajra, Shri Simha, Manjushrimitra, Jnanasutra, and other miraculously amassed substances. Tertön Sogyal further quoted Padmasambhava (Ibid., pages 158–159) as saying, "What is the benefit of placing this statue in the Jokhang and making offerings and meditating before it? You will certainly be reborn in a pure land, and in Tibet, all beings and the land will be placed in happiness and benefit, and the Dharma will not diminish but rather flourish, and it will prevent the Jowo Shakyamuni Buddha statue from being taken to the underworld. If you look at it with devotion one time, within seven lifetimes your realization will be equal to mine, and with one prostration you will soon become a vidyadhara, so whoever believes in me should make offerings to this statue and you will achieve accomplishment."

Page 104 *"Regent Demo presented Tertön Sogyal . . .":* Tsultrim Zangpo 1942, pages 148–149.

Page 106 *"Locals said that even the water . . .":* Nyoshul Khenpo 2005, page 244.

Page 106 *"Tertön Sogyal stayed for some months with Nyoshul Lungtok . . .":* Tsultrim Zangpo 1942, page 148. Nyoshul Lungtok bestowed the Oral Transmission Lineage of the Nyingma *(rnying ma bka' ma).* Tulku Thondup (1996, page 225) writes, "Throughout his [Nyoshul Lungtok's] life he shared the teachings of Paltrül [Patrul] with all who came to him, and especially after the age of fifty he gave Dzogpa Chenpo teachings. However, like Paltrül Rinpoche, he hardly gave any transmissions of empowerments."

Page 106 *"In Tertön Sogyal's 35th year . . .":* For the revelation of the statue, see Tsultrim Zangpo 1942, pages 146–153.

Pages 109–110 *"To the Lotus-born Guru of Oddiyana, we pray! . . .":* Rigpa 2004, pages 240–241. This is the last verse from chapter seven of *Sampa Lhundrupma: The Prayer to Guru Rinpoche That Spontaneously Fulfills All Wishes (bsam pa lhun grub ma).*

Page 110 *"The potency of Padmasambhava's wisdom intent . . .":* Tsultrim Zangpo 1942, pages 187–188.

Page 111 *"Hum Hum Hum . . .":* Nechung 2004, pages 23–26.

Translation courtesy Adam Pearcey. The conclusion of the *Guru Yoga of the Profound Path* (*zab lam bla ma'i rnal 'byor*) liturgy states, "For this profound treasure of Orgyen Tertön Sogyal, the great Dharma-King Nechung has prophesied that the seal of secrecy should be released in the Iron Hare [1891]."

Pages 111–112 *"In the year of the Iron Tiger . . .":* Tsultrim Zangpo 1942, pages 163–164.

Page 113 *"They named him Rigdzin Namgyal . . .":* Ibid., page 139. Lama Wangde told the author that Tertön Sogyal and Khandro Pumo had a second boy who died as an infant, but there is no mention of this in Tsultrim Zangpo 1942. Nyoshul Khenpo Rinpoche (2005, page 514) writes that Tertön Sogyal had another son, named Adin Peltsa Lodrö. Tromge Tulku Khachö Dechen Dorje, who lives near Yachen Gar in eastern Tibet, is the son of Adin Peltsa Lodrö, and a lineage holder of Tertön Sogyal termas. Tsultrim Zangpo does not write about Adin Peltsa Lodrö.

Page 114 *"Bantahor was a region . . .":* Nechung 2004. Some sources consider Bantahor to have been a region in current-day Gansu Province.

Page 115 *"One of the monks from Nechung Monastery . . .":* This monk, Orgyen Trinley Chöphel, was the seniormost incarnate lama at Nechung Monastery.

Pages 1115–116 *"Many people in Kham think . . .":* Nechung 2004; Khamtrul Rinpoche interviews 2008, 2013.

Page 116 *"After a month, the statue was returned to its throne . . .":* Thereafter on the tenth lunar day of each month, eight monks from Nechung Monastery would perform a ritual feast offering before the Guru Statue, and the Dalai Lama would send a white offering scarf. And every Monkey year, the Guru Statue was taken to Nechung Monastery for a ritual feast offering and prayers, and at this time other mediums gathered and were possessed by the various oracles that the Tibetan government consulted.

Page 117 *"But while in central Tibet, he was sure to connect . . .":* Tertön Rangrik was an emanation of Terdak Lingpa of Mindroling. Tertön Rangrik had a close relationship with the Thirteenth Dalai Lama, though it never matured to the degree of Tertön Sogyal's.

The Thirteenth was the patron of Lumorap Monastery, which Tertön Rangrik built. Tertön Rangrik Dorje's grandson, Gyurme Dechen Chokdrup, became the ninth throne holder of Mindroling.

Page 118 *"At one point, Tertön Rangrik and Tertön Sogyal . . ."*: Lodi Gyari Rinpoche interview 2008. Lodi Gyari Rinpoche (b. 1949), also known as Gyari Gyaltsen, was born in Nyarong, Tibet, and was recognized as the reincarnation of Khenchen Aten Jampal Dewe Nyima of Lumorap. He is the former Special Envoy of His Holiness the Dalai Lama and chief interlocutor with the Chinese government, and currently resides outside of Washington, D.C.

Page 118 *"Tanglha presided over the entire Himalayan . . ."*: One of the heavenly court ministers for Tanglha is Kawalurig, Heights of Eternal Snow, who resides in northern Nyarong.

Page 122 *"As their relationship deepened, Kongtrul acknowledged . . ."*: Jamgön Kongtrul 2003, pages 217–219, 249–250, and 393. Kongtrul referred to Tertön Sogyal as the "Tertön of Dzarkha."

Page 122 *"Padmasambhava uncharacteristically entrusted . . ."*: Tsultrim Zangpo 1942, page 190. *The Razor,* consisting of a cycle of terma teachings and material treasures, was entrusted to five of Guru Rinpoche's disciples—Kharchen Palgyi Wangchuk, Langchen Palgyi Senge, Nubchen Sangye Yeshe, Dorje Dudjom, and Shübu Palgyi Senge—but circumstances decreed that Tertön Sogyal, the emanation of Nanam Dorje Dudjom, would be the tertön to actually reveal the terma.

Page 124 *"Kongtrul had gone to that secret location . . ."*: Tsultrim Zangpo 1942, pages 215–217.

Page 126 *"This treasure is the one and only revival . . ."*: Tsultrim Zangpo 1942, page 191. See also Dalai Lama, 14th, 2007, pages 253–265. Khamtrul Rinpoche (interview 2008) described *The Razor* as follows: "What we have here is the teaching itself from the Guru Padmasambhava. It was revealed by Jamgön Kongtrul Lodrö Thaye, who was the incarnation of the great translator Vairocana. It was decoded by Tertön Sogyal Lerab Lingpa, who was the incarnation of Nanam Dorje Dudjom. So what you have is a terma that was produced through the combined efforts of the Great Guru, the Great Translator, and the Great Disciple, which combines the blessing of all three, and this is the terma that we have which is *The Razor of the Innermost Essence.*

Page 126 *"Ho! Through the power of generation and completion phases . . ."*: From the aspiration prayer of *The Razor of the Innermost Essence.* Translation courtesy Rigpa.

Page 126 *"Padmasambhava prophesied two holders . . ."*: Thupten Jampa 1998, page 691.

Page 127 *"The Gelug teachings will be strengthened . . ."*: Ibid., page 691.

Page 129 *"The Nechung Oracle issued a prophecy . . ."*: Tsultrim Zangpo 1942, page 221.

Page 130 *"Tertön Sogyal relied on Khandro Pumo's advice . . ."*: Ajam Rinpoche interview 2001.

Page 133 *"Tertön Sogyal took up residence . . ."*: This refers to *The Deepest Heart Essence of Vajrakilaya.* Khenpo Jikme Phuntsok on August 27, 1993, said that the three main Vajrakilaya termas of Tertön Sogyal are *Yang Sang Tropa (The Most Secret Wrathful Vajrakilaya),* which is very long; *Yang Nying Pudri (The Razor of the Innermost Essence),* which is of medium length; and *Yang Zab Nyingpo (The Deepest Heart Essence of Vajrakilaya),* which is the most concise.

Page 135 *"Just as the Abbot . . ."*: Thupten Jampa 1998, pages 582–583; also, Akester (forthcoming) points out that the name Tertön Padma Lingpa "was evidently an alias (gTer ming) for one of the highest dignitaries in the dGe lugs pa order, the ninth 'Phags pa lha incarnation mKhas grub ngag dbang blo bzang 'jigs med bstan pa'i rgyal mtshan [Ngawang Lobsang Jigme Tenpai Gyaltsen] (1849–1900)."

Page 137 *"At one campsite in the lush forests . . ."*: Tsultrim Zangpo 1942, page 233; Thupten Jampa 1998, pages 225–226.

Page 137 *"You, protectors, by the power of this offering . . ."*: Translation courtesy Rigpa.

Page 137 *"Part of the prophecy called for the construction . . ."*: Akester (forthcoming) outlines what is in Tsultrim Zangpo 1942, pages 231–233: "The *Nyi ma'i 'od phreng* [*Garland of Sunlight*] prophecy called for the construction of a series of geomantic temples, one devoted to Guru Padma in each of the three 'Chos skor' or royal temples of the Yar lung Dharmaraja-s (lHa sa, bSam yas and Khra 'brug, to suppress the rGya 'dre), and two groups of five temples each, one above gTsang gi Sil ma thang, at the western foot of Jo mo Kha rag (the holy mountain on the border between dBus and gTsang, to suppress the Dam sri), and one above Khams kyi Sha ba thang (at lHang brag in Nyag rong, to suppress the 'Phung 'dre). On arrival in lHa sa, gTer ston bSod rgyal [Tertön Sogyal] duly presented his revelations to His Holiness, who took a great interest in the prophecy, writing it out in his own hand from the gTer ston's reading and (supported by gNas chung and his official tutor Gling rin po che) authorised the necessary construction, which began the following year. The chapels added to the Parikrama precincts (Bar skor) of the three great Chos skor temples each had central images of Guru Padmasambhava, Guru drag po and Seng gdong ma, surrounded by 100,000 clay-mould figures of Guru Padma. The five chapels at Sil ma thang contained Buddha statues and five thousand volumes of scripture." See also Thupten Jampa 1998, pages 225–226.

Pages 138–139 *"Kyema! Profound, peaceful, and free . . ."*: Translation courtesy Rigpa, from booklets prepared for His Holiness the Dalai Lama's visit to Lerab Ling, September 2000.

Page 145 *"The cryptic message mentioned death. . ."*: The narrative of this assassination episode is based on Nyarong oral history and interviews with the late Sherab Ozer Rinpoche, Khamtrul Rinpoche, Tashi Tsering, Lodi Gyari Rinpoche, and the late Lama Wangde. Gelek Rinpoche was very generous to speak to me. Also, see Tsultrim Zangpo 1942, pages 243–245; Thupten Jampa 1998, pages 239–242. English sources that deal with parts of the episode are found in Goldstein 1991, pages 42–43; Kawaguchi 1979, pages 374–382; Tsepon Shakabpa 1967, pages 195–196. Matthew Akester provided me with Tibetan sources, which include *Hor khang bSod nams dal 'bar, Ram pa rNam rgyal dbang phyug* and *bShad sgrva dGa' ldan dpal 'byor* in *Bod kyi lo rgyus rig gnas dpyad gzhi'i rgyu cha bdams bsgrigs,* volume 8, and *Blo bzang rgya mtsho* in volume 19. Mullin (1988, pages 37, 40–45) erroneously writes that Tertön Sogyal and Lerab Lingpa are two different people; Lerab Lingpa was an alias of Tertön Sogyal.

Page 147 *"Tibetan government documents . . ."*: Tsepon Shakabpa 1967, pages 195–196.

Page 148 *"But it is more likely that Demo was exiled . . .":* Demo's previous incarnations are unclear. Khyentse Wangpo and others held that he was the incarnation of Shantarakshita. The Fourteenth Dalai Lama suggested in Laird 2007 (page 403, note 38) a more complicated situation, saying that Demo was the incarnation of a former Tibetan government minister (Garwa Tongtsen) who had suffered at the hands of King Songtsen Gampo.

Pages 151–152 *"Rigdzin Namgyal would follow in the tradition . . .":* Lama Wangde interview 2004.

Page 152 *"The Dalai Lama gave the name to the new temple . . .":* Sherab Ozer and Changchub Gyamtso 1996, pages 30–31.

Page 152 *"Nyoshul Lungtok was ill . . .":* Tsultrim Zangpo 1942, page 254. Adam Pearcey has pointed out in www.lotsawahouse.org/ tibetan-masters/terton-sogyal/biography that the biography of Khenpo Ngawang Pelzang mentions that Nyoshul Lungtok gave detailed teachings on the preliminaries to Tertön Sogyal around this time. Khenpo Ngawang Pelzang himself was present and took notes during the teaching which was to become his famous *A Guide to the Words of My Perfect Teacher (kunzang lama'i shyalung zindri)*. See Khenpo Ngawang Pelzang 2004.

Page 154 *"Inspire us with your blessings in this life . . .":* Translation courtesy Rigpa; from *The Prayer in Seven Chapters to Padmakara (le'u bdun ma).*

Page 154 *"As he was praying . . .":* Tsultrim Zangpo 1942, pages 255–256.

Page 156 *"It is known as* Tendrel Nyesel *. . .":* for the elaborate *Tendrel Nyesel (rten 'brel nyes sel gyi gdams pa zab mo)* revelation, see Tsultrim Zangpo 1942, pages 255–266. *Tendrel* means "interdependence." *Nye* means "something gone wrong"; *sel* means "to remove or to eliminate inauspiciousness."

Pages 158–159 *"For us and those who need protection . . .":* Translation courtesy Rigpa. Verse from the section *Dakini Ciphers: The Method Employing Air* found within the *Tendrel Nyesel* revelation.

Pages 159–160 *"All these momentary thoughts, perceptions . . .":* Translation courtesy Rigpa. Verses are from the medium-length *Tendrel Nyesel (nyes sel gyi cho ga 'bring po).*

Page 162 "*Pacify all outer, inner and secret inauspicious circumstances
. . .*": Translation courtesy Rigpa. Verses are from the concise-
length *Tendrel Nyesel (rten 'brel nyes sel gyi don bsdu)*.

Page 163 "*To be immersed in genuine, unfettered . . .*": Nyoshul
Khenpo 2005, page 245.

Page 163 "*The knots of the eight worldly concerns . . .*": Ibid., page
238.

Page 165 "*In the fourth month of the Water Hare year . . .*": Tsultrim Zangpo 1942, pages 220–222; Thupten Jampa 1998, pages
194–198 and 283.

Page 167 "*Both the Dalai Lama and Tertön Sogyal agreed . . .*": Tsultrim Zangpo 1942, pages 275–279.

Pages 169–170 "*Qing troops arrived in 1904 in Litang . . .*": Sperling
1976; Wim Van Spengen, "Frontier History of Southern Kham,"
and William M. Coleman IV, "The Uprising at Batang," in Epstein
2002.

Page 170 "*The age of degeneration will come . . .*": Ibid., page 283.

Page 170 "*The formless demon will enter . . .*": Tsultrim Zangpo 1942,
page 285; prophecy by Shiba Lingpa, Chökyi Gyalpo Garwang Rigdzin (1524–1588).

Page 170 "*The prophecies were confirmed . . .*": Tsultrim Zangpo
1942, page 341.

Page 171 "*The Fifth Dalai Lama called Dogyal a malicious spirit . . .*":
The most authoritative source in English on the origins of Dogyal
(Dorje Shugden) is Dreyfus 1998. Also see Bultrini 2013. The Great
Fifth Dalai Lama wrote in his biography (Dalai Lama, Fifth, n.d.,
Volume Kha, folio 239), "He is referred to as Dogyal because he is
a Gyalpo (king demon) from Dol Chumig Karmo. Gyalpo is a class
of interfering spirit. Since Shugden belongs to this group, he is
also called Gyalchen (the great Gyalpo), a very powerful perfidious
spirit (damsi), born from distorted prayers, who has been harming
the teachings of the Buddha and sentient beings."

Page 172 "*I bow down to you . . .*": Bultrini 2013, page 271.

Page 172 *"One of the foreign forces . . .":* Teichman 2000, pages 36–37. See also Epstein 2002 and Ho 2008. The epithet "Butcher Zhao" for Zhao Erfeng (Pinyin: Zhao Tufu) was coined around 1904 when he allegedly ordered the slaughter of 3,000 innocent people in Gulin county. See Zeng Guoqing, *Qingdai Zangshi Yanjiu* (*Studies of Tibetan history during the Qing dynasty*) (Lhasa: Xizang Renmin Chubanshe, 1999), as cited in Ho 2008.

Pages 172–173 *"They reported atrocities by Qing troops . . .":* Tripartite Conference between China, Britain, and Tibet 1940. See also Sperling 1976, page 87.

Page 173 *"Tertön Sogyal said . . .":* Tsultrim Zangpo 1942, page 286.

Page 173 *"In deep meditative states . . .":* The acts of vanquishing, whether by the sword of Butcher Zhao or the dagger of Tertön Sogyal, may appear similar in that they both remove an opponent; however, the crucial difference lies in the motivation. Butcher Zhao's motivation was violent conquest and a willingness to harm anyone obstructing him. Tertön Sogyal was a different kind of warrior: his motivation was to prevent such violence and aggression, not allowing the aggressor to incur negative karma for himself and not to harm others. No trace of anger could be found in Tertön Sogyal's motivation or actions, while his wrathful compassion gained intensity.

Page 174 *"Despite the many termas he had revealed . . .":* Tsultrim Zangpo 1942, page 242.

Page 174 *"There, in Pemakö, my followers . . .":* Ibid., page 291. Also see Khamtrul Rinpoche 2009 and Baker 2004.

Page 175 *"Two weeks later, Tertön Sogyal encountered . . .":* For the discussion of hidden lands, see Tsultrim Zangpo 1942, pages 293–300.

Page 179 *"The brutal accounts of destruction . . .":* Zhao was an imperialist, and he knew that he had to break the influence of the monks and Buddhism among the Tibetans. The plan that Zhao laid out included (1) appointing Chinese officials to take over from the local authority (2) training more soldiers for security, (3) bringing in Chinese settlers to work the land, (4) opening mines and exploiting the mineral resources of the area, (5) instituting commerce on a scale capable of doing away with the problems of securing and transporting goods to and from the borderlands, and (6) promoting education so as to change the "barbaric customs" of the local people and make them civilized. See Sperling 1976, pages 76–77.

Page 180 *"They told Tertön Sogyal they had to flee . . ."*: Lama Wangde interview 2003.

Page 180 *"Yet Tertön Sogyal was told he could remove . . ."*: Tsultrim Zangpo 1942, pages 321–325.

Page 181 *"In the final vision, Tertön Sogyal understood . . ."*: Ibid., pages 328–336.

Page 181 *"It was as Khyentse Wangpo had once said . . ."*: Jamgön Kongtrul 2012, page 16.

Page 182 *"He met the throne holders of Dzogchen . . ."*: Tsultrim Zangpo 1942, page 355. The Fifth Dzogchen Rinpoche, Thubten Chökyi Dorje, bestowed the empowerments of the Treasury of Precious Termas (*rin chen gter mdzod*), while the associated transmissions and instructions were granted by Gemang Choktrul.

Page 182 *"As he flowed in and out of these dream-like experiences . . ."*: Tsultrim Zangpo 1942, pages 356–365.

Page 182 *"On the 29th day of the tenth month of the Earth Bird year . . ."*: Tsultrim Zangpo 1942, pages 392–393. Thanks to Matthew Akester for original translation.

Page 185 *"Still, thousands of Chinese soldiers invaded . . ."*: Richardson 1984, page 99. See also Tsepon Shakabpa 1967, page 228; British Parliamentary Documents; FO 535/13, Further Correspondence Respecting the Affairs of Thibet; "Government of India to Viscount Morley," enclosure 1 in no. 37 (March 3, 1910): 27.

Page 185 *"Although Padmasambhava has been so compassionate . . ."*: Tsultrim Zangpo 1942, pages 411–413.

Page 186 *"Though Zhao experienced a gruesome death . . ."*: Teichman 2000, page 36, speaks of the death. Tsultrim Zangpo 1942, page 170, tells us that when Tertön Sogyal was informed about the death, he commented that Zhao Erfeng had been reborn in the pure land of Karma Heruka.

Page 186 *"The Dalai Lama wrote during this period . . ."*: Tsepon Shakabpa 1967, pages 246–248.

Page 190 *"Soon after Tertön Sogyal arrived in Golok . . . "*: The Wangchen Bum tribes battled with the other two main Golok tribes of Akyong Bum and Padma Bum.

Page 192 *"The time and conditions now presented themselves to bring . . ."*: Tulku Thondup 1996, page 237.

Page 192 *"After the teaching, Patrul Rinpoche . . ."*: The Way of the Bodhisattva (*Bodhicharya-avatara*), Nyoshul Khenpo 2005, page 324; Tulku Thondup 1996, page 206.

Pages 192–193 *"As lightning struck, Dodrupchen felt ill . . ."*: Nyoshul Khenpo 2005, page 325; Tulku Thondup interview 2007; Tulku Thondup 1996, page 242. Among the few visitors who were received for teachings were Tertön Sogyal, Rigdzin Chenpo of Dorje Drak, Katok Situ, Jamyang Khyentse Chökyi Lodrö, Garwa Tertön Long-yang, Terthang Choktrul, Tsultrim Zangpo, and Sera Ringtreng.

Page 194 *"It is raised as the crown of a high mountain . . ."*: Tulku Thondup 1996, pages 242–243.

Page 194 *"Crystalline lakes in the uplands are surrounded . . ."*: Tsultrim Zangpo 1942, page 456.

Page 195 *"If the people of Tibet have no devotion . . ."*: Tsultrim Zangpo 1942, page 412.

Page 196 *"Tertön Sogyal was told that he needed to find . . ."*: Ibid., page 415. See also Ju Mipham's *Kagye Namshe* (Ju Mipham Gyatso 2000).

Pages 196–197 *"With Dodrupchen's encouragement, Tertön Sogyal departed immediately . . ."*: Ibid., pages 466–476. See also Dilgo Khyentse Rinpoche teaching 1990.

Page 200 *"With stable meditative concentration that did not waver . . ."*:

Tsultrim Zangpo 1942, pages 469–472. See also Ju Mipham's *Kagye Namshe* (Ju Mipham Gyatso 2000).

Page 202 *"In 1912, the Northern Warlords Alliance appointed Ma Qi . . ."*: See Lipman 1984.

Page 202 *"Tertön Sogyal snarled at the warlord's message . . ."*: Lama Wangde interview 2001; Khamtrul Rinpoche interview 2008.

Page 202 *"Alak Gurong was a charismatic polymath . . ."*: For a brief biography of Alak Gurong, Orgyen Jikdrel Chöying Dorje (1875–1932), known also as Gurong Tsang, see Schaeffer 2013, pages 711–714. It was Alak Gurong who taught the French explorer Alexandra David-Néel about Tibetan mysticism when they met in Amdo and Peking. David-Néel had requested Dzogchen teachings when they met. Gen Pema Wangyal of Washington, D.C., is currently researching the cultural nexus between Tibetan/Hui/Salar/Mongolian/Monguor/Han peoples of northeastern Tibet in the late 19th and early 20th centuries, focusing on the lives of prominent people such as Alak Gurong, Tertön Sogyal, Dodrupchen Rinpoche, Lap Chamgon, the Ma family, and others.

Page 203 *"Alak Gurong and the yogis . . ."*: Secret Essence Tantra *(Guhyagarbha Tantra; ryud gsang ba'I snying po).*

Page 203 *"Devotees and yogis sought his meditation instructions . . ."*: It was during this time that the scholar-poet Gendün Chöphel, then in his youth, met Tertön Sogyal. The young boy went with his mother to seek Tertön Sogyal's blessing during an Avalokiteshvara empowerment for the public. Tertön Sogyal's stern but magnificent presence initially startled the young boy; he saw the tertön's face with its bluish complexion, his long cheekbones, and the crowned dreadlocked hair tied by a red string. During the empowerment, Tertön Sogyal saw Gendün Chöphel in the crowd and said, "Bring that boy to me." When they came face-to-face, Gendün Chöphel asked Tertön Sogyal to guide his recently deceased father in the states in between death and his next rebirth. Tertön Sogyal tenderly held the young boy's hands and told him he would do so and that he and his mother should return the next day. Tertön Sogyal bestowed an empowerment upon them the following day and placed a protection amulet around Gendün Chöphel's neck. He told the mother that the boy was an incarnate lama from the Nyingma tradition, and that he should study Padmasambhava's teachings, "but the Gelug will probably take you away." Years later, after Gendün Chöphel traveled to India and returned with progressive ideas he wanted to share with the county, narrow-minded Tibetan government officials in Lhasa imprisoned him on charges of sedition. See Mengele 1999. See also Stoddard 1985; Schaedler 2005; and Lopez 2007.

Page 204 *"Back at Gurong's residence of Mandigar . . .":* The small encampment of Mandigar, situated above the Yellow River in the area of Drakkar Nankar of Jentsa, was blessed in the past by Je Tsongkhapa's teacher, the great Kadam master Choje Dondrub Rinchen, when he did retreat in the caves and Shachung Temple along the river.

Page 204 *"With a flash the photo was taken . . .":* Regarding the story about the photograph, I collected oral histories from the late Gurong Gyalse (Alak Gurong's son) via Humchen Chenakt-sang in Xining, as well as from Alak Sertar in Rebkong and Kham-trul Rinpoche in Dharamsala. See also Orgyen Dongkawa 2000. Thanks to Gen Pema Wangyal in Washington, D.C., Gray Tuttle, and Matthew Kapstein for their assistance in researching Alak Gurong. For more information and photographs of Alak Gurong and family, see Da lta ba 2005, Gurong Tsang 1994, and Humchen Chenaktsang and Yeshe Ozer Drolma 2005. There is said to be at least one other photograph of Tertön Sogyal that is currently in the possession of Gurong Tsang, Orgyen Tenzin, of Jentsa, who is the reincarnation of Alak Gurong Orgyen Jikdrel Chöying Dorje.

Page 206 *"On the advice of his most trusted confidant . . .":* Li Dan (1871–1938) was from a traditional Chan Buddhist aristocratic family from Hunan. According to Ma Rong, a student of Li Dan, who has written for the Qinghai Cultural History Research Bureau, Li Dan's grandfather was governor of Yunnan-Guijo and a highly regarded scholar whose calligraphy was sought throughout China, a skill Li Dan inherited. Li Dan was sent to Gansu (at the time Qinghai was part of greater Gansu) and there he met Ma Qi. They immediately established mutual respect because of their similar political views. Ma Qi admired Li Dan for being soft-spoken, for having profound knowledge of spiritual and political matters, and for his stable advice. Li Dan admired Ma Qi for his openness and frankness. Ma Qi took Li Dan as his principal advisor. Li Dan told Ma Qi, "In order to control Qinghai, you must get along well with the Tibetans and Mongols." On the advice of Li Dan, Ma

Qi started what would become the annual Offering Ceremony to Lords of Lake Kokonor, which the Tibetans and Mongolians greatly appreciated. When the news of Ma Qi's friendship with the locals became known in Peking, he received praise and was eventually appointed Governor of Qinghai. Ma Qi continued to consult with Li Dan on all matters, including the military, education, and development. Li Dan was close to Alak Gurong of Jentsa and Lap Chamgon of Yushu, a prominent Gelug lama. Soon after Li Dan came to Qinghai, he translated Tsongkhapa's *Praise of Dependent Origination (rten 'brel bstod pa)* and Mipham Rinpoche's *Treatise on Advice to Rulers: Specifically the King of Derge (rgyal po'i lugs kyi bstal bcos)*. Li Dan's Tibetan name was Dame Dorje (Egoless Vajra). In 1920, at the Old Temple in Xining, he established the "Tibetan Xining Research Center," where many scholars would eventually train; and he composed a Tibetan grammar book, a Tibetan-Chinese dictionary, a Tibetan medical and herbal remedy book, and treatises on Abhidharma, the Paramitas, Madhyamaka, and Tibetan proverbs. Li Dan would go on to influence Chinese foreign policy, including China's withdrawal from the Simla Accord. Li Dan recommended maintaining harmonious relations with the Thirteenth Dalai Lama and was close to Geshe Sherab Gyatso, a Tibetan lama who, after falling out of favor with the Lhasa political establishment, worked with both the Nationalist Government of the Republic of China and later the Communist of the People's Republic of China. Thanks to Gen Pema Wangyal for his assistance in Xining and Washington, D.C. For a biography of Ma Qi, see Funchen Fun 2013.

Page 206 *"Ma Qi had even taken an interest in reading Li Dan's translation . . .":* See Hartley 1997 for comments on Mipham Rinpoche work. Mipham Rinpoche enumerated the seven constituents of political organization: the king, the king's officials and ministers, the country or rural regions, the fortified urban zones, the treasure, the army, and foreign allies.

Pages 206–207 *"Of all the Ma family warlords . . .":* Bulag (2002, pages 41–44) argues that Ma Qi's support of Tibetan Buddhist ritual offerings to land and lake spirits at Kokonor Lake was merely pandering to the Tibetan and Mongol imagination: "Controlling Tibetans and Mongols on behalf of the Center [the new Republican government, which] was the crucial way to maintain his power."

Page 208 *"Not to be outdone by Gurong . . .":* The oral history of the audio recording is from interviews with Khamtrul Rinpoche 2008, 2013. The audio recording of Tertön Sogyal has not been found. According to Ge 2009, page 48, the earliest gramophone recording in China was made in Shanghai in 1903; the recording of Tertön Sogyal is said to have taken place in 1914.

Page 211 *"The boy would be known as Pema Chöpel Gyatso . . ."*: Tsultrim Zangpo 1942, pages 555–556. Earlier, when Tertön Sogyal was in Achung Namdzong, the One-Eyed Protectress appeared to him and told him that his grandson would carry the blessing of the great master Ju Mipham Rinpoche. Rigdzin Namgyal's wife, Sonam Drolma—the child's mother—was of the Horshul Choyu tribe of Golok.

Page 211 *"Tertön Sogyal spent increasing amounts . . ."*: Ibid., page 522.

Page 212 *"The commentary was entitled . . ."*: Tertön Sogyal requested Dodrupchen Rinpoche to compose the commentary, *Key to the Precious Treasury: A Concise Commentary on the General Meaning of the "Glorious Secret Essence Tantra"* (*mdzod kyi lde mig*). See Dodrupchen Jikme Tenpa'i Nyima 2010.

Page 212 *"While Dodrupchen was not known publicly as a tertön . . ."*: Tulku Thondup 2007; see also Tulku Thondup 1996, pages 243–244. Tulku Thondup 1986, part four, contains a complete translation of Dodrupchen's *Wonder Ocean: A Brief and Clear Explanation of the Transmission of Termas* (*las a'phro gter brgyud kyi rnam bshad nyung gsal ngo mtshar rgya tso*).

Page 212 *"Soon after he met Tertön Sogyal, Tsullo invited . . ."*: Tsultrim Zangpo 1942, pages 486, 499. Tertön Sogyal gave the empowerments from the Northern Treasures tradition (*gshin rje* and *rig 'dzin gdung sgrub*) as well as those of the outer practices from his own revelations. Shukjung Monastery was established by the First Dodrupchen, Jikme Trinle Ozer (1745–1821).

Page 214 *"Khandro Pumo told Tertön Sogyal . . ."*: Tulku Thondup 1996, pages 213–214, 248.

Page 214 *"While staying at Puchung House, Tertön Sogyal received . . ."*: Tsultrim Zangpo 1942, page 496. The main focus was from the Jonang Jodrup (*sbyor drug*), the six-fold Kalachakra yogic practice.

This temple is likely where Choklung Repa Damtsik Dorje had once founded a hermitage in the 18th century; as Nyoshul Khenpo (2005, page 409) writes, "Repa Damtsik Dorje . . . spent a long time in Golok, caring for students in these northern reaches; he also founded a hermitage, which in later times Tertön Sogyal Rinpoche restored."

Page 214 *"Tertön Sogyal appointed the Dzogchen yogi Pushul Lama . . .":* Tulku Thondup said that practice continued until tribal fighting broke out in the 1950s and everyone departed from the warring area, and the temple was destroyed in the early 1960s.

Page 215 *"While staying at the temple, Tertön Sogyal had a pure vision . . .":* Tsultrim Zangpo 1942, page 523.

Page 215 *"For as long as space exists . . .":* Shantideva 1997, chapter 10, verse 55.

Page 218 *"Tertön Sogyal never wasted a moment . . .":* The text of Tertön Sogyal's teaching that forms the basis for this narration is in the personal library of Sogyal Rinpoche.

Page 221 *"Tertön Sogyal's ability to transmit experientially . . .":* It was as Nyoshul Khenpo writes on page xxx of a marvelous *Garland of Rare Gems* (2005) regarding "the transmission of the realization of this ultimate wisdom mind by the master to the student . . . this does not happen for just any ordinary person. A number of circumstances have to come together, in terms of how the master and the student interact: there are the *authentic* teachings, or pith instructions; there is the master, who has the *authentic* blessing of the lineage; and there is the student, who has *authentic* faith and devotion. When these three 'authentics' come together, the realization of Dzogpachenpo, the Great Perfection, can awaken in the student's mindstream."

Page 223 *"They asked Tertön Sogyal . . .":* Tsultrim Zangpo 1942, page 493.

Page 225 *"He knew that these were the blessed substances . . .":* For Dodrupchen's blessing from afar, see Tulku Thondup 1996, page 248; Nyoshul Khenpo 2005, page 327.

Page 225 *"During the ceremony, Tertön Sogyal again saw many dakinis . . .":* Tsultrim Zangpo 1942, pages 509–519.

Page 228 *"If I can teach the* Secret Essence Tantra *to His Holiness . . ."*: Khenpo Jikme Phuntsok teaching 1993. Also, Nyoshul Khenpo (2005, page 325) writes that Jamyang Khyentse Wangpo prophesied that if Dodrupchen "went to central Tibet, he would not only ensure benefit for the teachings and for beings, but also dispel obstacles to his life. However, circumstances supportive of such a journey did not materialize."

Page 229 *"With devotion, there is no difference between me and the prophecies . . ."*: Tsultrim Zangpo 1942, pages 519–520.

Page 229 *"For the next three years, Tertön Sogyal moved . . ."*: In autumn of 1917, according to Chögyal Namkhai Norbu 2012 (b), page 25, Tertön Sogyal received from Adzom Drugpa Rinpoche the *Direct Revelation of Samtabhandra's Mind (kun bzang dgongs pa zang thal)*.

Page 229 *"The removal of obstacles for everyone . . ."*: Tsultrim Zangpo 1942, pages 580–582. The prophecy was given to Tertön Sogyal by the dakini Mandarava in the form of White Vajravarahi.

Page 230 *"After a few weeks, the protectors led Tertön Sogyal . . ."*: Ibid., pages 568–569. The *Names of the Thousand and Two Buddhas of This Fortunate Age (sangs rgyas stong rtsa gnyis)*.

Page 231 *"Tertön Sogyal immediately redacted the meaning . . ."*: Ibid., page 584.

Page 231 *"While Tertön Sogyal was staying in the area . . ."*: Soon afterward he granted the empowerments and transmissions of *yongs rdzogs 'dus pa, phur pa rgya chen rol pa*, and the brief and medium versions of *rten 'brel nyes sel* to Khandro Pumo and his son Rigdzin Namgyal, Tsullo, and Atrin. Jamgön Kongtrul recognized Chökyi Lodrö as the incarnation of Jamyang Khyentse Wangpo. There were other incarnations of the great Khyentse Wangpo's body, speech, mind, qualities, and activities, but it was Chökyi Lodrö who was eventually enthroned at Dzongsar and carried on his predecessor's work to the greatest degree. Khyentse Chökyi Lodrö recognized the son of the Lakar family in Trehor—Sonam Gyaltsen—as an incarnation of Tertön Sogyal. Sonam Gyaltsen would become known as Sogyal Rinpoche and later founded Rigpa Fellowship and authored *The Tibetan Book of Living and Dying* (Sogyal Rinpoche 1992).

Pages 231–232 *"Greatest among teachers, Buddha and lord of sages, Shakyamuni . . .":* From the concise *Tendrel Nyesel.* Translation courtesy Rigpa.

Page 232 *"With Chökyi Lodrö's encouragement . . .":* Nyoshul Khenpo (2005, page 300) writes, "Terchen Lerab Lingpa [Tertön Sogyal] conferred on him [Chökyi Lodrö] the cycle *The Heart Drop of Freedom: The Natural Freedom of Enlightened Intent,* as well as his own profound termas, including the cycle of Vajrakilaya, the three levels—outer, inner, and secret—of *Dispelling Flaws in Interdependence.* He also bestowed on him the empowerments and teachings for *The Heart Drop of Chetsun [Heart Essence of Chetsun]* and authorized him to pass on all of these termas."

Page 232 *"The auspicious circumstances for the transmission . . .":* Khenpo Jikme Phuntsok teaching August 24,1993.

Page 233 *"He expelled his last breath . . .":* Tsultrim Zangpo 1942, page 585. Tertön Sogyal confirmed that Atrin had been reborn in the pure realm.

Pages 235–236 *"Stories swirled in Lhasa . . .":* Zemey Tulku 1973.

Page 236 *"How utterly mistaken are the minds . . .":* Translation courtesy Rigpa. Verse from the *na rak skong bshags (Emptying the Lower Realms from Their Very Depths).*

Page 236 *"And whenever he was unclear . . .":* Tsultrim Zangpo 1942, page 574.

Page 237 *"Tertön Sogyal continued using the two life-force stones . . .":* Ibid., page 575.

Page 237 *"As he continued his effort . . .":* Ibid., page 579.

Page 238 *"Tertön Sogyal was trying to single-handedly resupply the whole of Tibet . . .":* Ibid., page 625.

Page 238 *"One early spring evening in the Water Pig year . . .":* Tsultrim Zangpo 1942, pages 586–588.

Page 239 *"Each master repeated the same phrase . . .":* The *Complete Gathering of Teachings* is *ka yongs rdzogs bde 'dus.*

Page 240 *"There was a prophecy regarding this episode . . ."*: Tsultrim Zangpo 1942, page 603.

Page 241 *"Such a practice was the ultimate antidote . . ."*: Ibid., pages 603 and 626.

Page 243 *"But this devoted student . . ."*: Ibid., page 630.

Page 244 *"While staying in Shukjung Monastery . . ."*: Kunzang Nyima (1904–1958), also known as Sungtrul Rinpoche or Nuden Dorje, was the grandson and speech emanation of Traktung Dudjom Lingpa. See Nyoshul Khenpo 2005, pages 515–516.

Page 245 *"At this, the time for discovering Buddha directly . . ."* :Translation courtesy Adam Pearcey.

Page 245 *"Tertön Sogyal approached his two-room stone house . . ."*: Tsultrim Zangpo 1942, page 630.

Page 246 *"We pray to you who are like the moonlight . . ."*: Translation courtesy Rigpa.

Page 246 *"Tertön Sogyal thanked him for offering . . ."*: Tsultrim Zangpo 1942, page 541.

Page 246 *"He would later say . . ."*: Tulku Thondup interview 2007.

Page 247 *"At the end of the Wood Ox year . . ."*: Jamphel Sherab Rinpoche interview 2008. Tashe Lama, Lama Gendun, Wupho Lodi, and Yumtrul Dorje Gyamtso accompanied Tertön Sogyal and escorted him to his residence in the upper floor of the three-level Nubzor Temple. Nubzor, also known as Nubzur or Nizok, takes its name from a tribe in Golok.

Page 248 *"Buddha, Dharma, and Sangha . . ."*: Translation courtesy Rigpa.

Page 248 *"On the tenth day of the first month . . ."*: Tsultrim Zangpo 1942, pages 718–719.

Page 250 *"The innermost, profound meaning is crystallized here . . ."*: Translation courtesy Rigpa; from the brief *Tendrel Nyesel*.

Page 252 *"When the cremation stupa had cooled . . ."*: Regarding the five wisdoms, see Sogyal Rinpoche 1992, page 157; and Khenpo Ngawang Palzang 2004, pages 104–105.

Page 252 *"Tertön Sogyal's devotees rebuilt . . ."*: See Pistono 2011, pages 200–218.

Page 252 *"Woodblocks of Tertön Sogyal's 20 volumes . . ."*: The incarnation of Gurong Tsang, Orgyen Tenzin of Jentsa Township in northeastern Tibet recently published Tertön Sogyal's collected terma revelations and unpublished writings in 24 volumes; see Tertön Sogyal 2013.

Page 254 *"At a teaching at Reting Monastery. . ."*: See Tsering Shakya's biography of the Thirteenth Dalai Lama in Brauen 2005, pages 136–161.

Page 255 *"Tsullo says it was Rigdzin Namgyal who delivered it . . ."*: Tsultrim Zangpo 1942, page 621; Keutsang Trulku Jamphe Yeshe 2001, page 256.

Page 255 *"The Dalai Lama came down from Keutsang Monastery . . ."*: Dilgo Khyentse Rinpoche teaching 1990.

Page 256 *"His Holiness recalls . . ."*: Dalai Lama interview 2007.

Page 256 *"She said that seven incarnate lamas. . ."*: Ama Adhe 1997, pages 108–113.

Page 259 *"He also predicted that there would be . . ."*: In another prophecy found in Tertön Sogyal's *Hayagriva* treasure revelation, it is stated:

> *Lerab Lingpa, the one with infinite activities,*
> *In the next life will be born in Jakhyung and Taktsang;*
> *The first will show behavior difficult to assess*
> *And will grant blessings to all who come in contact,*
> *Be it positive or negative contact.*

It is believed that Ju Mipham Rinpoche's brother, born in Jakhyung Namdzong, was an incarnation of Tertön Sogyal. And regarding the other incarnation from Taktsang from the *Hayagriva* treasure prophecy, Pistono (2001, page 234) states, "Dilgo Khyentse Rinpoche told the story of how, when the meditation master Sonam Zangpo journeyed to the Dugsta Temple in Bhutan in the 1960s, he came across a philosophical discourse by the monk Gendun Rinchen from the famed Tiger's Lair. Sonam Zangpo was struck by the similarities in tone and content to the writings by Tertön Sogyal, whom Sonam Zangpo had met some decades before in eastern Tibet. Sonam Zangpo asked that Gendun Rinchen be brought to him, and it is said that at this time he recognized him as one of three incarnations of Tertön Sogyal. Gendun Rinchen, also known as Geshe Drakpukpa, was born in the same year Tertön Sogyal died. He was the 69th successive holder of the title Je Khenpo, the supreme head of Buddhism in Bhutan. According to this version, it is said of these three reincarnations of Tertön Sogyal, one would be a strict monk (Khenpo Jikme Phuntsok), one a learned hermit (Gendun Rinchen), and one a yogi with unconventional 'crazy wisdom' (Sogyal Rinpoche)." See also Nyoshul Khenpo 2005, page 514.

Page 260 *"In August 1993, the two principal reincarnations . . ."* See Khenpo Jikme Phuntsok teaching, August 27, 1993. *The Tathagata Practice of the Gathering of Drolö: gro lod bde gshegs 'dus pa.*

# GLOSSARY

**bardo** (Tibetan) The intermediate or transition states between death and rebirth. More broadly, the term refers to any of the junctures at which the possibility of awakening is heightened. Thus, bardos are occurring continuously throughout both life and death.

**barkhor** (Tibetan) Literally, middle circuit; in central Tibet, the walkway used for circumambulating Jokhang Temple in Lhasa; also refers to the neighborhood surrounding the Jokhang.

**bodhichitta** (Sanskrit) *Bodhi* means "enlightened essence" and *chitta* means "heart" or "mind." Hence, "the essence of enlightened mind/heart"; the compassionate wish to attain enlightenment for the benefit of all beings.

**bodhisattva** (Sanskrit) One who has realized bodhichitta, the compassionate wish to attain enlightenment for the benefit of all beings, and who engages in actions that bring them to that state; bodhisattvas vow to delay their own entrance into nirvana until all other beings have attained enlightenment.

**buddha nature** (Sanskrit *sugatagarbha)* The all-pervasive, primordial purity innate in every living being.

**Buddha of Compassion.** *See* Avalokiteshvara (page 267).

**chakra** (Sanskrit) Literally, wheel; focal center of subtle energy.

**chö** (Tibetan) Literally, cutting; a Vajrayana practice that seeks to destroy or "cut" demonic forces, namely, the self-cherishing ego.

**dakini** (Sanskrit; Tibetan *khandro*) Embodiment of enlightened energy in female form, manifesting sometimes as a human being, at other times as an ethereal being who protects the Buddhist teachings. *See also* khandro.

**dakini script** A symbolic script used by the dakinis, which can only be decoded by treasure revealers (tertöns).

**damsi** (Tibetan) A demon or evil spirit who has corrupted or broken its samaya commitments.

**deity** (Tibetan *yidam*) A tutelary or chosen meditational deity whose practice is the root of spiritual accomplishment. Deities can represent specific enlightened qualities (such as compassion, wisdom, or power), which are developed through the yogic practice of uniting with the essence of the deity. Deities are often classified according to whether they appear in peaceful or wrathful form.

**demon** (Sanskrit *mara*) A malevolent spirit; a negative force or obstacle on the spiritual path.

**Dharma** (Sanskrit) The Buddha's teachings; truth or reality; the spiritual path.

**Dzogchen** (Tibetan) *See* Great Perfection.

**Dzogpachenpo** (Tibetan) *See* Great Perfection.

**empowerment** (Sanskrit *abhisheka*; Tibetan *wang*) A ceremony performed by masters and lineage holders that transmits or awakens primordial wisdom, the power of realization, in the mind of the disciple; empowerments are a prerequisite for the practice of tantra in the Buddhist tradition; sometimes referred to as initiation.

**emptiness** (Sanskrit *shunyata)* The absence of inherent existence in self and all phenomena.

**enlightenment** (Sanskrit *bodhi)* Synonymous with buddhahood, the ultimate accomplishment of spiritual training; the perfect realization of the nature of mind and the understanding of reality. *See* nirvana.

**experiential-oriented instruction** (Tibetan *nyongtri)* A teaching method that is direct and practical and conveys the most essential elements to be put into practice immediately by the disciples so that they can experience nakedly the truth of the teaching; a teaching style in which instructions are given according to the progress of the individual meditator's experience.

**feast offering** *See* tsok.

**four kinds of (tantric) activity** To pacify, increase, magnetize, and subjugate; tantric practitioners train in the context of deity yoga to 1. pacify conflict, sickness, and famine, 2. increase longevity and merit, 3. magnetize auspicious circumstances, and, 4. subjugate hostile force. Highly realized yogis perform these four activities for the benefit of others.

**garuda** (Sanskrit) Mythical bird-like creature with various meanings; the Dzogchen Tantras indicate that garuda represents an individual's primordial perfection.

**Gelug** One of the four main traditions of Tibetan Buddhism, and the latest school of the Sarma, or New Translation, schools; founded by Je Tsongkhapa in the 15th century on the basis of the Kadam tradition. Followers of the Gelug tradition are called Gelugpas.

**Golok** A region in eastern Tibet.

**Great Perfection** (Sanskrit *mahasandhi* or *atiyoga*; Tibetan *Dzogchen* or *Dzogpachenpo)* The most ancient and direct stream of wisdom within the Buddhist tradition of Tibet.

**guru** (Sanskrit; Tibetan *lama*) Literally, heavy or weighty in positive qualities, vast knowledge, wisdom, and skill. *See* lama.

**guru yoga** (Sanskrit) A meditation practice that focuses on merging the disciple's mind with the wisdom mind of the teacher (guru), who is often visualized in an enlightened form.

**heruka** (Sanskrit) One of the names for wrathful enlightened deities.

**ignorance** (Tibetan *ma rigpa*) Misknowing; veiled awareness; the failure to recognize one's true nature, which is the basis for all other destructive emotions such as attachment, aversion, anger, jealousy, and pride.

**incarnate lama** *See* tulku.

**Jokhang Temple** Considered the most sacred temple in Tibet; home to the Jowo Shakyamuni Buddha statue; founded in Lhasa in the 7th century.

**Kalzang Temple** Founded by Nyala Pema Dündul in 1860, in Nyarong; later became the seat of Tertön Sogyal.

**Kama** (Tibetan) The Oral Transmission Lineage of the Nyingma; together with the terma lineage are the two modes transmissions of the sutrayana and the vajrayana teachings in the Nyingma School.

**Kham** A geographical area, also called eastern Tibet; in between the present-day Tibet Autonomous Region and Sichuan Province, parts of the southern areas of Qinghai Province, and part of Yunnan Province. Traditionally, Kham was referred to as the "Four Rivers, Six Ranges," because the gorges of the Ngul Chu (Chinese *Salween*), Dri Chu (Chinese *Yangtze*), Da Chu (Chinese *Mekong*), and Dza Chu (Chinese *Yalung*) Rivers all originated and flowed from the six parallel mountain ranges. People from Kham are called Khampas.

**khandro** (Tibetan; Sanskrit *dakini*) Literally, sky-goer, indicating one who traverses the sky of the expanse of wisdom. *Khandro is* often used as a title for a female lama or the consort of a male lama or yogi.

**Khenpo** (Tibetan) A title for one who has completed the major course of studies of more than ten years' duration, covering the traditional branches of Buddhist philosophy, logic, monastic discipline, and ritual. A khenpo can also be the abbot of a monastery.

**lama** (Tibetan) Spiritual teacher; contraction of the Tibetan *bla ne med pa,* meaning unsurpassed or nothing superior. *See* guru.

**Lhasa** The capital and largest city in Tibet; traditional home of the Dalai Lamas.

**life-force** (Tibetan *bla*) Subtle energy within the body that supports the consciousness and relates directly to one's vitality and strength.

**life-force stone** (Tibetan *bla rdo*) Stone that contains energetic qualities to enhance or strengthen a person's life-force; some stones naturally possess these qualities while other stones are imbued with the qualities by a tantric master.

**liturgy** (Sanskrit *sadhana*) A text presenting the ritual, contemplative, and meditation instructions to develop fully in oneself the enlightened qualities of a deity.

**mandala** (Sanskrit) Literally, center and surrounding; the sacred environment and dwelling place of a buddha, bodhisattva, or deity, together with the proximate environment, which is visualized by the yogi in tantric practice. A mandala can be a two-dimensional representation of a buddha or deity's environment on cloth or paper, or a three-dimensional representation made of sand, wood, or other material; a mandala can also be an offering of the entire universe visualized as a pure land with all the inhabitants as pure beings.

**mani** *See Om Mani Padme Hum.*

**mantra** (Sanskrit) Sacred syllable(s) spoken, chanted, or written to protect the mind from negativity and ordinary impure perceptions; used to invoke meditational deities.

**mara** (Sanskrit) *See* demon.

**meditation** The practice of familiarization with the mind and reality as it is; distinction is made between analytical meditation and contemplative meditation: analytical meditation is used for study and to develop qualities such as love and compassion; contemplative meditation is used to recognize the ultimate nature of the mind (rigpa) and to remain within the realization of that nature, which lies beyond conceptual thought.

**mind** (Tibetan *sem*) The ordinary mind whose condition is characterized by ignorance and delusion; distinguished from rigpa in the Dzogchen teachings.

**naga** (Sanskrit) Serpent-like spirits that live beneath the surface of the earth or in water.

**nature of mind** *See* rigpa.

**nirvana** (Sanskrit) Literally, extinguished. Beyond suffering; enlightenment itself; the state of peace that results from the cessation and total pacification of all suffering and its causes.

**Nyagar** An encampment in Golok, a day's horseback ride from Sertar, where Tertön Sogyal and his family lived the last two years of his life.

**Nyarong** Region in eastern Tibet where Tertön Sogyal was born.

**Nyingma** The oldest school of Tibetan Buddhism, which follows the original translations of the teachings of the Buddha into Tibetan, carried out up until the late 10th century; sometimes known as the Old Translation or Earlier Translation school, which is distinguished from the Sarma or New Translation schools (Kadam, Kagyu, Sakya, and Gelug).

**Old Translation school** *See* Nyingma.

***Om Mani Padme Hum*** The six-syllable mantra of Chenrezik; also known as the *mani* mantra.

**One-Eyed Protectress** (Sanskrit *Ekajati*) An important enlightened protectress of the Dzogchen teachings; depicted with a single tuft of hair, a single eye, and a single breast.

**oral transmission** (Sanskrit *agama*; Tibetan *lung*) The reading of a tantric text to a disciple by a master who holds the lineage of transmission, originating from the author of the text; considered essential for the blessing of the lineage to be conveyed and for the disciple to fully understand the text; also known as reading transmission.

**pandita** (Sanskrit) Title used for scholars who have mastered the five sciences of craftsmanship, logic, grammar, medicine, and the inner science of Dharma.

**phurba** (Tibetan; Sanskrit *kila*) A three-bladed, single-pointed dagger representing the skillful means of compassion and the destruction of the self-cherishing ego; the principal ritual implement of the meditational deity Vajrakilaya.

**Potala** The principal palace and residence of the Dalai Lamas, constructed in Lhasa by the Fifth Dalai Lama in the mid-17th century upon the ruins of an old palace and hermitage erected more than 1,000 years before by the kings of Tibet. Up until the Chinese invasion, it housed much of Tibet's central government. Namgyal Monastery is located within the massive 1,000-room compound.

**protector** (Sanskrit *dharmapala*) A deity or spirit whose role is to protect the Buddhist teachings and practitioners. Some protectors are emanations of buddhas or bodhisattvas; others are spirits and demons who have been subjugated and bound under oath by great practitioners such as Padmasambhava.

**rainbow body** Dissolution of the corporeal body into light through the practice of Dzogchen; outward sign of the yogi's supreme spiritual attainment.

**reincarnation** The successive existences that are experienced by the mind-stream, marked by birth and death; also called rebirth.

**rigpa** (Tibetan) In general, means intelligence or awareness; in Dzogchen terminology, it means the innermost, nondual nature of mind; one's ultimate nature, which is devoid of delusion.

**Rime** (Tibetan) Ecumenical, nonsectarian movement inspired by Jamyang Khyentse Wangpo and Jamgön Kongtrul and their disciples in eastern Tibet in the 19th century.

**Rinpoche** (Tibetan) Literally, precious one; an honorific title used for spiritual teachers, often denoting their having been recognized as an incarnate lama. *See* Tulku.

**sadhana** (Sanskrit) *See* liturgy.

**samaya** (Sanskrit) A set of precepts and vows taken between disciples and teachers, pledged to one another, when receiving or bestowing tantric empowerments.

**samsara** (Sanskrit) Continuous cycle of the conditioned existence of birth and death, characterized by suffering; the cause of samsara is ignorance of the true nature of reality.

**Samye** The first Buddhist monastery in Tibet, built during the time of King Trisong Detsen (8th century). *Samye* means limitless, as in beyond the conceptual realm.

**smoke offering** Ritual offering of aromatic plants, medicines, and wood, such as juniper and cedar, that are moistened and placed on a fire to create smoke that cleanses the external environment of pollution and purifies the yogi's internal channels from psychic knots; also made to local deities out of respect for entering or using their land.

**stupa** (Sanskrit) A reliquary monument symbolizing the enlightened mind of the buddhas. Stupas can vary in size and shape but often have a wide square base, a rounded middle, and a tall conical section at the top.

**tantra** (Sanskrit) Literally, thread or continuity. *Tantra* refers to both the texts of Vajrayana Buddhism and the tantric tradition in general, which teach the natural purity of the mind. Tantra begins with the view that the final attainment or result has been within the nature of mind from the very beginning, but has been obscured by ignorance.

**Tara** (Sanskrit; Tibetan *Drolma*) Female deity associated with compassion and enlightened activity.

**terma** (Tibetan) A spiritual treasure concealed by Padmasambhava and Lady Yeshe Tsogyal in the earth, sky, water, or in the mind-stream of certain individuals. Termas are discovered, or revealed, at a specified time for the benefit of beings, by tertöns, or treasure revealers, who are the incarnations of Padmasambhava's 25 closest disciples. Termas may be texts containing liturgies, religious practices, spiritual advice, and scrolls inscribed with dakini script, or may be blessed objects such as statues, ritual implements, medicine, or relics.

**tertön** (Tibetan) Treasure revealer; one who reveals *terma*s that were hidden in his or her mind-stream or as physical objects in Tibet and throughout the Himalayas during the 8th century by Padmasambhava and Lady Yeshe Tsogyal; incarnations of Padmasambhava's 25 closest disciples. See *terma*.

**Tibet** The nation composed geographically of three main provinces: U-Tsang (central and western Tibet), Kham (eastern Tibet), and Amdo (northeastern Tibet).

**torma** (Tibetan) Ritual cake, usually hand molded from butter, roasted barley flour, and spiritual medicine, and colored with dyes, to symbolize a deity, a mandala, an offering, or a weapon.

**tsok** (Tibetan; Sanskrit *ganachakra*) Tantric feast assembly to accumulate merit and purify samaya commitments; practiced regularly, especially on significant lunar days or to mark an auspicious occasion.

**tulku** (Tibetan)  Literally, emanation body; the reincarnation of a previous spiritual master who, at the time of death, was able to direct his next rebirth. Used in common speech to refer to any incarnate lama who is also often addressed as "Rinpoche." Chinese publications often incorrectly translate *tulku* as "living buddha."

**vajra** (Sanskrit; Tibetan *dorje*) A ritual scepter symbolizing compassion and skillful means. In Vajrayana rituals, the vajra represents the masculine principle and is the counterpart of the bell, which represents the feminine principle and the wisdom of emptiness; the union of skillful means and wisdom is the awakened mind.

**Vajrayana** (Sanskrit) The Diamond (*vajra*) Vehicle (*yana*); the tantric branch of Mahayana Buddhism, which utilizes a wide variety of methods, including mantra and visualization of deities, and which gives great emphasis to the role of the teacher.

**view** The genuine nature of phenomena; sustaining the realization of emptiness; first in the common triad of view, meditation, and action.

**wind** (Sanskrit *prana*) The wind-energies or psychic-wind that moves through the subtle channels of the body's psychophysical system; normal wind perpetuates the movement of dualistic thought patterns of ignorance, hatred, and desire; normal wind can be transmuted through yogic practice into wisdom wind.

**yogi** (Sanskrit; feminine, *yogini*) A practitioner of yoga; one in union with the natural state. The term implies a practitioner who has some degree of spiritual realization.

# REFERENCES

Akester, Matthew. Forthcoming. "The rJe 'bum sgang lha khang and Other Follies: rNying ma pa Ritual Architecture in the Resurgence of the Modern Tibetan State." *Journal of the International Association of Tibetan Studies.*

Alexander, Andre. 2005. *The Temples of Lhasa: Tibetan Buddhist Architecture from the Seventh to the Twenty-first Centuries.* Serindia.

Ama Adhe. 1997. *The Voice that Remembers: A Tibetan Woman's Inspiring Story of Survival.* Wisdom Publications.

Aten Dogyaltshang. 1993. *A Historical Oration from Khams: The Ancient Recitation of Nyag Rong.* Tibetan Literature Series No. 1. Edited by Tashi Tsering. Amnye Machen Institute.

Baker, Ian. 2004. *The Heart of the World: A Journey to the Last Secret Place.* Penguin Press.

Baker, Ian. 2000. *The Dalai Lama's Secret Temple: Tantric Wall Paintings from Tibet.* Thames & Hudson.

Bell, Charles. 1987 (reprint). *Portrait of a Dalai Lama: The Life and Times of the Great Thirteenth* (1946). Wisdom Publications.

Bell, Charles. 1931. *The Religion of Tibet.* Oxford. Clarendon Press.

Brauen, Martin (editor). 2005. *The Dalai Lamas: A Visual History.* Serindia.

Bshes gnyen tshul khrims [Shenyen Tsultrim]. 2001. *The Precious Ornamental Heaping of the Lhasa Monasteries.* Sichuan Nationalities Publishing House. Chengdu.

Bulag, Uradyn E. 2002. *The Mongols at China's Edge: History and the Politics of National Unity.* Rowman & Littlefield.

Bultrini, Raimondo. 2013. *The Dalai Lama and the King Demon: Tracking a Triple Murder Mystery through the Mists of Time.* Tibet House.

Byrom, Thomas. 1993. *Dhammapada: The Sayings of the Buddha.* Shambhala Publications.

Cantwell, Cathy, and Robert Mayer. 2013. "Representations of Padmasambhava in Early Post-Imperial Tibet." *Tibet after Empire: Culture, Society and Religion between 850–1000.* Lumbini International Research Institute. Volume 4.

China Tibetology. 1991. *History of Monasteries in Kandze, Kham: A Clear Mirror of Buddhism.* Volume 1. China Tibetology Center Publishing House.

Chögyal Namkhai Norbu. 2012 (a). *The Lamp that Enlightens Narrow Minds: The Life and Times of a Realized Tibetan Master, Khyentse Choki Wangchuk.* Shang Shung Publications.

Chögyal Namkhai Norbu. 2012 (b). *Rainbow Body: The Life and Realization of Togden Ugyen Tendzin.* Shang Shung Publications.

Coleman, William M. IV. 2002. "The Uprising at Batang: Kham and Its Significance in Chinese and Tibetan History," in Epstein 2002.

Da lta ba [Da Tawa]. 2005. *dGu rong tshang gi zhabs rjes.* Volume 2. Xining.

Dalai Lama, Fifth (Ngawang Lobsang Gyatso). n.d. *Autobiography: Dukulai Gosang* (Lhasa edition). Volume Kha.

Dalai Lama, Fourteenth (Tenzin Gyatso). 2000. *Dzogchen—The Heart Essence of the Great Perfection: Dzogchen Teachings Given in the West.* Snow Lion Publications.

Dalai Lama, Fourteenth. 2007. *Mind in Comfort and Ease: The Vision of Enlightenment in the Great Perfection.* Wisdom Publications.

Das, Sarat Chandra. 1988 (reprint). *Journey to Lhasa and Central Tibet* (1970). Cosmo Publications.

Do Khyentse. 1997. *Autobiography of Do Khyentse Yeshe Dorje.* Sichuan Nationalities Publishing House.

Doctor, Andreas. 2005. *Tibetan Treasure Literature: Revelation, Tradition, and Accomplishment in Visionary Buddhism.* Snow Lion Publications.

Dodrupchen Jigme Tenpa'i Nyima. 2010. *Key to the Precious Treasury: A Concise Commentary on the General Meaning of the "Glorious Secret Essence Tantra."* Translators: Lama Chönam and Sangye Khandro of the Light of Berotsana Translation Group. Snow Lion Publications.

Dreyfus, George. 1998. "The Shuk-den Affair: History and Nature of a Quarrel." *Journal of the International Association of Buddhist Studies,* Volume 21, Number 2.

Dudjom Rinpoche. 1991. *The Nyingma School of Tibetan Buddhism: Its Fundamentals and History.* Translators: Gyurme Dorje and Matthew Kapstein. Wisdom Publications.

Epstein, Lawrence (editor). 2002. *Khams pa Histories: Visions of People, Place and Authority.* PIATS 2000, Tibetan Studies: Proceedings of the Ninth Seminar of the International Association for Tibetan Studies. Brill.

Ferrari, Alfonsa. 1958. *Mk'yen Brtse's Guide to the Holy Places of Central Tibet.* Editor: Luciano Petech. Istituto Italiano per il Medio ed Estremo Oriente.

Funchen Fun. 2013. *Ma Zi Zhum (Ma Qi Biography).* Qinghai Peoples Publishing House. Xining.

Gardner, Alexander. 2006. "The Twenty-five Great Sites of Khams: Religious Geography, Revelation, and Nonsectarianism in Nineteenth-Century Eastern Tibet." Ph.D. dissertation, University of Michigan.

Ge, T. 2008. "Shanghai EMI—The Development of Shanghai EMI during the Modern Period." *History Review.* (5), pages 26–41.

Ge, T. 2009. *Records and Modern Shanghai Social Life.* Lexicographical Publishing House. Shanghai.

Goldstein, Melvyn C. 1973. "The Circulation of Estates in Tibet: Reincarnation, Land and Politics." *Journal of Asian Studies,* Volume 32, Number 3.

Goldstein, Melvyn C. 1991. *A History of Modern Tibet, 1913–1951: The Demise of the Lamaist State.* University of California Press.

Gurong Tsang. 1994. *Dgu rong sku phreng snga phyi'i rnam thar* (Biography of Gurong Gyalse). Nationalities Publishing House of Gansu.

Hartley, Lauran Ruth. 1997. "A Socio-Historical Study of the Kingdom of the Sdedge (Derge, Kham) in the Late Nineteenth Century: Ris-Med Views of Alliance and Authority." M.A. thesis, Indiana University.

Ho, Dahpon David. 2008. "The Men Who Would Not Be Amban and the One Who Would: Four Frontline Officials and Qing Tibet Policy (1905–1911)." *Modern China*, Volume 34, Number 2, pages 210–246.

Humchen Chenaktsang and Yeshe Ozer Drolma. 2005. *A Collection of Histories Concerning the Ngak Mang Rebkong Monastery.* Nationalities Press. Beijing.

Jacoby, Sarah H. 2007. "Consorts and Revelation in Eastern Tibet: The Auto/Biographical Writings of the Treasure Revealer Sera Khandro (1892–1940)." Ph.D. dissertation, University of Virginia.

Jagou, Fabienne. 2009. "The Thirteenth Dalai Lama's Visit to Beijing in 1908: In Search of a New King of Chaplain-Donor Relationship." In *Buddhism between Tibet and China.* Editor: Matthew Kapstein. Wisdom Publications.

Jamgön Kongtrul. 2003. *The Autobiography of Jamgön Kongtrul: A Gem of Many Colors.* Translator: Richard Barron. Snow Lion Publications.

Jamgön Kongtrul. 2012. *The Life of Jamyang Khyentse Wangpo.* Translator: Matthew Akester. Shechen Publications.

Jamyang Norbu. 1986. *Warriors of Tibet: The Story of Aten and the Khampas' Fight for the Freedom of Their Country.* Wisdom Publications.

Ju Mipham Gyatso. 2000. *Kagye Namshe (dpal sgrub pa chen po bka' brgyad kyi spyi don rnam par bshad pa dngos grub snying po: Explanation of the Eight Logos).* Provisional English translation by Zach Beer and Dharmachakra Translation Committee. Sichuan Nationalities Publishing House.

Ju Mipham Gyatso. n.d. *Treatise on Advice to Rulers: Specifically the King of Derge (rgyal po'i lugs kyi bstan bcos).*

Kapstein, Matthew T. 2004. "The Strange Death of Pema the Demon Tamer." Chapter 6 in *The Presence of Light: Divine Radiance and Religious Experience.* University of Chicago Press.

Kawaguchi, Ekai. 1979 (reprint). *Three Years in Tibet* (1909). Ratna Pustak Bhandar.

Keutsang Trulku Jamphe Yeshe. 2001. *Memoirs of Keutsang Lama: Life in Tibet after the Chinese "Liberation."* Paljor Publications.

Khamtrul Rinpoche. n.d. "A Brief Biography of the Great Treasure Revealer [Tertön Sogyal] Lerab Lingpa Known as the Drop Thread of Purity, He Who Is Freed from the Cloud Covering of the Two Obscurations, Who Has Thoroughly Completed All Clear Light Appearances of Wisdom and Compassion, Who Showers the Beneficial and Blissful Rays of the Profound and Highest Secret Tantra."

Unpublished manuscript. Translator: Acharya Nyima Tsering (Mike Gilmore). Dharamsala.

Khamtrul Rinpoche. 2009. *Memories of Lost and Hidden Lands: The Life Story of Garje Khamtrul Rinpoche*. Translator: Lozang Zopa. Chime Gatsal Ling. Dharamsala.

Khenpo Namdrol. 1999. *The Practice of Vajrakilaya*. Snow Lion Publications.

Khenpo Ngawang Pelzang. 2004. *A Guide to the Words of My Perfect Teacher*. Translators: Padmakara Translation Group. Shambhala Publications.

Khenpo Sodarjey. 2001. *Biography of His Holiness Jigmey Phuntshok Dharmaraja*. Translator: Arnaud Versluys. Hua Xia Cultural Publishing House.

Laird, Thomas. 2007. *The Story of Tibet: Conversations with the Dalai Lama*. Grove Press.

Li, John Fangjun. 2011. "The Development of China's Music Industry during the First Half of the Twentieth Century." *NEO: Journal for Higher Degree Research in Social Science and Humanities*.

Lipman, Jonathan. 1984. "Ethnicity and Politics in Republican China: The Ma Family Warlords of Gansu." *Modern China*, Volume 10, Number 3.

Longchenpa Rabjam. 2002. *The Practice of Dzogchen*. Translator and annotator: Tulku Thondup. Snow Lion Publications.

Lopez, Donald S. Jr. 2007. *The Madman's Middle Way: Reflections on Reality of the Tibetan Monk Gendun Chopel*. University of Chicago Press.

Lotsawa House. www.lotsawahouse.org.

Mayer, Robert. 1991. "Observations on the Tibetan Phurba and the Indian Kila." *The Buddhist Forum*, Volume 2: 163–192.

McGranahan, Carole. 2001. "Arrested Histories: Between Empire and Exile in Twentieth-Century Tibet." Ph.D. dissertation, University of Michigan.

Mengele, Irmgaard. 1999. *dGe-'dun-chos-'phel: A Biography of the Twentieth-Century Tibetan Scholar*. Library of Tibetan Works and Archives. Dharamsala.

Mullin, Glenn H. 1988. *Path of the Bodhisattva Warrior: The Life and Teachings of the Thirteenth Dalai Lama*. Snow Lion Publications.

Nebesky-Wojkowitz, René de. 1993. *Oracles and Demons of Tibet: The Cult and Iconography of the Tibetan Protective Deities*. Tiwari's Pilgrims Book House.

Nechung. 2004. *An Anthology containing an exposition of the "Tenth Day, Fifth Month, of the Monkey year," the birth anniversary of the embodiment of all buddhas of the three times, mahaguru Padmasambhava: an account of how the wish-fulfilling nirvana-granting statue retrieved as a hidden treasure by Orgyen Lerab Lingpa was conveyed to Lhasa; and a brief account of the glorious deeds of Nechung, the great Dharma protector.* Nechung Dratsang. Dharamsala.

Ngawang Senge (Sarkis Vermilyea). 2013. "The Vajra Heart Essence of the Luminous Expanse: The Recitation of the Common Preliminaries." Unpublished translation.

Ngawang Zangpo. 2001. *Sacred Ground: Jamgön Kongtrul on Pilgrimage and Sacred Geography.* Snow Lion Publications.

Ngawang Zangpo. 2002. *Guru Rinpoche: His Life and Times.* Snow Lion Publications.

Noetic Sciences Institute. 2002. "The Rainbow Body." *Institute of Noetic Sciences Review*, Number 59 (May).

Nyoshul Khenpo. 2005. *A Marvelous Garland of Rare Gems: Biographies of Masters of Awareness in the Dzogchen Lineage.* Translator: Richard Barron. Padma Publications.

Orgyen Dongkawa. 2000. *The Life Story of Gurong Gyalse, Reincarnation of Mipham: A Cloud of Offerings to Delight Manjushri.* Gansu Nationalities Publishing House.

Orgyen Tobgyal Rinpoche. 1982. *The Life and Teachings of Chokgyur Lingpa.* Translators: Tulku Jigmey and Erik Pema Kunsang. Rangjung Yeshe Publications.

Petech, Luciano. 1973. *Aristocracy and Government in Tibet, 1728–1959.* Istituto Italiano per il Medio ed Estremo Oriente.

Pistono, Matteo. 2008. "Master Scholar of Fearless Sublimity: A Biography of the Lord of the Dharma, Choje Jigme Phuntsok Rinpoche." *The Fifth Anniversary of Choje Jigme Phuntsok Jungne Journal.* New Delhi.

Pistono, Matteo. 2011. *In The Shadow of the Buddha: Secret Journeys, Sacred Histories, and Spiritual Discovery in Tibet.* Dutton.

Rangjung Yeshe Wiki. www.rywiki.tsadra.org.

Ricard, Matthieu. 1996. *Journey to Enlightenment: The Life and World of Khyentse Rinpoche, Spiritual Teacher from Tibet.* Aperture.

Ricard, Matthieu (compiler and editor). n.d. "The Enlightened Vagabond: Images of Episodes in Patrul Rinpoche's Life." Unpublished manuscript. Padmakara Translation Group.

Richardson, Hugh. 1984. *Tibet and Its History.* Shambhala Publications.

Rigpa. 2004. *A Great Treasury of Blessing: Book of Prayers to Guru Rinpoche to Celebrate the Wood Monkey Year 2004–2005.* Dharmakosha for Rigpa.

Rigpa International. 2000. "On an Island of Wish-Fulfilling Jewels." *The Rigpa Journal.* Tertön Sogyal Trust.

Rigpa Shedra Wiki. www.rigpawiki.org.

Ringu Tulku. 2006. *The Ri-me Philosophy of Jamgön Kongtrul the Great: A Study of the Buddhist Lineages of Tibet.* Shambhala Publications.

Rockhill, William Woodville. 1891. *The Land of the Lamas: Notes of a Journey through China, Mongolia and Tibet.* The Century Company.

Ronis, Jann Michael. 2009. "Celibacy, Revelations, and Reincarnated Lamas: Contestation and Synthesis in the Growth of Monasticism at Katok Monastery from the Seventeenth through the Nineteenth Centuries." Ph.D. dissertation, University of Virginia.

Ruegg, D. S. 1991. "Nchod-yon, Yon-chod and chod-gnas/yon-gnas; on the Historiography and Semantics of a Tibetan Religio-social and Religio-political Concept." *Tibetan History and Language: Studies Dedicated to Geza Uray on His Seventieth Birthday.* University of Vienna.

Schaedler, Luc (director). 2005. *Angry Monk: Reflections on Tibet* (DVD).

Schaeffer, Kurtis, Matthew Kapstein, and Gray Tuttle (editors). 2013. *Sources of Tibetan Tradition.* Columbia University Press.

Shantideva. 1997. *The Way of the Bodhisattva: A Translation of the Bodhicaryavatara.* Translators: Padmakara Translation Group. Shambhala Publications.

Sherab Ozer. 1981. "A History of Nyarong Gonpo Namgyal." In Sherab Ozer and Changchub Gyamtso 1996.

Shes rab Od zer/Byang chub rgya mtsho (Sherab Ozer and Changchub Gyamtso). 1996. *A Mirror Clearly Reflecting the Buddhist Teachings: A Clear Explanation of the History of the Various Monasteries of Kardze in Kham* (*shar rgyal ba bskal bzang dgon gyi byung ba rags bsdus*). Sichuan Nationalities Publishing House. Chengdu.

Smith, E. Gene. 1970. "Jam mgon Kong sprul and the Nonsectarian Movement." *Kongtrul's Encyclopedia of Indo-Tibetan Culture.* International Academy of Indian Culture. New Delhi.

Smith, E. Gene. 2001. *Among Tibetan Texts: History and Literature of the Himalayan Plateau.* Wisdom Publications.

Sogyal Rinpoche. 1989. *Dzogchen and Padmasambhava.* Rigpa Publishing.

Sogyal Rinpoche. 1992. *The Tibetan Book of Living and Dying.* HarperCollins.

Sperling, Elliot. 1976. "The Chinese Venture in K'am, 1904–1911, and the Role of Chao Erhfeng." *Tibet Journal,* Volume 1, Number 2 (April/June), pages 10–36.

Stoddard, Heather. 1985. *Le Mendicant de l'Amdo.* Societé d'Ethnographie.

Stoddard, Heather. 2006. *The Great Phi gling dmag zlog of 1888.* International Association for Tibetan Studies. Bonn.

Tarthang Tulku (general editor). 1995. *Masters of the Nyingma Lineage.* Crystal Mirror Series, Volume 11. Compilers: Leslie Bradburn and the staff of the Yeshe De Project. Dharma Publishing.

Tashi Tsering. 1986. "Nag-ron mgon-po rnam-rgyal: A Nineteenth-Century Khams-pa Warrior." In *Soundings in Tibetan Civilization: Proceedings of the 1982 Seminar of the International Association for Tibetan Studies.* Editors: Barbara Nimri Aziz and Matthew Kapstein. South Asian Books.

Teichman, Eric. 2000 (reprint). *Travels of a Consular Officer in Eastern Tibet: Together with a History of the Relations between China, Tibet and India (1922).* Cambridge University Press.

Terrone, Antonio. 2010. "Bya rog prog zhu: The Raven Crest—The Life and Teachings of Bde chen 'od gsal rdo rje, Treasure Revealer of Contemporary Tibet." Ph.D. dissertation, Leiden University.

Tertön Sogyal. 2013. *The Collected Treasure Revelations and Writings of Tertön Sogyal, Lerab Lingpa.* Private publication. Xining.

Tertön Sogyal. 1985. *The Collected Visionary Revelations and Textual Discoveries of Lerab Lingpa [Tertön Sogyal].* Published in Bylakuppe [Karnataka, India] by Pema Norbu Rinpoche, reproduced from a set of the Nyarong block prints from the library of Dilgo Khyentse Rinpoche.

Thupten Jampa Tsultrim Tendzin. 1998. *The Wondrous Garland of Precious Gems: A Brief Summary of the Ocean-like Life and Liberation of the Thirteenth Incarnation of the Incomparably Gracious Lord of the Victorious Ones, the Crowning Ornament of All Samsara and Nirvana Including the Heavens* [Biography of His Holiness the Thirteenth Dalai Lama]. Sherig Parkhang.

Thupten Jinpa. 2005. *Mind Training: The Great Collection.* Wisdom Publications.

Treasury of Lives: Biographies of Himalayan Religious Masters. www.treasuryoflives.org.

Tripartite Conference between China, Britain, and Tibet. 1940. *The Boundary Question between China and Tibet: A Valuable Record of the Tripartite Conference between China, Britain, and Tibet held in India, 1913–1914.* Peking.

Tsepon Shakabpa. 1967. *Tibet: A Political History.* Yale University Press.

Tsering Shakya. 1999. *The Dragon in the Land of Snows.* Columbia University Press.

Tsong-kha-pa. 2000. *The Great Treatise on the Stages of the Path to Enlightenment [Lamrim Chenmo].* Translators: Lamrim Chenmo Translation Committee. Snow Lion Publications.

Tsultrim Zangpo. 1942. *The Secret Biography of the Great Tertön Sogyal Lerab Lingpa: The Marvelous Garland of White Lotuses.* Printed from woodblocks from Kalzang Temple, Nyarong, eastern Tibet.

Tsultrim Zangpo. 1974 (retraced and printed). *The Secret Biography of the Great Tertön Sogyal Lerab Lingpa: The Marvelous Garland of White Lotuses.* Published in New Delhi by Sanje Dorje from the library of Dudjom Rinpoche.

Tulku Thondup. 1986. *Hidden Teachings of Tibet: An Explanation of the Terma Tradition of Tibetan Buddhism.* Wisdom Publications.

Tulku Thondup. 1996. *Masters of Meditation and Miracles: The Longchen Nyingthig Lineage of Tibetan Buddhism.* Shambhala Publications.

Tulku Thondup. 2011. *Incarnation: The History and Mysticism of the Tulku Tradition of Tibet.* Shambhala Publications.

Tulku Urgyen Rinpoche. 2005. *Blazing Splendor: The Memoirs of Tulku Urgyen Rinpoche.* Rangjung Yeshe Publications.

Tuttle, Gray. 2005. *Tibetan Buddhists in the Making of Modern China.* Columbia University Press.

United Front. 2004 (June). *Qinghai Provincial Documents. Ma Family Genealogy.* Xining.

Yeshe Dorje. 2013. *The Cloud of Nectar: The Life and Liberation of Nyagla Pema Düdul*. Translator: Oriol Aguilar. Shang Shung Publications.

Yeshe Tsogyal. 1978. *The Life and Liberation of Padmasambhava*. Dharma Publishing.

Yeshe Tsogyal. 1993. *The Lotus-Born: The Life Story of Padmasambhava*. Translator: Erik Pema Kunsang. Shambhala Publications.

Younghusband, Sir Francis. 1910. *India and Tibet*. John Murray.

Yudra Nyingpo. 2004. *The Great Image: The Life of Vairochana the Translator*. Translator: Ani Jinba Palmo. Shambhala Publications.

Yudru Tsomu. 2006. "Local Aspirations and National Constraints: A Case Study of Nyarong Gonpo Namgyal and His Rise to Power in Kham (1836–1865)." Ph.D. dissertation, Harvard University.

Zemey Tulku Lobsang Palden. 1973. *The Yellow Book: An Account of the Protective Deity Dorje Shugden, Chief Guardian of the Gelug Sect, and of the Punishments Meted Out to Religious and Lay Leaders Who Incurred His Wrath*. Delhi, India.

# INTERVIEWS
*and* TEACHINGS

Ajam Rinpoche interviews 2001, 2007. Nyarong, eastern Tibet.

Ama Adhe interviews 2006. Dharamsala, India, and Washington, D.C.

Dalai Lama XIV interview 2007. Washington, D.C.

Dilgo Khyentse Rinpoche teaching, August 19, 1990. Prapoutel, France.

Gelek Rinpoche interview 2007. Washington, D.C.

Jamphel Sherab Rinpoche interview 2008. Golok, eastern Tibet.

Khamtrul Rinpoche teaching, August 12, 1992 (a). Lerab Ling, Roqueredonde, France.

Khamtrul Rinpoche teaching, January 14, 1992 (b). Dzogchen Monastery, Kollegal, India.

Khamtrul Rinpoche interview, April 2008. New York City.

Khamtrul Rinpoche interview, January 2013. Dharamsala, India.

Khenpo Jikme Phuntsok teaching, August 24, 1993. Lerab Ling, Roqueredonde, France.

Khenpo Jikme Phuntsok teaching, August 27, 1993. Lerab Ling, Roqueredonde, France.

Khenpo Jikme Phuntsok interview, November, 1999. Larung Gar, eastern Tibet.

Khenpo Namdrol Rinpoche teaching, May 2007. Alameda, California.

Lama Wangde interview 2001. Nyarong, eastern Tibet.

Lama Wangde interview 2004. Nyarong, eastern Tibet.

Lodi Gyari interview, April 2008. Washington D.C.

Matthieu Ricard interview, March 2004. Kathmandu, Nepal.

Nyoshul Khenpo Rinpoche teaching, September 22, 1985. Rigpa, London.

Orgyen Topgyal Rinpoche teaching, August 18 and 23, 1996. Lerab Ling, Roqueredonde, France.

Sherab Ozer Rinpoche interview, June 1998. Washington, D.C.

Sherab Ozer Rinpoche teaching, July 1998. Lerab Ling, Roqueredonde, France.

Tashi Tsering interview, December 2002. Dharamsala.

Tulku Thondup interview, November 2007. Boston.

# INDEX

Cremation ritual, 252

Crystal Lotus Cave, 49, 74–75, 76, 103, 240

# D

Dakinis, 12, 15, 17, 21, 34, 41–42, 51–52, 53, 78, 82, 106, 110, 126, 138, 152–156, 159, 163, 180–182, 196, 225–228, 238–239, 241, 244

Dakini script, 12, 15–17, *23*, 24, 37, 43, 49, 75, 76, 103, 106, 197, 212, 229

Dalai Lama

    incarnation lineage, 91

    regents, 92–93

    role of, 88, 90–91

Dalai Lama, 5th, 91–93, 97, 171, 189

Dalai Lama, 13th, *89*

    ascendancy to throne, 141–142

    assassination attempt, 141–149

    death of, 255

    death prophecies, 180, 182–184

    declaration of independence from China (1912), 186–187

    *The Deepest Heart Essence of Vajrakilaya,* 133

    *Dispelling Flaws in Interdependence,* 162

    Hayagriva-Vajravarahi life-force stone, 194, 196, 199, 255–256

    Kalzang chapel statutes, 163–164

    Life-Force Phurba, 138

    as lineage holder of Tertön Sogyal's treasure teachings, 253

    *Luminous Garland of Sunlight* prophecy, 138

    Peking journey, 182

    Phabongka reprimand, 171–172

    as *The Razor of the Innermost Essence* holder, 126–128, 138–139

    refuge in India, 184–185

    Tertön Sogyal's first summons from, 87–96

    Tertön Sogyal's influence on, 161–162

    Tertön Sogyal's last meeting with, 166–167

    at Tertön Sogyal's public treasure revelation, 99–102

    treasure revelations by, 103

    warning about hostile forces attacking Tibet, 254–255

    *Wish-Fulfilling Jewel Guru Statue That Liberates Upon Seeing,* 116

Dalai Lama, 14th, 256

# PHOTO CREDITS

Page 9: photo by Matteo Pistono

Page 23: photo by Matteo Pistono

Page 29: photo by Matteo Pistono

Page 30: photo by Matteo Pistono

Page 77: courtesy of Dzongsar Monastery, Tibet

Page 89: courtesy of the Jacques Marchais Museum of Tibetan Art, Staten Island, NY

Page 117: photo by Matteo Pistono

Page 123: courtesy of Dzongsar Monastery, Tibet

Page 125: courtesy of Sogyal Rinpoche

Page 131: photo by Matteo Pistono

Page 153: photo by Matteo Pistono

Page 157: courtesy of Sogyal Rinpoche

Page 193: photo by Matteo Pistono

Page 205: photo by Alak Gurong, Orgyen Jikdrel Chöying Dorje, circa 1913

Page 213: photo by Matteo Pistono

Page 217: photo by Matteo Pistono

Page 253: photo by Jurek Schreiner

Page 258: courtesy of Khenpo Jikme Phuntsok

Page 261: courtesy of Rigpa

# ABOUT *the* AUTHOR

Matteo Pistono is a writer, photographer, and practitioner of Tibetan Buddhism. Pistono lived and traveled throughout Tibet and the Himalayas for a decade, bringing to the West graphic accounts and photos of China's human rights abuses in Tibet, detailed in his memoir, *In the Shadow of the Buddha* (Dutton 2011). Pistono's writings and photographs about Tibetan and Himalayan cultural, political, and spiritual landscapes have appeared in *The Washington Post,* BBC's *In-Pictures, The Global Post, Men's Journal, Kyoto Journal,* and *HIMAL South Asia.* He is the founder of Nekorpa (www.nekorpa.org), a nonprofit foundation working to protect sacred pilgrimage sites around the world, and he sits on the executive council of the International Network of Engaged Buddhists, and the board of directors of Rigpa Fellowship and the Conservancy for Tibetan Art and Culture. Pistono and his wife, Monica, divide their time between Wyoming, Washington, D.C., and Asia. www.matteopistono.com

# Hay House Titles of Related Interest

*YOU CAN HEAL YOUR LIFE*, the movie, starring Louise Hay & Friends
(available as a 1-DVD program and an expanded 2-DVD set)
Watch the trailer at: www.LouiseHayMovie.com

*THE SHIFT*, the movie, starring Dr. Wayne W. Dyer
(available as a 1-DVD program and an expanded 2-DVD set)
Watch the trailer at: www.DyerMovie.com

*THE DALAI LAMA AND THE KING DEMON: Tracking a Triple Murder
Mystery Through the Mists of Time,* by Raimondo Bultrini

*A DROP FROM THE MARVELOUS OCEAN OF HISTORY:
The Lineage of Lelung Pema Zhepai Dorje, One of the Three Principal
Reincarnations of Tibet,* by Lelung Tulku Rinpoche XI

*IN MY OWN WORDS: An Introduction to My Teachings and Philosophy,*
by His Holiness the Dalai Lama

*WHY MEDITATE: Working with Thoughts and Emotions,*
by Matthieu Ricard

All of the above are available at your local bookstore,
or may be ordered by contacting Hay House (see next page).